Lust for Life!

A note on the author

John Neil Munro lives in Laxdale, Isle of Lewis. His previous books are *The Sensational Alex Harvey* (Firefly Books, 2002, and Polygon, 2008), *Some People Are Crazy: The John Martyn Story* (Polygon, 2007) and *When George Came to Edinburgh* (Birlinn, 2010).

Lust for Life!

Irvine Welsh and the *Trainspotting* Phenomenon

John Neil Munro

Polygon

First published in Great Britain in 2013 by
Polygon, an imprint of Birlinn Ltd.

Birlinn Ltd
West Newington House
10 Newington Road
Edinburgh
EH9 1QS

www.polygonbooks.co.uk

ISBN 978 1 84697 242 3
eBook ISBN 978 0 85790 664 9

British Library Cataloguing-in-Publication Data
A catalogue record for this book is available
on request from the British Library.

Typeset in Sabon by Hewer Text UK Ltd, Edinburgh
Printed and bound by Bell & Bain Ltd, Glasgow

Contents

This book is dedicated to Hannah.

Acknowledgements

Whenever you write a book like this, you are reliant on people who were actual witnesses to the events taking time out of their busy schedules to help you, invariably for no financial reward. Special thanks go to Irvine, of course, for not only writing such a brilliant book in the first place but also for giving lots of invaluable fresh input to this book. Also, special mention goes to Duncan McLean for nursing me through a nasty hangover, answering all my dumb questions and scouring through his home in Orkney to find long-lost letters from Irvine. Harry Gibson took the time to write me a majestic seven-page letter (one paragraph ran for three and a half pages) with his memories of adapting *Trainspotting* for the stage. Alan Warner also deserves special mention. I had been trying to get him to make a contribution for months, but his own writing deadlines made that increasingly unlikely. Then, with just a few days to spare, a 4,000-word email arrived from Alan which gives a great insight into the whole Edinburgh writing scene in the early 1990s.

A lot of his old friends from the 1960s and 1970s have taken a strict vow of *omertà* where Irvine is concerned, so gratitude goes to Sandy Macnair, Dave Todd and Dave Harrold – three guys who knew Irvine long before *Trainspotting* was published and all the hangers-on and glory-hunters appeared on the scene. All three were unstinting in offering advice, memories and old photos. Thanks also go to David Aukin, Dame Gillian Beer, Ian Brown, Lesley Bryce, James Cosmo, Lisa Dowdeswell at the Society of Authors, Janice Galloway, Giles Havergal, Duncan Jones of the Association for Scottish Literary Studies, Jack Lechner, Colin Leslie, Grant Mason, Rob O'Connor, Hugh Reed, Robin Robertson, Dr Roy Robertson, David Stewart, Mike Wilson and Hamish Whyte.

One of the more disappointing aspects of researching this book has been dealing with unhelpful or unresponsive agents and press officers, so praise goes to those who actually took the time to help set up interviews, especially Arthur Carrington at United Agents, Sarah McNair at Alan Brodie Agency and Paula Rabbitt at the West Yorkshire Playhouse.

Help and advice came from Allan Brown, Keith Bruce, James Kelman, Roddy Lumsden and Aleks Sierz. The staff at Stornoway Library, Kirkwall Library, the National Library of Scotland and Muirhouse Library all helped out too, as did Stephanie Faugier, Carol Kearney High, Russell Leadbetter, Calum Angus Macdonald, Mary McElhinny, Sandie MacIver, Robin Macmillan and Neville Moir, Alison Rae, Jim Hutcheson, Sarah Morrison and Vikki Reilly at Birlinn.

Just for taking the time to ask how things were going – Suzy Harper, Joanne MacLennan, Innes Morrison and Hannah Onstad.

John Neil Munro
Laxdale
August 2013

Introduction

I love it when people write things about me that aren't true . . . I've no wish to put any of it right. The more contradictory nonsense written about me the better.

In the autumn of 1991, the literary journal *New Writing Scotland* (*NWS*) published a short story by an unknown Edinburgh writer. Buried away on page 145 of the annual anthology, 'The First Day of the Edinburgh Festival' certainly made for interesting and unusual reading. Focusing on a desperate day in the life of a junkie in Scotland's capital city, it was powered by vernacular language coarse enough to make a horse bolt. Promising as the debut story was, though, the consensus was that the writer's best hope was to make his name as a Scottish Bukowski, a cult author writing for a small if devoted readership. Commercial success seemed unlikely for Irvine John Welsh.

Yet just six years later, Welsh's debut novel *Trainspotting*, a dazzling ragtag collection of loosely connected stories, including the one that had first appeared in *NWS*, was voted the best book of the twentieth century in a poll of over 15,000

readers throughout the UK, leaving established classics like
Lord of the Rings, *Nineteen Eighty-Four* and *Catcher in the
Rye* trailing in its wake. By then Welsh was well into a career
that would see him write a string of bestselling follow-up
books.

One of the early editions of *Trainspotting* had an eye-
catching quote on the front cover, courtesy of counter-culture
literary journal *Rebel Inc.*: 'The best book ever written by
man or woman ... deserves to sell more copies than the
Bible'. Although it probably won't ever do that, the sales
figures for *Trainspotting* are seriously impressive. It has sold
over a million copies in the UK alone and has been translated
into 30 languages. The acclaimed stage adaptation has been
produced around the world, and directly inspired the stunning, award-winning film that rebooted the UK film industry, enhanced the careers of a squad of young Scots actors
like Ewan McGregor, Ewen Bremner and Peter Mullan, and
introduced the world to Kelly Macdonald. The author, meanwhile, having created the greatest Scottish cultural phenomenon of the age, was living in exile, a millionaire by all
accounts.

How on earth did that happen? How did a guy who had
seemingly never shown any inclination to be an author write
the most talked-about, most controversial book of a generation – a book that transcended cult status to become required
reading for everyone from couch-bound schemies to high-
flying politicians? Irvine in the early 1980s seemed destined
for a life of anonymity. Having failed to achieve his ambitions to become a footballer or a rock star, he was stuck in a
nine-to-five work routine he hated. People who knew him
back then feared the worst. He was always great company,
very bright and funny, a very clever man pretending not to be
knowing, but he had a certain capacity for self-destruction

and was always chasing oblivion . . . and that was before he tried heroin. How he managed to turn it around, how he went from amiable also-ran with a drink problem to millionaire author with a drink problem is a story that's never been fully told.

Initially, my idea for this book was to write it as a conventional biography. Irvine's an old friend, and when I've read some of the profiles of him over the years, they didn't seem to ring true to the guy I used to know. My impression is that when his first book was published, Irvine, for a laugh, gave out some biographical information full of half-truths and exaggerations, which over the years have become endlessly repeated until they became accepted as fact. *Independent* writer John Walsh summed up eloquently how the press cuttings gave a false image: 'He appears, even after repeated inspections, to be the damnedest thing: a pure writer, an *enfant sauvage*, a literary Kaspar Hauser, raised in darkness, schooled in depravity, unread, unlettered and unlearned but capable, given pen and paper, of producing staggering feats of storytelling.' In fact, the Irvine Welsh I knew back in the 1970s and 1980s was a successful academic who came from a respectable, educated working-class family.

As the critic Elizabeth Young noted, right from the start Irvine was very canny in his dealings with the press: 'He never really gave anything away – particularly regarding drug use. Thus, considering the nature of his fiction, he has been able to avoid becoming a cartoon and been able to maintain his dignity and integrity and get on with his life.' On occasion Irvine would hint that the press profiles bore little similarity to the truth, and often gleefully added to the misinformation by throwing contradictory titbits into an interview. Sometimes he just told lies. There's an interesting line in *Skagboys* that offers some insight into the playful approach he brings to autobiographical revelations in his novels. 'By writing, you can use your own experience but detach it from yourself. You nail certain truths. You make up others. The incidents you invent clarify and explain as much as, sometimes more than, the ones that actually occurred.' I read once that he said he could barely write his own name to sign on the dole in the early 1980s. In fact, he was studying for a degree in social sciences at Essex University around then. To add to the confusion, Irvine is notoriously protective of his private life, refusing to speak in any great detail about his family and friends to outsiders.

And so the man became a bit of a mystery even to those who considered him a friend. He's always had this enigmatic side to his personality, always keen to keep people guessing. I was speaking recently to a mutual friend who has known Irvine for over 30 years, and I asked him what Irvine's brother was up to these days. 'Irvine has a brother?' was the reply. Another old friend recalled: 'When I first met him in 1978 he told me he had a sister, and for years after that I used to ask him how his sister was doing, and he would spin out some elaborate tale about her. Needless to say, I was pretty miffed years later when I mentioned his sister to another of his pals and he said, "What sister? He doesn't have one; he's only got a brother!"' The consequence of all this misinformation is, inevitably, confusion. In 1997 the Edinburgh *Evening News* reported that neither of Irvine's parents had ever spoken about their son's success; yet his father died eleven years before *Trainspotting* was published. Another misguided reporter, this time from the *Western Mail*, stated that Welsh was born in 1961 and grew up in the 'Morningside housing projects' in the city. Wrong, wrong, wrong.

I thought it was about time that a book was written that corrected a few of these myths and gave some accurate biographical details on the man. I wrote to Irvine, back in November 2007, asking if he would contribute to this book.

His reply was polite but firm. 'One thing I've never done and will never do is expose family members, close friends or even ex-work colleagues in any way. My family have always wanted to be private, and I've kept them out of the way of everything with my writing life. I've extended that same right to everyone else in my life, whether they like it or not. Anyway, I can't even begin to express how dull my life is, that's why I get on with my fiction.' So, if you bought this book in the hope of finding out about Irvine's marriages, his mum, his brother, his pets, etc, then I'm afraid you are going to be disappointed. Maybe it's best to leave that story to the man himself, though I doubt he will write an autobiography soon. Neither is this book some scholarly analysis of the meaning of *Trainspotting* – best to leave that type of thing to scholars, I think.

Rather, this is a book that I hope explains how the *Trainspotting* book, stage play and film were made, and the remarkable impact each had. Again, Irvine was less than keen about this idea, and initially said that, though he would not try to block it, he would not contribute in any way. Despite these initial protestations, Irvine gradually began to take an interest and send corrections and contributions when time allowed. His reluctance to get involved was partly because of his heavy workload. At the time, he was finishing a new novel, judging a fiction prize and about to start preparatory work on a new film, which would be followed by a promotional tour for his book in the US and the UK.

Another reason for him not getting involved is that Irvine genuinely tired of talking about *Trainspotting* many years ago. He told me: 'I'm highly flattered, but it's not for me at the moment. I've had a couple of approaches, and to be honest the whole *Trainspotting* thing is a bit of a drag, and I feel that I've read, talked and discussed it a hundred times more than I ever want to. So, you'll forgive me if I don't get

involved – I really have said more than I would have wanted
to in a million lifetimes about it, most of it nonsense made up
on the spot in response to daft questions, basically to avoid
sounding like a parrot. I'm still surprised that people are so
fascinated by it – not that I'm complaining. I think people in
Scotland maybe see *Trainspotting* as something a lot bigger
and more important than it really is. Anyway, it's hard to be
objective and honest about your own journey in life, especially if you're programmed to go relentlessly forward.' It's
undeniable that the book has cast a big shadow over his life,
and there must be a sense of frustration that he will for ever
be known as the '*Trainspotting* author'; on the other hand,
that cross must get a little easier to bear when the royalty
cheques drop through his letterbox twice a year.

Irvine believes that, even though they never gained the same
level of commercial success or critical acclaim, some of his subsequent books – such as *Marabou Stork Nightmares* and *Filth* –
have been stronger than *Trainspotting*. He may be right. I remember, when I first read *Trainspotting*, being amazed that someone
I knew could write something so powerful and downright good.
I read it again recently, and of course this time around it didn't hit
me quite as hard. There are parts of the book that are still pretty
terrifying and also quite beautiful. *Trainspotting* is best when
Irvine writes about the things he knows most about – football,
violence, music, sex, boozing and drugs. It takes you to some
pretty dark and scary places, but it also makes you laugh until
you ache. But there are also long passages that are much weaker,
and short stories that add nothing to the overall narrative. (It's
also questionable whether *Trainspotting* is even the best book
that emerged from the new wave of Scots writing in the 1990s.
Morvern Callar, by Alan Warner, would certainly run it close.)

Even so, it remains a remarkable, powerful read, and
surely worthy of a book that explains – twenty years on –
how Irvine came to write it and the impact that it had.

There are plenty of critics who will nip away at Irvine's reputation, who will tell you that James Kelman and Tom Leonard wrote in the vernacular long before Irvine did, or that Alexander Trocchi wrote about heroin addicts while Irvine was still a toddler. But that kind of misses the point. Prior to 1993 I had never read Leonard or Trocchi. Now, for the first time, someone was writing in a non-judgemental way about a culture and people that I knew very well. I think that was the same for countless other *Trainspotting* aficionados; the whole 'shock of the new' aspect blew them away. Suddenly they were witnessing characters they thought they recognised from their everyday lives in literature for the first time, and they were being written about in a stylish, funny and impartial way in a language they understood. Irvine turned an awful lot of people on to reading (and some even to writing) when he wrote *Trainspotting*.

This book is divided, roughly, into four parts. The quotes which open each chapter are all by Irvine Welsh, unless indicated otherwise. The first few chapters centre on Irvine prior to the publication of the book, his obsession with Hibs and rock music, his wilderness years and the gradual interest in writing. Hopefully these chapters will, at last, provide some accurate biographical detail about the man. The second section details Irvine's own history of drug abuse and the social problems in communities like Muirhouse in Edinburgh that were the background for the tales told in *Trainspotting*. There's also a chapter on the writers who influenced and emboldened him. The third part explains how he broke on to the literary scene, firstly through football and literary fanzines before finally winning a book contract with one of the most famous publishers in the UK. The final few chapters centre on the subsequent stage play and film and the influence they have had. The focus of this book is primarily on Irvine's debut novel and the unfolding of the associated *Trainspotting* phenomenon up until 1997, when he made a triumphant return to the US, the land where he first started writing what was to become *Trainspotting*. To go further or to write about Irvine's later works would need another 76,000 words, and I wouldn't wish that even on my worst enemy.

1

Second maisonette on the right

There was a sense of being trapped when I was a teenager. I always wanted to be somewhere else. Not because I hated where I came from – the reverse, in fact, I loved where I came from – just because I wanted to see different things. But I sensed I didn't have the social ammunition to function in another environment.

In 2002, Irvine Welsh travelled to Afghanistan. Almost a decade on from the release of his debut novel *Trainspotting*, Irvine was in the permanently war-torn land to report on work being done by the children's charity Unicef. Walking through the pot-holed streets of Kabul, which were littered with rusting tanks and ancient cars, he came across a large housing scheme dotted with five-storey flats. As he surveyed the poorly maintained, ramshackle homes his first thoughts were that this grindingly poor society where everyone seemed to have access to a Kalashnikov reminded him strongly of just one place – Muirhouse, the notorious Edinburgh housing estate where he had grown up during the 1960s and 1970s.

*

It takes under half an hour on the number 14 bus to get from
Edinburgh's bustling, affluent city centre to Muirhouse, but
it feels like you have travelled to another world. Even at
quarter past ten on a beautiful, sunny August morning,
Muirhouse has an air of menace about it. Outside the shopping centre, three winos who look like they have staggered
off a *Trainspotting* stage set are conducting an earnest
conversation over an al-fresco round of Super Lager. As I
walked quickly past one of them, a stout bespectacled woman
of indeterminate age, wearing a shellsuit, yelled: 'Ah telt the
cow she wiz a cow.' For a second I considered introducing
myself and asking them their opinion of Irvine Welsh, but a
glower from the female persuaded me that the better part of
valour was, as ever, discretion.

In the neat and tidy local library, the friendly staff were
working on a display informing the locals of the latest attempt
to improve the area. Part of the 21st Century Homes for
Edinburgh regeneration scheme, the project will see the
construction of nearly 800 new homes. Up on Muirhouse
Avenue, where Irvine grew up, work was already under way
tearing down the existing maisonettes.

Hopefully the revamp of the area will include the bulldoz-
ing of the 'mall'. Aside from the ubiquitous Co-op, the only
stores that seem to be doing good business are Gregg's the
baker, a chip shop, a couple of bookies, a Salvation Army
charity shop and, of course, the Gunner pub, arguably one of
the most intimidating hostelries in the western world. The
covered walkway that leads to the library is equally grim, and
probably best not entered after dark. The aim of the regeneration project is to create a 'viable and sustainable community',
and with luck they'll get it right this time around. The long-
suffering people of Muirhouse certainly deserve better.

Like many post-war Scottish council housing estates,
Muirhouse was a project founded on good intentions but

crippled by fatal design flaws. The development, to house families who had been uprooted by the slum clearances from the city centre, was started in 1953 on land once owned by the Duke of Buccleuch and covered by fields of corn and wheat. Within a couple of years this bucolic idyll was transformed into a sprawling mess of new housing, a mix of maisonettes and high-rise blocks, the biggest of which was the towering 23-storey Martello Court. Though some of the projects had state-of-the-art underfloor heating, a combination of post-war financial constraints, use of poor-quality building materials and timber shortages meant that the planned dream homes eventually ended up as basic, flat-roofed, metal-window-framed flats which were always going to be vulnerable to the ravages of the cold and damp Scottish climate. The estate was also bereft of decent shops and amenities; essentially, it was just lots of cheap housing where families had very little to do. Simple, life-enhancing things like phoneboxes, adequate street and walkway lighting, and play areas for kids seemed to have been forgotten by the planners.

Still, Irvine recalls how the 1960s was a time of optimism, with young working families moving into the area. For a while morale was high and there was a real community spirit, with most locals in regular employment and eager to make the best of where they lived. Anyone interested in finding out more about what went wrong in Muirhouse is well advised to check out *Never Give Up*, an excellent book brought out by the North Edinburgh Social History Group. A community that could once rely on well-paid work from the local brickworks, wireworks and ironworks was gradually hit by de-industrialisation and soul-sapping high levels of unemployment. By the late 1970s, Muirhouse was cut adrift from the rich tourist traps of the city centre and the New Town and was beset by a sadly familiar chain of interlinked social problems: lengthy dole queues, poor health, rising crime levels, vandalism, backcourts strewn with refuse, smashed windows and boarded-up empty homes.

But it would be wrong to depict Muirhouse as a lost cause. Reading through back issues of the neighbourhood newspaper *Commune*, it's plain that this was a strong community with an open, generous spirit, ready to campaign vigorously against poor housing and poor health. It wasn't unknown for activists to occupy the City Chambers to protest over council rent rises or the council policy of selling off homes cheaply to private-sector companies, which then did up the homes and sold them off at prices locals could never afford. The activists' struggle got much harder in the 1980s, with Thatcherism at its peak and an influx of cheap heroin from Pakistan. Within a matter of years, the community was floored by the drug, and Muirhouse became the estate worst hit by a scourge that saw Edinburgh branded the drugs and Aids capital of Europe. Crime and gang violence became commonplace. The community's centrepiece, the Martello Court high-rise, became known as 'Terror Tower', and the Gunner earned a reputation for being one of the toughest pubs in Scotland, with a fearsome clientele. There's a great line in *Laidlaw*, one of the books which inspired Irvine to start writing, where William McIlvanney describes a similar Glasgow scheme as an 'architectural dump where they unloaded the people like slurry'. Irvine would no doubt have recognised the description from his own experience.

The fog of misinformation that surrounds Irvine once threw up a tale that he actually grew up in Silverknowes, the leafy, middle-class district near Muirhouse. Irvine set the record straight when he proudly told the *Evening News* in March 1996: 'I come from Muirhouse, the Avenue. Turn left at the doctor's surgery on Pennywell Road, second maisonette on the right. It's bad enough being an old punk from Muirhouse, but an old hippie from Silverknowes . . . no way!

They'll be saying I'm a Jambo next. Now that would be damaging!' A flick through the valuation roll for 1971 proves Irvine right. The Welsh family resided at 30/6 Muirhouse Avenue, a thin-walled, three-bedroomed apartment. *Trainspotting* fans will be amused to discover that among the family's close neighbours on the avenue were a Mr Renton and a Mrs Frances Begbie.

So, yes, Irvine was brought up in Muirhouse, though as ever with Mr Welsh the story is not quite so straightforward. Irvine was born in Edinburgh's Elsie Inglis Maternity Hospital on 27 September 1957. It might surprise readers to find out that the fanatical Hibs fan's first words were 'God bless Willie Bauld'. Irvine's paternal grandfather was a Hearts fan who forlornly tried to set Irvine on the same path by teaching him words of praise for the Hearts striker, one-third of the legendary Terrible Trio of the 1950s. The misinformation trail will tell you that at the time of Irvine's birth, his dad was a Leith docker. Again, not strictly true. Peter Ronald Welsh, Irvine's father, did work for a while on the docks – as had Irvine's grandfather – but he gave it up after a bout of tuberculosis, and by 1957 he was working as a carpet salesman. (Incidentally, the only time I met Mr Welsh senior was in the early 1980s, when he was working as a civilian employee of Lothian and Borders Police.) Peter Welsh hailed from Newhaven, a quiet, picturesque former fishing village that neighbours Leith. Irvine recalls his dad telling him that when he was courting Irvine's mum, Jean, he persuaded her to walk around the narrow ledge that surrounded the local lighthouse. Only when she had successfully negotiated the perilous walk would he ask her to marry him. Mr Welsh was apparently keen on such tests, once playfully suspending Irvine upside down by his ankles over the River Forth.

At the time of Irvine's birth, Peter and Jean (née Lamb) were living at 13 Canonmills, a district some distance from

Leith on the edge of the New Town. The family then lived for a few months with Irvine's aunt Betty and uncle Willie in Prince Regent Street, Leith. They subsequently moved to a prefab in Pilton for a couple of years until, when Irvine was aged just four, they moved up the coastline that fringes the Firth of Forth to Muirhouse. By the mid-1970s though, the Welsh family had moved to a slightly more upmarket council estate on the western periphery of the city. When Irvine started raking in the cash from his writing, one of the first things he did was shell out £19,000 to buy the council property for his mum, who opted to stay there rather than move into a plush new home elsewhere.

Psychologists searching for clues of an unhappy childhood that might explain some of the shocking storylines Irvine later dreamed up in his books are set to be disappointed. By all accounts Irvine had a remarkably stable childhood, albeit one that was clouded by his father's ill-health. His parents were, in Irvine's own words, 'very much in love', although there were plenty of arguments, mostly about politics. From the little Irvine has spoken about his early years, it would seem to have been an unremarkable working-class Scottish childhood. The social calendar for Muirhouse kids was limited, with only a scabby patch of rough ground outside their home for them to play on. The local chip shop was the place where he went to meet pals and girls. Otherwise, apart from football, there were trips to a nearby wood, where you could swing on branches and collect wood for building bonfires. (In fact, these woods were where Irvine had his first clumsy sexual encounters.) There were also times spent on the nearby golf course, and 'tormenting the occupants of police cars by banging sticks on railings', to keep the kids amused. Probably the most exciting times were trips made to an old haunted house near Silverknowes beach, where a dead cat was strung up in one of the rooms. While at the beach

Irvine and his pals would smash crabs caught in pools and poke at jellyfish. At home he watched exploitation films and crap TV shows like *Crossroads*. His fascination with the legendary Midlands soap remains strong to this day, and he considers it 'ten times funnier and more surreal than *Twin Peaks*'. For many years he kept a scrapbook featuring *Crossroads* stars such as Noele Gordon and Jane Rossington. Irvine told me that Bruce Forsyth was another unlikely favourite back then. 'I remember finding a Conservative Party rosette during an election and wearing it in pubs on the [Leith] Walk, claiming to be the Tory candidate, with my mate Willie McDermott acting as my agent. I spoke in a loud Bruce Forsyth accent and was roundly abused in every boozer we hit.'

Under-age drinking was de rigueur in Muirhouse. As to when Irvine first got drunk, this depends on which article you read. In one interview he talks of imbibing poisonous home-brews made by friends at the age of twelve. According to another cutting, he got drunk for the first time two years after the home-brew experiment, when he went camping with some pals on the Isle of Arran. Back then, drugs were a no-no, and although he discovered the hallucinogenic effects of Airfix glue at the age of nine, one suspects that was just from constructing model planes rather than any wilful attempt to get wrecked. It wasn't until his late teens that he first tried dope, speed or acid.

Irvine's mother worked in a restaurant frequented by Sean Connery (whom she described as a real gentleman and a good tipper). Even so, Irvine's diet, as for most Scottish kids back in the 1960s, was a nutritionist's nightmare, with lots of pies, mince and tatties, and, as a special treat, battered fish on a Friday. Holidays were rare events for the Welsh family, though Irvine fondly recalls trips to Blackpool for the September weekend, where the hours were spent building sandcastles and going on donkey rides. In his later teenage years Irvine went to Great Yarmouth on a drunken lads' holiday, and it was there that he got the skull-and-dice tattoo on his forearm. Slightly more exotic breaks came when he was packed off on summer holidays to visit relatives in Dublin, Nairn, Wolverhampton and Southall, west London. The latter destination, where he stayed with his aunt Jessie, was a favourite with Irvine. 'I'd spend loads of time there from an early age, and stayed there with my aunt for a while. It ingrained London and travel into my psyche from an early age. And as I was staying with relatives, it made moving to a new place to live, rather than just for a holiday, seem like a comfortable option.' His first proper overseas holiday came when, aged sixteen, he and some mates went to Lloret de Mar on the Costa Brava for a break, later saying: 'I couldn't wait to get away. I had such a desire for independence. We were just scabby, spotty young guys, getting up to all kinds of drunken *Ibiza Uncovered* mischief ... chasing women, drinking excessively, puking up.'

According to Irvine, Muirhouse was a community where everyone was a storyteller but no one wrote. Both his parents had an interest in reading, though their small council apartment had few books and was bereft of a bookcase or shelf space. Books were not seen as something to hold on to. Instead, friends and relatives would give the Welsh family tatty paperbacks by writers like Catherine Cookson, and those books would then be passed on to neighbours or acquaintances. The idea that a working-class kid like Irvine would one day write novels was just a fantasy, though Mrs Welsh would later encourage Irvine to persevere with his writing when he started to take it up seriously. Irvine's dad died before his son's writing success, but his mum is by all accounts proud of her son's achievements; she reads Irvine's books and apparently loves them. As Irvine told the

Guardian's School's Out page: 'She's quite broadminded. She used to get on to me about the swearing, but she doesn't even do that any more.' After a few years of reluctance, she now attends launches and readings, and 'stalks' her son when he is back in Edinburgh to do a reading or a book signing.

Both parents were supportive of their son. Welsh senior, who Irvine says came from a family of scammers, told him that 'you can do anything, but make sure you get away with it'. But as with any parent–child relationship, there were bound to be tensions. Welsh recalls his father recoiling at the sight of T. Rex performing 'Get It On' on *Top of the Pops* in 1971. This, of course, served to reinforce Irvine's growing infatuation with pop music, and like most kids back then he used music as a way of alienating adults. He soon had posters of Iggy Pop and Debbie Harry on his bedroom wall. Like any young male in the 1970s with a pulse, Irvine had a crush on the Blondie lead singer, so when he was a successful writer and met Debbie Harry he told her that he had 'stiffened a few sheets' staring at her poster. Harry apparently looked him up and down and replied: 'I can't say the same about you, Irvine.'

Both his parents were lifelong Labour voters, and Irvine soon developed a distrust of the middle and upper classes. (As a teenager Irvine's political hero was Tony Benn.) When Margaret Thatcher came to power he grew to despise the Tories, and it wasn't until he became a successful writer that he came into contact with genuinely decent upper-class people like the *Daily Telegraph* columnist Bill Deedes. When he admitted to enjoying their company, one erroneous newspaper report said Welsh would be happy to see David Cameron's Tories take power. Irvine's indignant reaction was the classic line: 'Apart from calling me a paedophile or a Hearts supporter, describing me as a Tory is the worst thing anybody can say about me.' Just to reinforce the point, he told another reporter that he would be the first to party when Margaret Thatcher should die. When the Iron Lady finally pegged it in April 2013, Welsh's hatred of her politics remained undimmed, and he tweeted that 'as heinous as she was, Thatcher, just by the simple virtue of being dead, is nowhere near as offensive as the cunts currently in power'. He maintains a healthy dislike for all mainstream political parties and considers nearly all politicians to be manifestly insincere. He hasn't voted since casting his X for Labour in 1983. He isn't indifferent to politics; he just finds it difficult to select a party that represents his views.

Ainslie Park Secondary School, where Irvine toiled away during the first half of the 1970s, was an establishment always struggling to survive. In 1972 it had 1,430 pupils and 100 staff, but even back then future prospects were bleak after the local council's decision to deprive it of three of its feeder primary schools. Some of the school buildings were seriously sub-standard, with pupils being taught in rows of concrete and wooden huts. The Parents' Charter of the 1980s, which saw parents opting to send their kids to schools with a higher reputation, further reinforced the image of Ainslie Park as a no-hope school, and despite a vigorous campaign by the parents of pupils the school eventually closed. Yet, in its heyday, it was an excellent school, with the motto 'Guid in Need'. The school magazine, *The Dolphin*, ran from 1964, and a swift perusal shows it to have been a thriving school with its own orchestra and successful fencing, rugby, football and hockey clubs. Frustratingly, the magazine was discontinued in 1969, just before Irvine's arrival, so denying us the pleasure of reading his embryonic writings. By then though, the rot had set in, and Irvine recalls his alma mater as being 'pretty crap'.

Irvine never really enjoyed academic life at Ainslie Park. The whole thing seemed a trial, starting with the morning walk to school, when he was regularly chased by semi-feral dogs. He hated most school subjects and always had an eye on escaping the drudgery. One report card stated that he would never amount to anything as he was too much of a dreamer. Irvine told the *Guardian*: 'This was meant as scornful condemnation; even at the time I instinctively felt it was positive, and it provided me with a great deal of affirmation. It often seemed easier to retreat into my head rather than deal with what was going on around me. For such a child, a book is a godsend. Sitting with one in front of me gave me permission to dream and enriched and defined my creative landscape.'

If they had allowed him to just paint and write stories all day he would have been much happier, but he left school aged just sixteen. He cites two teachers as standing out from the rest. His English teacher Irene Tait – who would read excerpts from Lewis Grassic Gibbon to the class – always believed Irvine had a flair for writing, and introduced him to challenging books like Melville's *Moby-Dick* and George Orwell's *Keep the Aspidistra Flying*. Another positive influence was his art teacher, Mrs Cameron, who let him escape the confines of still-life drawing and encouraged him to 'draw all of the weird shit that was in my head and didn't judge me. But the fact is they were both very good-looking and I had massive crushes on them. They made me want to be a mature young man and not a drooling adolescent.'

Away from the classroom, the boy known as 'Taz' or 'Welshy' found the social aspect of school life much more fun, forging and losing friendships and alliances in the playground, always on his guard and trying to avoid the nutters and the bullies, while simultaneously making life a misery for those pupils lower down the chain. In comparison to the nice quiet wee primary school he attended, Ainslie Park was a jungle. He discovered that the only ways to get status were to be a good fighter, which was never an option for Welsh, or to be the class joker or a great footballer. He felt that fellow pupils thought him a bit of a weirdo, always fooling around and joking. Classmates recall a boy with a feathered haircut, which he dyed when Ziggy Stardust first beamed down on to Planet Muirhouse. It is also rumoured that he wore a cream-coloured trench coat on occasion.

With all the other football-mad kids from the area, Irvine took part in epic night-time matches on the wasteland beside the maisonettes on Muirhouse Avenue. Irvine was an enthusiastic player but soon realised his limitations, especially when he came up against a wee kid who lived at 4/4 Muirhouse Grove. Even in the mayhem of those forty-a-side, jumpers-for-goalposts games, played out on a pitch littered with dog mess and broken bottles, a diminutive, flame-haired boy stood out. Gordon Strachan was a couple of years older than Irvine, so the pair were never close mates, though they were both avid Hibs fans. Welsh says he was merely one of the nondescript traffic cones that Gordon would effortlessly weave past during the Muirhouse matches. Strachan went on to win 50 Scottish caps and had a glittering career, most notably at Aberdeen, Manchester United and Leeds (though sadly not for his beloved Hibs, who, astonishingly, thought he was too small to make a telling impact).

Recalling his days in Muirhouse, Irvine gave his verdict to the *Sunday Herald*: 'There was a sense of being trapped when I was a teenager. I always wanted to be somewhere else. Not because I hated where I came from – the reverse, in fact, I loved where I came from – just because I wanted to see different things. But I sensed I didn't have the social ammunition to function in another environment. A lot of that was a kind of self-sabotage, which I think is quite common. Through a convoluted set of circumstances, I realised that I actually could do it, and in a way I've been travelling ever since.'

2

Telford daze

The only two things that I ever wanted to do, seriously, was to play football and to make music and I was shit at them both. So this, the writing game, was very much a third choice for me.

Looking back on his life recently, Irvine described the years between eighteen and twenty-five as a period where he lost his way and led an excessively nihilistic lifestyle. Coincidentally, I'm sure, those were the years when he was one of my closest friends. I first met Irvine on 10 January 1977. I had just escaped off the Isle of Lewis and was sleeping on the floor of my brother's student flat on Inverleith Row in Edinburgh. I was seventeen, and my ambition in life amounted to some vague notion that I could become a roadie for Led Zeppelin. I wasn't really into the whole concept of a nine-to-five job, but after a couple of weeks aimlessly wandering the streets of Edinburgh I was ordered by Jobcentre bosses to work as an audiovisual aids technician at Telford College, out at Crewe Toll, where Irvine was already employed.

We worked in a tiny room called TO3, down in the basement. Our boss was the avuncular Steve Marsden, a good guy who put up with a lot of crap from me and Irvine (who accurately described Steve as a 'placid, pipe-smoking Englishman'). There was also an elderly guy called 'Snowy' Whiteside, who I think was a war veteran from Newcastle and who, along with Steve, was the brains of the operation. They actually knew how to repair the TV and projectors on the numerous occasions when they broke. Irvine probably knew more than I did about fixing the equipment, but that's much the same as saying Bucks Fizz were a better band than Paper Lace. In reality, we were both clueless.

After leaving school, Irvine studied on a City and Guilds electronics technician course at the college before joining the staff. A big presence at just under six foot two, back in those days Irvine had a mess of short hair, roughly cut in a proto-punk style. Unkind critics would later be disparaging about Irvine's appearance, Teddy Jamieson of the *Herald* even going so far as to liken him to 'Shrek's better-looking, fitter brother'. His old friend Sandy Macnair thought Welsh, with a hangover, looked like an 'ageing bloodhound that had been run over by a truck'. The writer Nigel Farndale was equally unimpressed by Irvine's looks, saying he had a head like 'a large lightbulb screwed into his neck'. With his high forehead and slightly chubby face, he might not have been convention-ally good-looking, but even as a gangly, somewhat awkward youth Irvine never had many problems pulling girls. Sometimes, though, things went badly wrong. I recall how one day when he was waiting alone for the lift doors to close, down in the college basement, a particularly attractive female student got into the lift beside him. Irvine asked which floor she wanted and then emitted a rather loud and noxious invol-untary fart just as the doors shut, resulting in an awkward ride up to the fifth floor for both of them. Back when I first met him, though, he didn't have a steady girlfriend, and he often affected a camp, Larry Grayson-style comic manner.

This, though, was just done as a wind-up to confuse 'hard' mates. He later wrote in the *Guardian* how 'growing up in Edinburgh, we had a very black-and-white understanding of people, so women were naturally divided into virgins and whores. That was what I grew up with: there were some lasses that you didn't take home to Mummy . . . Even when I was at my most angsty teenage point, where I desperately wanted as much sex as possible with as many women as possible, I still thought there must be something else. I still had this elusive notion of romance, usually swathed in some kind of tragedy, so I tended to attract unrealistic lasses who were a bit like me. I was never really comfortable with one-night stands; I don't actually think a lot of guys are. I was always more relationship-orientated, and I think that came from my background, where there was a lot of visible love.'

In *Skagboys*, Irvine describes the character Sick Boy as having a smile which when it 'gits turned oan ye, ye feel pure thit you're the chosen yin'. He might well have been writing about himself. Like his hero Iggy Pop, Irvine has a dazzling, transformational smile that can light up a room. Even in his pre-druggie days, he usually spoke in a lazy, low, monotonal Edinburgh accent, and a stranger might have mistaken him as being a shy and diffident individual. But when he had a drink inside him, or when he had an audience, he switched to being the main attraction, a cruel mimic, loud and incredibly funny. Back then he had a liking for screeching *Monty Python* imitations that tended to bring a deathly silence to a busy pub. Occasionally his madcap act would cause offence or lead to confrontations. Mostly, though, Irvine was a popular character with a wide circle of friends. He told me how 'it's a strange thing, but I've always had different scenes and different groups of friends – football mates, people I grew up with, people I worked with, drug-takers and non-drug-takers, musical genres etc. I could never work out why this was.

Sometimes there was a bit of crossover between the groups, but usually not. I suppose that's understandable in London, but it was quite strange and unusual in a smaller city like Edinburgh.'

The day I met Irvine, I scribbled in my diary: 'This may not be the best job in the world but it pays and I'm penniless. Good times are coming!' They certainly were. Irvine might have been a year older than me, but any notion that he could have been a stabilising influence on me was a forlorn one. To put it bluntly, an inebriated Irvine Welsh, full of nervous, chaotic energy, was a genuine nutter.

Back in the late 1970s, Telford College was a bleak, functional building not far from two of the capital's toughest housing estates, Granton and Pilton, and also close to – by way of complete contrast – Tony Blair's alma mater, the ultra-posh Fettes College. Telford's student population was mostly made up of young guys who had messed up at school and now had to study to get back on the career ladder. They were not the friendliest of people, and soon took an instant dislike to the effete, long-haired wastrel whose job it was to try to set up film projectors. On my second day at work, I was left alone in charge of a projector showing a film about contraception to 30 of the most threatening youths in the capital. I survived, and was soon happy to find out that Irvine was just as bored and terrified by the job as I was. Equally welcome was the realisation that we shared similar musical tastes and a fierce thirst for the demon alcohol.

Irvine was a year older than me, but even in his late teens he was set firm on a lifelong devotion to the bevvy. At first we drank separately with our own friends at the weekends, but by Monday lunchtime we were both ready for a livener. On occasion we would travel uptown on the bus and visit Rose Street pubs or Mather's bar in the West End. Another regular lunchtime hangout was the Ken Buchanan Hotel, a

short bus journey away from the college at the other end of
Ferry Road. There the welcome was never really that warm,
as the former world lightweight boxing champ was less than
keen on the two wasters noisily gulping down pints of lager
and annoying the other clientele. The hour-long lunch-break
allowed for five or six pints to be guzzled before we ambled
back to work. Pretty soon the college bosses were on our
case, and I was hauled in before them and asked bluntly
when I last had a bath. This caused Irvine great amusement.

Work at the college usually involved setting up audiovisual
machinery in lecture theatres and then collecting it an hour
or two later. So, there was lots of time to waste. Irvine was
the saving grace; he had a wicked, anarchic sense of humour,
and we soon invented a parallel fantasy college society where
quiet, innocuous lecturers and janitors were reinvented as
dissolute rock stars. I was quite adept at this, but Irvine was
the real instigator, spending hours inventing bands like The
Obnoxious Builders and Willie and the Introverted Janitors.
And he didn't stop at names: vast tour itineraries and back
catalogues of albums were dreamed up. Irvine is a very
talented cartoonist and would add brilliant visuals to the
fantasies. On regular occasions during 1977 the print unions
would go on strike, leaving huge blank spaces on the pages
of the *Sun*. Irvine would spend hours filling the gaps with
spoof stories of the alleged sexual proclivities of some of the
Telford College staff. Back in the late 1970s this was as far
as Irvine's writing ambitions went. And if I had ever predicted
that he would one day become a successful novelist, he would
no doubt have laughed me out of court. But Irvine later
recalled that the seeds of his literary success were probably
sown when he was walking home from Telford College one
day and bumped into Irene Tait, his old English teacher from
Ainslie Park. She asked him whether he was still writing and
encouraged him to do so. Irvine recalls being amazed that

this smart, educated woman, whom he still had a crush on, actually believed that he had the potential to succeed as a writer.

For a man who later made his name and fortune depicting the lives of heroin addicts, Irvine was – back in 1977 – vehemently against any form of illegal drug abuse. Smoking hash, in particular, was treated with disdain: for Irvine, this was the preserve of middle-class bores. Still, you could sense that underneath the stern exterior was a drug fiend in the making. After much persuasion he eventually tried drawing on some of the pleasant Red Leb which dominated the Edinburgh drug scene back in the late 1970s. Predictably, he loved it, and our lunchtime drinking bouts were soon being enhanced by a smoke or two. Once, as we ambled back to work, we stopped off at Fettes College's playing fields to soak up the sun and watch some cricket. It took a couple of minutes to realise that we were actually watching Lothian and Borders Police First Eleven playing and they were watching us puffing away. Time for a quick exit back to the safety of Room TO3.

I lasted six months working at Telford College. Lord knows how. My ineptitude led me to quit on 1 July 1977, after which I took the easy option of enrolling as a student at Stevenson College. Irvine lasted a few more months before moving briefly to London, where he lived in a squat in Shepherd's Bush. In January 1978 he started work as a clerical officer in the General Register Office in Ladywell House, Corstorphine, Edinburgh. His new job was one of unremitting tedium, endlessly checking figures in the Census and Statistics Branch. To counteract the boredom, Irvine picked out a couple of like-minded workmates – Dave Todd and Sandy Macnair – for some fun and games. Dave Todd recalls how 'just about everybody from the bosses down went for a bevvy every lunchtime, so Irvine and I very quickly bonded on the obligatory pub crawl of Rose Street'. The pair's first outing together ended with Welsh vomiting copiously on the carpeted floors of the Ensign Ewart pub – they immediately re-christened the pub the Ensign Spewart – and Dave remembers that 'at least I had the decency to go outside to be sick'. As at Telford College, Welsh and his pals fought off the boredom by winding up work colleagues, sending cartoons to each other and constructing a parallel universe where ordinary employees became the most unlikely of rock stars, such as Eddie and the Messengers, all complete with detailed background biographies on each 'band member'.

My own friendship with Irvine continued after I left Telford College, with the following year punctuated by heavy boozing in the drinking dens of Sighthill and Wester Hailes, with Saturday trips to the east terracing of Easter Road for light relief. Irvine had a second short spell in London before he eventually got his act together and enrolled at the University of Essex in 1978. I drifted back to Stornoway none the wiser, but we kept in contact through letters and occasionally met up for shape-shifting, Edinburgh booze sessions. My diary from back then is full of tales of debauchery in dives like the Clan on Albert Street, Sneaky Pete's, Nicky Tams and the Diggers (the Athletic Arms). The entry for 26 July 1980 went thus: 'Irvine, Willie McD, Sandy and some guy with glasses help me on killer pub crawl of Leith and Easter Road . . . we drank among the prostitutes till 1 a.m. . . . . Willie carried out of the Spey Bar at one point, legless. Much hilarity.' Even with the aid of my diary, memories of those days are understandably sketchy, but they usually involve Welsh getting barred from pubs. We were sitting quietly in the Harp Hotel one Sunday evening when he said to me, 'I hope to God no one plays "You Were Always on my Mind" by Elvis on the jukebox.' A few minutes later he put 10p in the box and played that very song. He then proceeded to sing along very loudly while standing by the jukebox, in the style of Dean Stockwell's character in *Blue Velvet*. Not surprisingly, we were both barred from the Harp Hotel that evening.

Irvine's boyhood ambition was to play football for Hibernian FC. He was infatuated with the club, though he pretty quickly realised that he would never make the grade as a player. 'It was never an option. My gangly, all-legs build made me crap at football, and at fighting.' As a kid, he and his Muirhouse mates, who were mostly fellow Hibees, would make the pilgrimage to Easter Road every other Saturday on the number 16 bus, a trip complete with raucous singing, minor vandalism and under-age drinking. Irvine was lucky in that he grew up during the 1960s, when Hibs actually had a decent side; he idolised players like Peter Marinello, Peter Cormack and Colin Stein, all of whom were flogged off to bigger clubs once they started showing great promise. Such is always the way with Hibs, I'm afraid. Irvine's great hero, though, was Pat Stanton, a supremely talented defender/ midfielder who stayed loyal to the club until near the end of his career. When Irvine took part in kickabouts with his mates, he demanded to 'be' Stanton, hoping forlornly that some of the great man's skills would rub off on him. Stanton was the skipper of manager Eddie Turnbull's team of the 1970s, a quality side that for a brief time looked like it could permanently usurp the two big sides from Glasgow – Celtic and Rangers. It's almost incomprehensible now, but back then Stanton's Hibs went unbeaten in twelve successive games against deadly rivals Hearts. When he made it as a writer, Irvine was asked by the *Scotsman* newspaper what object he desired most in life. His answer was the green-and-white Hibs strip with the number four on its back, belonging to Stanton, whom Irvine also described as 'God without the faults'.

Anyone wanting to know more about Hibs should get a copy of Andy MacVannan's excellent book *We Are Hibernian*, which gives the fans, including Irvine, a platform to explain what the club means to them. Hibs was founded in 1875 by Irish immigrants, and for a long while – even up until the late 1970s – it wasn't uncommon to see Irish tricolour flags being waved and pro-IRA songs being chanted by fans. Irvine certainly knew the words to some of those songs. I vaguely recall both of us being asked, not very politely, to leave a Corstorphine hotel one evening in the early 1980s after Irvine gave vent at full volume to some arcane dirge about the Potato Famine. When I reminded him of that night, he said: 'In the interest of balance, and due to a Protestant, Hearts-supporting extended family, I'd like it recorded that I could also sing "Derry's Walls", "The Sash", "The Old Orange Flute" and "Dolly's Brae" verbatim – and I often did.' These days, though, he still takes some pride in Hibs' historic connection to Ireland; that's about as far as his feelings go. He gives short shrift to sectarianism, the ugly offspring of the Protestant–Catholic divide in central Scotland. Writing once in the *Big Issue*, he said: 'Sectarianism is just another bit of angst that people can grab a hold of to give their lives some kind of strange status. It's all part of the same shite that controls people and keeps them down.'

I was always under the impression that Irvine came from a solid, pure Hibs background. In fact, though his father was a Hibee, the rest of Mr Welsh's family were staunch followers of Heart of Midlothian. Irvine attributes his dad's support of Hibs to him just being awkward, but Mr Welsh left it open to young Irvine to decide which team to support. As was quite common in the early 1960s, he took the boy to both Easter Road and Tynecastle, though Irvine soon took an instant dislike to the latter, hating the stench from the nearby brewery and the maroon strip the Hearts boys played in.

When Irvine first clocked the green-and-white strips of the Hibs players it was love at first sight. His choice of Hibs is interesting, as they are usually portrayed – by their fans at least – as the plucky underdog, dedicated to playing expansive, entertaining football even if it means losing more games than they win. In comparison, city rivals Hearts are depicted as the club of the Edinburgh establishment, who play dour football that always gets them results. Such generalisations are, obviously, simplistic; Hearts have had many brilliant footballers over the years, and I've seen quite a few clubbers and donkeys don the Hibs strip. But Irvine's choice of Hibs tied in neatly with his own romantic, flamboyant outlook on life in the years after he left school.

Even to this day it is hard to overestimate just how much Irvine loves Hibs: he has a fierce, tribal loyalty to the club. As a teenager he obsessively attended every match, home and away, and a defeat would plunge him into a deep depression that would last for days. Now, living thousands of miles from Leith, he is a bit mellower and more Zen-like about the club's fortunes, admitting to me that 'there are times when I've been passionate and other times where I've not really given a fuck'. He's backed them for almost 50 years of underachievement punctuated by fleeting spells of brilliance, with three League Cups the sum total of major honours won. His writing gives him the frequent opportunity to praise the Hibs in print and also to take a sly kick at the Hearts. His early letters to me contained regular updates on the team's fortunes and showed his emerging talent as a humorous writer. Even in the darkest times he adopted the maxim, 'The worse they get, the more I love them'. So, in November 1978, still smarting from a defeat to Hearts, he predicted that 'the Scottish League seems in a state of flux right now, but once Hibs find some consistency, we've as good as won it'. A few months later they were relegated. At the end of that season, when Hibs made it to the Scottish Cup Final, he showed his devotion to the cause by hitchhiking up from Colchester while under the influence of a particularly strong dose of LSD. The journey was broken by a night in the cells in Grantham after 'an incident in a café', but Irvine eventually made it to Hampden, only to see Hibs fail again.

His letters contained occasional serious insights into Hibs' continuing misfortunes. In one missive, he stated: 'Was at Hibs v. Celtic game and I'm pleased to announce that despite only taking two points from the last three games, the picture is not as bleak as it superficially looks. The boys are actually playing interesting, attacking football and are far more watchable than the bad Auld days. Once Jackie Mac returns from suspension and he and Welsh link up in front of Roughie things will be sound. The embryonic midfield of Conroy, Callachan and Tommo (a nice-looking boy, but loves a scrap) looks promising. Once again it's up front that fucks things up.'

In November 1984 he wrote, after Pat Stanton had been replaced as manager by John Blackley: 'God has gone, long live God, meaning John B has taken over the helm from Paddy S. I like the look of our new boy, "Hot Shot" Gordon Durie, the "striking miner" from East Fife. He produced four strikes Art Scargill would've been proud of in two games against the Huns and Sons. We also recently outplayed Jambos whose usually pathetic, dour, stunted, Presbyterian play stole them a negative point and sent the crowd home sleeping. The [Hibs] team sheet still reads like the track listing of a Bucks Fizz album. The odd gem, but still a lot of dead wood to be chopped out and new releases to be included before greatest hits can be released.'

I always felt that his love of Hibs was perhaps only matched by his intense dislike of city rivals Hearts. In a letter in early 1981 he summed up his feelings towards them in an

alliterative frenzy. 'The Hearts are a penny-pinching
Presbyterian pack of putrid poofs. They disgust me with their
pathetic parochial Scottish traditionalism, and their chairman is a backwoodsman with a crappy newsagent shop.' But
one shouldn't read too much into this – much of Welsh's
perceived hatred of the Hearts was exaggeration, invariably
alcohol-fuelled. He told me: 'I never really disliked them that
much. I always took great delight in winding them up, but
my Jambo mates and family members always gave as good as
they got. "Hatred" in a youthful performative way is different from a deep personal hatred, which I never had.' He
wasn't brought up to despise Hearts, and still has a number
of friends who support the club, but he recalls bitter arguments over the merits of the teams even with family members.
As a youngster he was fascinated to see how mild-mannered
friends, full of drink, would turn on each other at the New
Year's Day derby match and engage in sometimes violent
arguments. It showed him the power of football for the first
time. With the introduction of segregation on the terraces in
the 1970s, things got a lot nastier at derby matches. Bizarrely,
as Sandy Macnair revealed in his book *Carspotting*, Welsh
once applied for the manager's job at Hearts in the summer
of 1977 after compiling an elaborate fake CV. The Tynecastle
bosses gave the job to the club's coach, Tony Ford, but Irvine's
rejection letter took pride of place on the wall of his home
for years.

The hatred between both sets of fans often spilled into
violence. I remember Irvine telling how he was walking away
from Tynecastle after a derby match, and as he walked under
a railway bridge he saw a group of Hearts fans baying for
blood. He had resigned himself to a kicking when from
behind he heard the raucous chanting of hundreds of Hibs
fans, a noise that sent the Hearts boys scurrying up a side
street like frightened rats. 'I have never been more happy in

my life to hear the sound of grown men singing badly,' Irvine said. I always felt that, at heart, Irvine had an almost visceral interest in violence. Like his alter-ego Renton, in *Skagboys*, he only really gets violent when he is scared and when his eloquence has failed to calm the crisis. We used to have a catchphrase when a friend was in danger of a kicking: 'Let's offer support, but just moral support, right?' Once at a derby game we spent the entire 90 minutes taunting the Hearts fans with the usual 'See you outside' nonsense. After the game, walking down Easter Road we spied a group of Hearts skinheads heading our way. I've never seen scarves removed from necks quicker, and we escaped unnoticed.

Irvine has written about having several 'half-arsed fights rolling around in gutters . . . I was a crap fighter who usually fought other crap fighters' as a youth, but I think that was the sum total of his involvement in the gang scene. Yet he had an almost encyclopaedic knowledge of the Edinburgh gangs and would talk knowledgably about the relative strengths and merits of outfits like the Clerry Derry, Young Niddrie Terror, The Bar-Ox, Young Mental Drylaw (YMD) and the Young Leith Team, whose YLT graffiti can still be seen on walls in Leith.

The YMD were known for violent forays into Muirhouse, leading to wild fights with sticks, knives and knitting needles. Observing the behaviour of these radges helped Irvine to write so accurately and skilfully about violence in *Trainspotting*. 'I was in some ways both fortunate and unfortunate regarding street gang/football stuff. Nutters who loved a scrap always liked having me around for some reason, even though I could be something of a liability in a brawl. But there were always mugs in the other squad too; you tended to pair off with them. One time I had such a crap fight with a guy in Lothian Road, the bams on both sides actually half-stopped it out of embarrassment. They pulled us apart and went down the road. My best mate threatened to kick my cunt in for such a poor show.

'I love the terrace football hooliganism. It was toy violence, just charging and flaying and swaying across a no-man's-land. You didn't have to be a great fighter to get involved. But when it went out into the streets I lost interest. I took a kicking up at Dundee once; I went down and couldn't get up. I woke up in Ninewells Hospital. After that, the enterprise became a bit too rich for my blood. In retrospect it was a good thing; it showed I was a rubbish, windmilling street-fighter with the balance of a newborn foal. Whenever I fought I generally came off second best. I was too gangly, all legs. When I went down it was game over. So I stopped.

'The only time I've ever been violent in the last 30-odd years is all damsel-in-distress stuff. I battered a guy who insulted Anne [Irvine's first wife], punched an acquaintance for insulting her in a Stoke Newington pub, and nutted a guy who was trying to harass Beth [Irvine's second wife] at a party. In my late thirties I took up martial arts, particularly boxing, generally as a way of keeping fit, but also with the intention of doing a charity celebrity fight which never materialised. I thought learning how to punch and take a punch would be a useful skill-set for the streets. I know, though, I would have to have a cause to be coldly effective in a fight, and if it came to a street rammy, I'd just panic and revert to flailing, ineffective type.'

3

If it hadn't been for the Pistols and The Clash . . .

Ah'm too poncy to be a proper Leith gadgie n too fuckin schemie tae be an arty student type.

Renton's self-analysis in Skagboys

Most post-*Trainspotting* profiles portray Irvine as a punk singing in bands such as Stairway 13 and wasting away the late 1970s and early 1980s on the dole in Edinburgh and London. In reality, Irvine enrolled as a social sciences undergraduate at the University of Essex in the autumn of 1978 and remained there until graduation in 1981. But he did mess around in a lot of bands with a variety of personnel during this period. Off the top of his head Irvine remembers outfits called Pubic Lice, Pollution, Hate, Crude Oil and The Unstoppables. But they never really amounted to much more than aimless, youthful fun. His long-term drinking buddy Sandy Macnair describes Pubic Lice and another group The Southside Wasters as being 'somewhat on the fictional side', the latter consisting of Welsh and Macnair composing spoof songs at home to the tune of well-known rock classics. Irvine

believes these early forays into songwriting laid the basis for
his later prose writing, as whenever he tried to write lyrics
they tended to lead to storywriting.

Contrary to what has been written in countless articles,
'Stairway 13' was a song rather than a band. As Irvine
recounts: 'It was written by Eric Ross from Duddingston, a
Rangers fan whom I farted around at music with. It was a
song about death-trap stadiums and fans being penned in
like animals. Eric had a friend or relative who was badly hurt
in the 1971 Ibrox disaster.' Pubic Lice recorded a demo of
'Stairway 13' along with a couple of other songs, 'Our Town'
and 'Iceland', though they weren't up to much. According to
Sandy Macnair, another song, 'Strictly Cowdenbeath', 'made
The Damned sound like the Mahavishnu Orchestra'. By his
own admission, Irvine was worse than hopeless as a musi-
cian, going 'from guitar to bass to fuck all'. As a bassist, he
was definitely more Sid Vicious than Jaco Pastorius.

Musically inept he may have been, but Irvine, then as now,
had an almost obsessive love of music and was a genuine
punk. I've read some profiles that say he was living in squats
in London and pogoing to bands like Slaughter and the Dogs
at the Vortex club in clothes smeared in dogshit when the
punk revolution happened. Maybe he did later, but back in
1976 and 1977 he was still living with his parents and working at Telford College in Edinburgh. But he did love punk
music, and I remember us both buying the Sex Pistols' 'God
Save The Queen' on the day of its release, on the Virgin label
in the summer of 1977, during a lunch break from the grind
of working at Telford College. He recalls that day as being
crucial in his decision to move on from Telford and do something more with his life. 'I think that was a really pivotal
moment in my life. I felt like something had shattered inside.
I remember looking at you, and us deciding that there was no
staying where we were. There's no question that day changed

my life. We just realised then there was no way we could stay working there. We had to take off and do what we really wanted to do. And about eighteen months later I was in London. If it hadn't been for the Pistols and The Clash I would never have written *Trainspotting*.' Irvine was certainly a music fan prior to punk rock, though he was always more in the glam-rock camp of Bowie and Iggy Pop as opposed to the long-hair-and-denim bands like Yes and Genesis. He did have quite wide-ranging musical tastes; the only two 'serious' bands I recall him saying he actively disliked were The Beach Boys and Steely Dan. He has since learned to love The Beach Boys, but he still has an unfathomable loathing for Becker and Fagen's band.

Once the *NME* rejected the old guard en masse, Irvine followed their lead, and when he moved south in 1978 he symbolically sold his copy of Pink Floyd's *Wish You Were Here* to Dave Todd. Irvine, incidentally, is also a connoisseur of bad 1970s pop, and revels in the awfulness of Boney M, David Soul and, in particular, the 1973 aural atrocity that is Barry Blue's 'Dancin' (On A Saturday Night). Dave Todd reminded me of the Barry Blue connection. 'It usually happened in a crowded bar like the Diggers or Sandy Bell's. He would belt out that song over and over again at the top of his voice. We would be putting our hands over his mouth trying to gag him, but then he was still singing it behind your hand. Sometimes he would be up on the chairs or a table singing it! By the thousandth verse it was not funny and even worse for the rest of the bar. Invariably it ended with the pub landlord shouting, "Right, lads . . . *out!!!*"' Irvine explained: 'This was more to annoy the fuck out of everybody rather than a genuine love of the music. But I still sing David Soul and Sheena Easton in karaoke. I've no singing voice, but I love to sing. With karaoke you have to be either very good or very bad at it for it to work.'

Back in the late 1970s, as he flirted with the idea of trying
for a career in music, there were few signs that he had any
real interest in literature. I certainly cannot remember him
citing favourite authors or books. Sandy Macnair does,
however, recall very early stirrings of interest. 'It would be
hard to pinpoint a time when Irvine definitively took a decision to try his hand at serious writing. I suppose my earliest
recollections of his interest would be around 1979–81, when
I was resident in the notorious Southside flat. I remember
Irvine, myself and another guy, Brocky, having a series of
weekly "literary" get-togethers when we kicked around ideas
for producing some sort of regular publication. We were
influenced by punk fanzines and satirical magazines and
were adopting a black-humour approach to the nascent ned
culture of that time, with articles sometimes written in the
first person, an approach Irvine developed to considerable
effect in *Trainspotting*. But at the time it was all very vague
and never amounted to anything concrete. Around this time
we put together *The Southside Wasters Songbook Volumes
One and Two*, which was hundreds of spoof rock songs we
had written. But I have no particular memories of him
expressing any interest in writing seriously at this stage – we
were both just having a laugh, basically.'

The other outlet for Irvine's writing talent back in those
days was his letters to friends. When he moved to London
and Colchester he would write regularly back home to
Scotland. Sandy Macnair recalls getting correspondence
from Welsh on an almost daily basis, though sadly these
letters have been lost over the years. I managed to hang on to
about twenty letters and cards, and reading them you can see
Irvine's latent talent breaking through. Mostly they consist of
wickedly funny satirical skits about people he knew or
worked with. Sandy says people of a violent and/or stupid
disposition featured highly in his usual output. And, of

course, there were more incredibly detailed spoof discographies and tour itineraries of the imaginary rock groups we used to dream up. It was always somewhat reassuring to discover that Willie and the Introverted Janitors were still filling stadiums in the States, at least in Welsh's weird imagination. Most of the time it was just juvenile banter between mates, but every now and then there was a classy bit of prose that hinted at future greatness.

Just prior to enrolling at the University of Essex, Irvine, along with Dave Todd and Sandy Macnair, travelled down from Edinburgh by bus to see Bob Dylan headline at the Blackbushe music festival. The gig on Saturday, 15 July 1978 saw around 200,000 music heads flock from all over the UK to the Hampshire airport for Dylan's near-three-hour-long epic show and a bill that also included Eric Clapton, Joan Armatrading and Graham Parker and the Rumour. Dave Todd recalls: 'We left on the Friday night on the overnight Citylink bus after a few pints in the grotty Highwayman pub in the bus station. All we were armed with for the whole weekend was our carry-out for the bus. We had no food, no change of clothes or anoraks. Sandy and me had the obligatory jeans, T-shirts and denim jackets. Irvine, though, wore a green sports jacket, checked shirt and jeans along with Doc Martens, which he said were for standing on the hippies' feet.'

The overnight bus to London was a rite of passage for just about every working-class Scots kid around then. It was a soul-sapping journey through the dark spine of England, surrounded by drunken, antsy Scots and the noxious stench of cigarette smoke and the chemical toilet. Irvine made the bus trip many times, and used his experience well in *Trainspotting* when the boys head to the Smoke to score dope. He told me: 'That fucking bus journey used to be the bane of my life. The one extravagance I have now is a

first-class Edinburgh to London railway ticket.' Dave Todd
remembers Irvine taking the lead in demolishing their massive
stock of Export, wilfully defying the Citylink staff's pleas of
'Nae drinking on the bus!' Near the end of the trip, Welsh,
inebriated and in madcap mode, covered his head with a
blanket and gave the fellow passengers a mock tour guide to
the delights of London's suburbs. He enjoyed Dylan's gig,
but the whole concept of open-air festivals never really
appealed to Irvine. At the 1979 Ingliston Festival outside
Edinburgh he was refused entry after trying to gatecrash
barriers with his carry-out of Export.

Back in those days, Irvine was seemingly always pushing
his luck with the custodians of licensed premises. Dave Todd
remembers Irvine entering Sandy Bell's pub one day, drinking
a can of Export. 'The bar manager told him, "Son, you
cannae drink a can in here, so just finish it and I'll put it in
the bucket for you." Irv finished it and handed it over without a word, and promptly takes a new can out of his pocket
and opens it at the bar!'

Irvine's musical tastes during his university days reflected
his own personality, an appealing mix of street-tough gang
culture and the outrageously camp. His holy trinity, all of
whom would influence his writing, were Iggy, Bowie and
Lou Reed – three men who were as likely to carry a tube of
mascara as a switchblade in their pockets. Irvine had an
almost freakish knowledge of Bowie's work and was prone
to grilling people in the pub with questions like 'Who played
violin on *Lodger*?' or 'Which English county was Bowie's
father from?' Irvine had been an avid fan of the Mainman
ever since seeing the Ziggy Stardust show on 6 January 1973
at the Empire Theatre in Edinburgh.

Only Iggy Pop rivalled Bowie as a source of inspiration for
Welsh's subsequent writing. He was a fan from the early
1970s onwards and saw him first on Iggy's *New Values* tour

in 1979, and then again in London in 1983. The influence Iggy has on Irvine is sometimes all too obvious – the Stooges' classic song 'Death Trip' has the line 'Sick boy, sick boy baby now learning to be cruel'. Irvine idolised and copied Iggy in the way a younger sibling would look up to a delinquent, crazy big brother. Welsh attributes many of his problems in the early 1980s to his fascination with Iggy and his desire to ape his hedonistic drugs-and-booze-fuelled lifestyle. Bizarrely, he now counts Iggy as a good friend, seeing him about four times a year. At the time of writing, Irvine and Iggy were working together on a film project in Miami. (Surely there can be no greater example of the radical way Irvine's life has been transformed by the success of *Trainspotting* than that!) A nervous Welsh gave Iggy a Hibs strip when they first met, and the two men are occasional drinking partners, much to Irvine's mum's disquiet. Apparently, when he was leaving to meet the star, Mrs Welsh issued the memorable line, 'Behave yourself with that fuckin' Iggy Pop!' The first meeting must have gone well, because a few months later, at T in the Park 2000, the great man was telling the crowd how fantastic it was to be in Scotland – 'the home of Irvine and Sick Boy!'

When Irvine became famous, critics were always trying to bracket him neatly alongside other authors and trace those writers' influence on *Trainspotting*. In fact, the writers who really inspired Welsh were lyricists like Bowie, Iggy, Lou Reed, Elvis Costello and Shane McGowan. Irvine was always drawn to the bohemian, seedy and camp lifestyle of rock stars. His early-1980s letters also raved about Orange Juice, whom he saw play at the Fed Up With Fat Futurists gig at Tiffany's in Edinburgh, and later at another Edinburgh club, Valentino's. He called the Glasgow band's song 'Poor Old Soul' his favourite single of 1981. There were also honourable mentions in his letters around this time for The Clash (Irvine attended the band's gig at the Brixton Academy in

1984, which was in support of striking miners), Grace Jones, Big Country, Wall of Voodoo and Linton Kwesi Johnson, alongside old-order acts like Randy Newman, The Beatles and Robert Plant (in one letter to me he opined bizarrely that the old Led Zeppelin screecher's latest solo album 'can still raise the knob up'.)

Irvine didn't make much of an impression at Essex University. When I contacted the press office to see if any of his old lecturers were still on the scene, they were unaware that Irvine had ever attended the university. The man himself has less than glowing memories of the place. When I mentioned that they might be interested in listing him as one of their high-profile alumni, he said the idea was 'about as appealing as having my nuts sawn off with a rusty hacksaw'. He's on record as saying that one of the reasons he enrolled there was to be near a girlfriend who lived in the south-east of England. His overall impressions of university life were lukewarm; the course work was manageable, though in his letters he preferred to write about a lecturer who hung out with a transvestite. Certainly his time there would have helped hone his writing skills, but he found life a bit dull. The self-contained university campus is situated a twenty-minute bus ride out of Colchester with its own bars, shops and accommodation. In November 1978 he lived briefly in room 14/11 in the splendidly named Bertrand Russell Tower Hall of Residence before escaping to a flat with fellow students at 14 St Monance Way, in a district he described as 'a really fucking snobbish area, no blacks or anything like that'. The social life in one of London's commuter towns was pretty good, and in the first term he enjoyed the varied delights of the Tom Robinson Band and AC/DC live in concert. But the campus bars were never going to be lively enough to satisfy the needs of the grade-A party animal from Edinburgh, and he was soon barred from one of them after an incident 'involving glasses'. Irvine and his friends found consolation in the Colchester town centre bars and the pubs of nearby Chelmsford. He confided that 'a lot of the students here are opulent bourgeois bastards who make me puke, but there are some good piss-artists'.

Often he escaped to London for the weekends, spending time with his latest girlfriend, Lesley Pavitt, whom he had met prior to enrolling at Essex. He made regular forays into the capital to watch West Ham games with Lesley's brother, Keith, who was a fanatical Hammers supporter. He also occasionally went to Stamford Bridge to see Chelsea with a Rangers-supporting pal, Jack Scott. A trip to Wembley in 1979, for the annual England v. Scotland game, ended with Irvine being fined £20 for pelting passers-by with bottles and using foul and abusive language to police officers. His trips to London became so regular that he was effectively half-living in a house on Lady Margaret Road in Southall. But when it came to football, Welsh's thoughts were always with his beloved Hibees, making regular hitchhiking trips north to support the cause even when his team nosedived to relegation in abject fashion during the 1979–80 season. He would later write about how he financed a trip north to see Hibs lose 3–1 to Rangers in a League Cup game. 'I visited my bank manager and hit him with the funeral story for the umpteenth time. I was running out of grandparents faster than Alex Miller was running out of excuses . . . anyway, Fort Ibrox here we come!'

The club's forlorn attempt to save itself by signing the Northern Irish genius George Best drew admiration from Welsh, and he wrote, 'George Best is fucking God – but his sex life is his own affair. No, honestly, the man is so far ahead of everyone else in Scottish football. I saw him against Rangers and Celtic. It was embarrassing watching Duncan Lambie and Ally Brazil trying to play one-twos with him.

Only young Mr McLeod* is anywhere near his wavelength.'

By the winter of 1980, Welsh had tired of the 'dreary satellite town the maps refer to as Colchester . . . I've been back in England for a week now, and I am getting worried about my complete inability to relate to the university course, or do any sort of work. I spend my day drinking, scoring "Robert"** and lying in bed dreaming of wild sexual adventures with hosts of beautiful women, which never seem to materialise.'

All of his letters are filled with typical youthful indiscretions, short-lived flings with girls who will remain anonymous, and tales of drink and drug-fuelled recklessness. Occasionally there was a flash of the wicked humour that runs through *Trainspotting*; speaking of one mutual friend from Edinburgh, Irvine commented that 'it's easier to get a tab of acid from Robert Runcie than a drink out of him'. In a later letter, after the departure of Pat Stanton as manager of Hibs, he wrote, 'the gang are stunned by the departure of Paddy which, as one witty pundit of the wasted fraternity put it, "makes the Lennon assassination seem like a good ride, ya cunt".'

Stressed out by the prospect of his final exams, his face disintegrating in acne, he confessed that 'these exams will tell whether I'm really the liberal intellectual or just another piece of teenage wildlife'. The answer came pretty soon afterwards. In October 1981, just a few months after graduating, he was back in Edinburgh working part-time in a bingo hall in Gorgie, calling out the numbers while standing on a stage twenty feet above a packed mass of bitching local housewives. Weekends were spent drinking with his old cronies in bars like the Harp Hotel and making dutiful trips to Easter

---

* Hibs striker Ally McLeod.
** Hash – Robert or Bob Hope was used as rhyming slang for dope.

Road to see the hapless Hibs. Soon afterwards he was working for the local parks department, and his university years
must have seemed like a real waste of time.

Things really began to change for Irvine in 1982. On 12
January his dad passed away in Edinburgh's Western General
Hospital, aged just fifty-two. Mr Welsh's death was related
to long-term damage to his lungs and other organs which
could be traced back to a childhood bout of TB. It was a long
and distressing period for the Welsh family; his father actually came out of a coma and rallied for a while before his
inevitable demise. Watching his father – who he always
thought was indestructible – waste away was a tough experience for Irvine, who admits now that he would have liked to
enjoy his dad's company more. Thereafter his letters seemed
different, more adult, I suppose.

I only met Mr Welsh once, on 29 July 1981. I know the
date because Irvine and I were in a pub suffering the
horrors of watching Prince Charles's wedding to Diana
Spencer. Irvine suddenly stood up and said, 'Come on out
of here and let's go and visit my dad.' At the time Mr
Welsh was convalescing in the Eastern General Hospital.
He was obviously not well, but he welcomed us and was
entertaining company. I remember him quickly finding
Irvine's weak spot by teasing him about Hibs attemping to
re-sign Bobby Smith from Leicester City. When I asked
him where he worked, Mr Welsh told me he was a civilian
employee with Lothian and Borders Police, before menac-
ingly adding, 'Ah ken what you're thinking, you're thinking filth . . . aren't you?' It took me a few seconds before I
realised that he shared Irvine's offbeat sense of humour. It
was a poignant visit, because it was obvious that Mr Welsh
was not going to recover. My diary entry for that day
concludes: 'Got drunk with Irvine to blot out the pain.' In
the summer following his dad's death, Irvine blotted out

the pain on a more regular basis by shooting up heroin (of which more later).

The month after his dad died, Irvine himself had a near-death experience when a coach packed with Hibs supporters from the Liberton Travel Club travelling to a Scottish Cup clash with Dundee United at Tannadice veered off an exposed section of the M90 outside Perth in high winds. One fan died, and others were badly injured, including Irvine, who spent a week in Perth Royal Infirmary with some cuts and scrapes, a few stitches in the head and ear, and severe concussion. While suitably sedated, Irvine tried to make an escape from the hospital in his nightgown, Basil Fawlty-style, and was caught at the main gate making his way to the nearest pub. Sandy Macnair was also injured in the crash, and spent a week in Bridge of Earn hospital with broken fingers (which needed skin grafts) and head injuries which required sixteen stitches. Both men were incredibly lucky as they had been sitting, drinking whisky, at the front of the top deck on the side of the bus that crashed into the ground. They celebrated their release from hospital with an all-day drinking bout in the notorious Clan on Albert Street, a session broken only by a trip to Easter Road to see Hibs beat Celtic 1–0.

In the autumn of that year Irvine took his chances on a big jet plane and flew to the US, departing on 12 October with California his ultimate destination. His parting shot was typically defiant and humorous. 'I plan to settle for as long as I can with some rich, thick-thighed Californian broad who'll send for Hibs videos and McEwan's Export in cans for me.' In the end he was back in Scotland for the winter, but his stay in California, and a visit to New York the following spring, can be seen as a liberating and life-changing experience for Irvine. He summed up the trip as one of 'lavish promiscuity'. Spending moonlit nights on Laguna Beach and basking under the Californian sun in Westwood with coke-snorting bronzed babes, who had a 'wonderful susceptibility to a bit of flannel in a strange accent', certainly beat hurried sexual encounters down alleyways off the Royal Mile. Equally, the nights in Rosie O'Grady's in 52nd Street, Manhattan, along with visits to Studio 54 and CBGB, were always going to edge it over all-day sessions in the Clan.

In a letter on his return from the first stateside journey, he wrote: 'I've been leading a low-key life since my return from my triumphant US tour . . . I won't bore you by telling you how magic it was, or how I intend to go back after the New Year for a more prolonged stay. Suffice to say that I wince when I look at my holiday snaps of a bronzed young Caledonian warrior surrounded by adoring, blonde, leggy Californian chicks and compare this to the current white ghostly face punctuated by the odd spot which greets me in the bathroom mirror every morning.' Another letter following his second trip to the US spelled out his frustration at having to haul himself back to the grim reality of Scotland. 'I won't bore you about my stateside experiences and my coast-to-coast Kerouacisms, it's over now and it's very painful to be back in this shitty country with its poxy weather. Still, as Joy Division would say.'

While in California he visited two sisters he had met in Edinburgh back in the late 1970s. The two girls had met Irvine and Dave Todd while they were on a Rose Street pub crawl. The Americans weren't put off by the sight of another member of Irvine's entourage vomiting into a rubbish bin, and the next day they were given a guided tour of some of Edinburgh's tourist delights by Dave and Irvine. In the States he was inexorably drawn to the bohemian flipside of the American dream, fraternising with some of the 'weirdoes and street-wise dudes' in downtown Los Angeles, which was back then distinctly down-at-heel and populated by disenfranchised bums and junkies. Irvine and his mate Terry Volk, whose family ran a huge depository in the district, used to while away time drinking in Cole's Bar on East 6th Street. His overall impression of Los Angeles was less than favourable. Unable to drive and desperately short of cash, he had to rely on his American pals to get him around. This made him feel a bit of an outsider in a city where everyone seemed to have a car. He thought the city was a soulless sprawl and later wrote: 'There I was, untanned and untravelled, a naive young laddie from the land of hills and heather . . . a sickly, furtive, troubled urchin, going through a dark time in my life, and in the brightest, gaudiest town in the world.'

The US trips involved long, laborious coast-to-coast Greyhound bus trips during which Irvine had plenty of time to kill, and it was on these journeys that the first sketches of what would become *Trainspotting* were written. I think his travels to the US also showed him that there was an alternative to the dull nine-to-five existence in Edinburgh, and he dreamed of returning there one day. He arrived back in Scotland just in time to catch his hero David Bowie playing Murrayfield Stadium as part of the *Serious Moonlight* tour on 28 June 1983. After just a few hours' sleep, Irvine braved the reality check of driving rain to meet up with Dave Todd and more mates for pre-gig drinks in the Diggers and the Green Tree on Gorgie Road. Strategically opting for a fish supper rather than watch support act the Thompson Twins, Dave and Irvine arrived at the stadium to find themselves positioned right at the back of the capacity 47,000 crowd. Dave recalls: 'I came up with the idea that I would use my work identity pass and pretend we were official bouncer-type guys. I flashed my pass and said "Excuse me" politely, gently shoving my way through with Irvine following behind. About three-quarters of the way to the front Irvine asked if he could take the lead. As soon as I gave him my pass he changed into LA cop mode and started pushing folk out of the way and shouting "*Security!*" in a loud American accent, and threatening one guy who refused to let us pass that he would "bust his ass!"' Amazingly, the sozzled pair got right to the front of the crowd just as Bowie came on stage. They later serenaded customers and staff in a Chinese takeaway with their version of Bowie's 'China Girl'. Dave's abiding memory of the day is of Irvine, only feet away from Bowie, fondly yelling obscenities at the star. In a letter to me soon afterwards, Irvine gave his verdict on Bowie's show in his own succinct, flamboyant way: 'The man is a gem, a pure gem.'

4

London crawling

I think work is a horrible thing. People should avoid it at all costs.

Stuck in a rut in his native Edinburgh, Irvine moved permanently to London in the winter of 1983. The move south was meant to bring a fresh start, but for a while he was living a Bukowski-esque itinerant existence, sleeping in seedy bedsits and working in one short-term job after the other. Writing novels was probably the last thing on his mind; indeed, he says, he was doing well just tying his shoelaces and getting out the door in the morning back in those days. In interviews Irvine has spoken about working as a dishwasher, road digger, clerk, waiter, cook, kitchen porter, TV repair man, builder, removal man, cook on the Harwich to Hook of Holland ferry, council training officer in equal opportunities, a housing manager, a club promoter and an industrial training consultant. Not bad for a man who despises the whole concept of nine-to-five drudgery. Suffice it to say that during his early twenties he was not cut out to last too long in a permanent job. 'I flew through a job every few weeks back then. I was a personable enough bullshitter to get something, but hopeless at keeping in employment,' he says.

The post-*Trainspotting* profiles often mention that he was a property developer back in the mid-1980s, conjuring up an image of Irvine as some kind of Thatcherite yuppie spiv. Although he never actually ran or worked for a property development agency, he did seem to have a happy knack of buying flats cheap, living in them while doing them up and then flogging them for profit. The combined total gain of the three London bedsits he bought and sold came to £50,000. In fact, if things had worked out differently it could have been an alternative career. At one point he did actually consider moving to Sydney, Australia, with the notion of setting up a property management company with a friend who was already living there. Irvine's dream back then was to earn enough from property dealing to allow him to retire when he reached the age of thirty.

Late in 1983, Irvine was sleeping on a friend's floor in a flat in Hackney before he made his first foray into the property market, snapping up a bedsit nearby at 79 Amhurst Road. It was a risky move, given his capacity for fucking up, but by then he had stumbled into a relatively well-paid job working for a community project for the unemployed. He started off doing admin work, but quickly ended up running the training programme for people on the dole. The monthly pay cheque allowed him to buy the tiny bedsit for £12,000. According to Sandy Macnair, the flat contained absolutely nothing other than a bed and a fridge with a seemingly inexhaustible cargo of McEwan's Export. Irvine told *Sunday Times* reporter Emma Wells how the flat had vile beige carpets and curtains, covered in grime and bluebottles: 'I hadn't even noticed them. Young guys are pretty minging, and when you've been on drugs, you get into slovenly, dirty habits.' The third-floor flat, which shuddered every time a train came and went from the nearby Hackney Downs train station, was in an area full of smack dealers, but Irvine resisted temptation and stayed clean. He eventually sold the Amhurst Road property for £26,000 in 1985.

He then moved to 345 Thornton Road in West Croydon, before settling at 270b Queensbridge Road in Dalston, from where he wrote to tell me, 'I've finally made it into the bourgeoisie, lower middle management, suit and tie, eight grand per annum etc. IT'S DOING MY FUCKIN BRAINS IN. I'm working as a personnel manager in an agency in Lower Clapton. Still, the bread, as the cliché goes, is good(ish).'

He might have eased off the drugs, but he was still prone to problematic booze binges which brought him into contact with the law. He has talked about fighting with police on picket lines during the miners' strike and the Wapping printers' dispute, and of smashing up a community centre in North London in a whisky-crazed frenzy. He also had a brush with the Stoke Newington police when he and Sandy Macnair were arrested for drunkenly singing Hibs songs. Each was eventually given a six-months conditional discharge.

His life took a turn for the better when he fell in love with Anne Ansty, a Clapham-born nurse, who later worked as a human rights activist. Post-*Trainspotting*, Irvine declined to speak much about Anne, leading to all sorts of nonsensical conjecture about her in the press, one report even going so far as to call her his 'secret wife'. In fact, anyone who knew them back in the 1980s will vouch for the fact that Irvine and Anne socialised together all the time. They were very much in love and inseparable, and were married at Croydon registry office on 12 October 1984. I recall Anne as being an unlikely choice – at five foot seven she was a lot smaller than Irvine, and was also much quieter, but she was attractive, with a lovely friendly disposition. She came along in his life at just the right time, helping to stabilise his chaotic lifestyle and encouraging his writing. Not for nothing is *Trainspotting* dedicated solely to Anne.

In a letter written shortly after he met Anne, he told me about the changes in his life:

'Dear John, Apologies in order for not penning back as quickly as I would have liked. The reasons;

1) A lazy fucker by nature;

2) So fucking busy doing shite all useful;

3) Such a boring fucker – I don't really think you want to know me these days.

'Yes it's all taking its toll, job, mortgage, even worse, engagement. Yes, I'm head over heels in love and there's nothing more boring for anyone than to hear about someone else like that.

'I felt a bit of a cunt when Sandy came down recently. I had to "second" the man to some like-minded wasters who got wrecked with him, while Anne and I held hands and gazed into each others eyes.

'I feel it's a lot to do with my age, 25 is a dangerous time for laddies. I just can't take the bevvy, the loud chanting and falling about. It physically does me in.

'I hate fuckin' working, having to suck the asses of people who I despise so much. I wouldn't fuck them for all of Michael Jackson's gold discs.'

In a letter from 345 Thornton Road, dated 21 November 1984, he wrote:

'Dear John,

Hello. A few details about your old mucker Irv

1) A married man.

2) Living in a suburb

3) A steady job

4) A wanker

'Yes, it's all true. I'm such a boring fucker now, but the horrible thing is, I don't really mind too much.

'How did I get to where I am from where I was? Well sit yourself down son, and let me tell you a tale . . .

'Once upon a time there was a spotty, sexually-repressed Hibby who having gorged on a diet of bronzed US chicks, Edina slags and strange substances (to which he was introduced to by a pale, bi-sexual, Highland Hibby) in an attempt to find the meaning of this sordid little acid trip somewhat tritely referred to as life, took off to the smoke.

'A job followed, then a flat, then a chick, then a better job, the chick became a wife, then a house etc . . . it is a bore, but love always is (other people's that is). Suffice to say I'm nutty about Anne (my Mrs) . . .

'Now I kept the fuss down to a bare minimum with only my old girl coming down for the shabby register office do. I caused a row between Anne and her family (who are not taken by yours truly moving in on their only daughter) as I didn't really want to get married, being happy to languish in co-habitation.

'It was a combination of psychological pressure on Anne and financial inducements (tantamount to bribery – but every man has his price) which persuaded me to have my love sanctioned by the state. I wouldn't go as far as to let the church bless us though . . . oh my god, fuck sakes . . . which caused more Elephant and Castle [hassle]. The do was tedious, I know it's not possible to be present at your own funeral, but this was the sort of atmosphere. It *really was* that horrific. For fuck sake . . . think once, think twice . . . think Dyke. (drawing of hand motion).

'Anyway, do not judge me too harshly. We had a do up in Scotland, the bears were all present.'

He settled down to married life in Croydon, but as he later told the *Herald* newspaper: 'I was more worried about myself then than I was at any other time of my life. You've fallen into something that's so ugly and terrible. Instead of My Drugs Hell it's My Suburban Hell . . . One thing I really fear is living that whole kind of home/garden/kids kind of suburban existence. DIY and all that. I'd much rather be selling my arse in King's Cross than living that kind of life. It's sick and sordid that people have set such limitations on themselves, thinking that's all they'll get.'

Though he was based in London, Irvine made regular trips back home to Edinburgh. He became increasingly aware of the crippling effect that heroin and the Aids epidemic was having on once strong working-class communities. He was called home to a number of funerals – many of the folk he had grown up with were getting drawn into alcohol and drug-related trouble. The deaths of old friends in Muirhouse were harrowing enough, but Irvine was also shocked at how the local communities were so accepting of the deaths. He saw that his old stamping-ground had taken such a battering that many of the locals had developed a horrible fatalism.

Irvine's response, just to try to make sense of the social phenomenon and the tragedy unfolding in his own backyard, was to start writing again. He has talked about a seven-year gestation period between the start of his writing and the eventual completion of *Trainspotting*. But, as with the doodling done on the Greyhound bus trips, Irvine says he never really had any ambition to write an actual book, telling the journalist Sue Wilson that his mid-1980s writings were just 'bits and pieces of things that had happened, scenarios and events . . . But I never really thought I was going to write this book. It just happened.' Clueless as to how to go about it, he bashed out 100,000 words ('just my launch pad to get into what I need to write about') on to a floppy disc and forgot about them. These stories would later resurface as part of *Skagboys*, the prequel to *Trainspotting*.

He might not have had a game plan to become an author, but as early as 1985 Irvine was writing prodigious amounts. His early pieces written in America, along with work put on to floppy disc, amounted to some 300,000 words. Dave Todd recalls: 'Sandy and I crashed at Irvine's house after [Bruce] Springsteen's 1985 Wembley gig. I was a bit worse for wear after the concert and woke up with an awful hangover next morning on the settee. Irvine gave me a strong cup of tea together with a huge typed manuscript to read. Looking at it did sober me up a bit, and I did say to him that nobody would possibly publish it. It was 1985, and who wanted to read about a bunch of Embra junkies? How wrong can you be?'

By December 1986 Irvine was back in his home city. He bought a five-bedroomed Victorian flat on Wellington Place, overlooking Leith Links. He loved living in a flat that had walls thick enough to let him blast out Iggy and the Stooges without bothering the neighbours *too* much (one of his neighbours was the Tory councillor Cornelius Waugh). It was in this Leith flat that *Trainspotting* as we know it was written. Welsh was now working as a training officer for Edinburgh City Council. He would live in Leith until September 1994, when his literary career started to take off – though this period included two years (1988 to 1990) when the council sent him to Heriot-Watt University's Edinburgh Business School to study part-time. He graduated with a MBA (Masters in Business Administration) which allowed him to become a management consultant with the council. A model student and a super member of the class, according to his supervisor, Irvine found the course work pretty easy and dull, so to beat the boredom he started seriously writing what was to become *Trainspotting*. He recalls that it was a make-or-break time in his life. He thought that his life up until then had been defined by mediocrity at best – working in middle-management in the public sector wasn't ideal for a guy who grew up wanting to lead the life of Bowie or Iggy Pop. Irvine had been told by friends and a former teacher that he could write, and, perhaps more importantly, he knew he had the ability to write well. 'Most of the stuff you see in Waterstone's is a waste of good trees ... most books are absolute shite', as he succinctly put it.

And he now had a subject matter – the heroin/Aids

epidemic – that he was knowledgeable about, and his domestic circumstances were good, especially in comparison to just a few years previously. He told me: 'I remember the early 1980s as fun but grim and bleak, but by the late 1980s I was getting into acid house, had a decent job and a stable relationship. So I felt I was actually writing the book from a position of (relative) strength.'

Irvine's mention of acid house is interesting as, in the late 1980s and early 1990s, he was drawn back into the drug scene through his love of rave culture. This time, though, the drug of choice was ecstasy as opposed to heroin, and like countless others around that time he balanced a mundane, nine-to-five work existence with the hedonistic rave culture at weekends. Although for a while his advocacy of ecstasy was strident, it was a different type of drug use to the dark old days of the early 1980s. The excitement of acid house energised his writing, while the comedowns – which lasted for days on end – made his writing more reflective. As he told the writer Kenny Farquharson in 1993, 'My finger isn't jammed on the self-destruct button any more – but I'll give it a wee flick every now and then just for a bit of intrigue. Maybe once in about six months I'll go through a miniature breakdown and I'll disappear for a few days at a time. People spend a lot of time justifying leading crap lives, saying they're getting too old for these things.' While not as pronounced as with other contemporary writers, the influence of his ecstasy use can be read in some of the more trippy sections of *Trainspotting* and his subsequent books. During the writing of *Trainspotting* he did experiment once with heroin but ended up feeling sick, and almost as if he had never stopped using. To the best of my knowledge he has never used the drug since. 'I wouldn't be interested. Once you've broken the physical addiction to the drug, there's got to be a psychological thing to make you go back. Whatever was driving me to heroin doesn't exist any more.'

As *Trainspotting* began to take shape, Irvine also had another outlet for his creative talents. Five years before he became a published author he – under the pseudonyms of 'Octopus' and 'Leith Lounge Lizard' – was a regular contributor to Hibs fanzines. Sandy Macnair told me how the Octopus name came about: 'He got his zine name after we tried to pull two young chicks at a party. Overt touchy-feely tactics from our chum caused his target (Pam, as I recall) to suddenly shriek, "Hoi, you've goat airms like a fuckin' octopus." Needless to say, we both failed to score.'

The late 1980s saw disgruntled football fans, fed up with the party line from the clubs they followed, bring out their own low-budget but highly amusing takes on the game. Celtic fans' *Not the View* was perhaps the best-known Scottish zine, but Hibs fans were also to the fore. They were an ideal outlet for supporters to question how their clubs were being run, and they provided opportunities for writers to trash opposing clubs and players. Irvine wasn't going to let this chance to have a laugh and a kick at the Hearts pass by, and in August 1988 he started making scurrilous and often hilarious contributions to *Hibees Glasgow Gossip*, *Hibs Monthly* and *The Proclaimer*. Sandy Macnair – alias 'Hibbie Hippie' – was also a regular contributor. Irvine used to write his fanzine pieces in Vittoria's on Leith Walk over a coffee and scone and submit them anonymously. Mike Wilson, who ran *The Proclaimer*, told me: 'He sent the material speculatively and under a pseudonym. I never met him, never knew his real name and never paid him.'

Irvine's satirical drawings were sometimes aimed at Hibs manager Alex Miller, but mostly they poked fun at Hibs' biggest rivals. 'Specky, the Short-Sighted Jambo' in *Hibs Monthly* showcases Irvine's acidic wit and not inconsiderable talent as a cartoonist.

Specky was a 29-nine-year-old, visually challenged virgin

who also happened to be a close friend of 'Hawrts' chairman 'Wallet Mercenary'. In one cartoon, Specky tells readers how Scottish Tory chairman Michael Forsyth, a personal friend, did him a good turn the other day. 'In response to my application for a post with the Conservative Party, he told me: "You're an obnoxious, pathetic, reactionary, boring, four-eyed, greasy little git . . . I can think of no one more appropriate for the post." I start on Monday.'

Leafing through back issues of *Hibs Monthly* gives an intriguing insight into the untried author's literary style. Given the scandalous content of many of the early football fanzines, some of Irvine's outpourings are surprisingly sober, especially given that he was writing anonymously. In one article he sternly warns fans that 'no club can survive such adverse financial ratios'. A few of the articles saw Irvine give eminently sensible opinions on Hibs' travails during the early 1990s – a time when the club was mired in debt and rumoured to be on the point of moving from its much-loved Easter Road home to a new out-of-town stadium. So, in the 'WE SHOULD NOT BE MOVED!' article, Irvine told of his trip to Los Angeles almost ten years previously, when he visited the 'ugly, soulless' California Angels baseball stadium in Anaheim. There he paid inflated prices to watch a match in sterile surroundings, with an MC trying in vain to encourage some atmosphere. After the game, fans just piled into their cars and took the freeway home. Irvine complained that there was no opportunity for pre- and post-match pints of ale, no room 'for debate, discussion, opinions, slaggings, laughter'. 'Octopus' feared that the same would happen if Hibs moved to the proposed new stadium at Straiton.

He loathed the idea of football becoming just another 'product', stating that such language is usually used by people who do not understand the game. 'They are generally board-room figures who wouldn't know what a terracing crush barrier was if it hit them in the nuts. With the game redefined as a product, the Wallace Mercers [Hearts' chairman] of this world get a stiff feeling in their trousers and the rest of us get what they give us.' Irvine warned that the greenfield fad was a fleeting diversion and that the move to Straiton would be a big mistake. Instead, he advocated the building of a new 30,000-capacity all-seated stadium at Easter Road. 'Following a team means more than sticking your weekly six quid in the coffers. Many life-long friendships are forged before and after these games, often between people who would never come into contact with each other in different circumstances.'

The more provocative and amusing pieces of 'Octopus''s output are detailed in full in Sandy Macnair's excellent *Carspotting*, but some are so good they merit inclusion here too. Some, though, such as his piece on 'Ugly Bastards of Scottish Football', are still probably libellous to this day. One unfortunate Rangers defender was described as looking like the bastard offspring of Myra Hindley. In some places there is early usage of the Leith rhyming slang that was used to such great effect in *Trainspotting*, for example, Mantovani for fanny and Salisbury Crag for shag.

It's in the 'Hungry Hibby's Good Grub Guide' that Welsh really hits his stride. In 1990 the very existence of the club was put in jeopardy when Wallace Mercer proposed a merger between the two Edinburgh sides which would have seen Hibs disappear for good. Mercer moved even higher up the Welsh hate parade. Tinelli's Italian restaurant on Easter Road was described as one of Irvine's favourite haunts, and spending a romantic evening there made him doubt 'that things like nuclear weapons, Aids [and] Wallace Mercer exist in the world'. Conversely, he wrote of Pepe's on Albert Street that 'grease, filth and pus impregnate the walls of this temple of bad taste. The council were able to close down their adjacent public toilet as this gastronomic sewer doubles up nicely.' Best of all, though, was his paean of praise to the late lamented 128 Café on Leith Walk: 'Fat, peroxide, tattooed women struggling with prams, shopping and screaming shell-suited brats who hurl chips at each other, compete for table space with hatchet-faced, stewed-tea-guzzling, varicose-veined old crones in a bizarre ritual of death.' He told readers how he preferred to eat his fish supper in the street outside the Albert Street Chippy, as 'it gives me an extra few precious minutes of sobriety'.

Another feature on pubs near Easter Road had some priceless gems. Skivvy's on Duke Street was described thus: 'The old designation of "an ashtray with lights" does not apply to this pub . . . there are no lights. The inhabitants of this pub are generally the type of punters you find in the casualty unit of the Western [General Hospital]. Everyone seems to be in the throes of some terminal disease. Sip a pint of slops then stick around until the next cardiac arrest, family feud or unprovoked assault breaks the monotony.' Much more acceptable was the Cooper's Rest: 'One of the most important institutions in western culture . . . the neighbouring sister-bar the Cedar Lounge is a seething cauldron of romance and decadence bringing to mind nothing less than the Berlin of the 1930s.'

Couples Bar on Leith Walk was 'a bit like being inside the lungs of a 75-year-old forty-a-day man'. About the Collie Dug on Leith Walk he wrote: 'Fine ale, tasteful decor, warm friendly clientele bubbling over with sparkling wit and intellect. All are conspicuous by their absence at the Collie Dug. Given this, it would appear to be a Jambo stronghold.' Last word, though, went to our favourite old haunt, the legend that was the Clan on Albert Street. Irvine waxed lyrically about a hostelry that 'has elevated tackiness to an art form. Its seemingly random mess is actually designed to be aesthetically pleasing. If heaven isn't like the Clan, I'll take my chances in hell.'

5

Chasing oblivion

I really would like for there to be no drugs at all – tobacco, alcohol, ecstasy, cannabis or whatever we need to get us into a spiritual relationship. I really would like it if we could get there without any drugs, but I think the kind of world we live in makes it very difficult for that to happen.

No matter what he does in the future, even if he finds faith and starts writing religious tracts, Irvine will, because of the subject matter of *Trainspotting,* for ever be associated with illegal drug use. But the extent of his own drug-taking, and in particular the degree of his heroin use over the summer of 1982, has been a subject of some conjecture. Not many genuine junkies emerge on the other side of their addiction as eloquent, focused and driven as Irvine has. Fewer still go on to become bestselling authors. The rumour persisted that, for whatever reason, Irvine was perhaps exaggerating his drug use. His assertion that the major problems he encountered through drugs were caused by procuring them, rather than the physical side-effects, would tend to suggest that he hadn't quite experienced the full horror of withdrawal on a regular basis. So, time for some clarity on the matter. But first we need a brief recap on the circumstances that led him to abuse smack.

1982 was Irvine's *annus horribilis*. His boyhood ambitions of becoming a footballer or a rock star were long since dead. The great Hibs team of the 1970s was a distant memory, and even Irvine's eternal optimism was put to the test watching a bunch of average players ply their trade in a green-and-white strip every week. His time at university was now over, and the only real option to earn money was to join the rat race he despised. His dad's death had hurt him badly, and he didn't handle the related trauma well. Irvine now sees his flight to heroin use as the result of his being in denial about the terminal nature of his father's illness.

He also seemed unable to tie down a lasting relationship. (An affair with the first girl he truly loved ended around this time.) Instead, he was increasingly drawn to seedy, drunken one-night stands. In a letter to me in the winter of 1983, after returning from his trip to America, he wrote: 'My sexual encounters since leaving the US consist of a blow job from a horror down Anderson's Close ... and a liaison with a woman who had a dodgy hip, down in old Haggerston E8. Hardly the stuff to give Warren Beatty sleepless nights eh?'

Stuck in a rut and without the emotional range to deal with the difficulties life was throwing at him, Irvine fell back into his old hard-drinking ways, which were occasionally punctuated by antisocial behaviour leading to court appearances. And by the early 1980s, drugs were playing an increasingly central role in his attempts to escape from the pain and tedium of everyday life. Like many bored, rootless youngsters at the time he was drawn to the escape route that drugs seemed to offer. He says he wanted the validation of drama in his dull, meaningless life, and so he turned to drugs, a decision he now describes as born out of stupidity and ignorance.

He told *Herald* writer Teddy Jamieson how he 'didn't have the emotional vocabulary to cope with these things. I didn't really have a way of getting over that pain. I didn't have a mechanism by which I could communicate my despair at all. If you're on that tendency towards self-destruction you're always going to meet up with and bond with a lot of damaged people ... Things weren't working out for me the way I wanted to. I got into a culture where I found people who were very much like myself and I remember my early twenties as quite a dark time. Probably the only time in my life that I felt like I'd gone off the rails so badly and I was out of control.' Speaking to Sean O'Hagan, he explained the depths he reached. 'I spent a lot of time chasing oblivion; that was the big thing for me ... I'd get up in the morning and it would be a beautiful day, and immediately I'd want to get out and get fucked up. It took me a long time to realise what I was actually doing was ending that feeling, killing the beauty. I couldn't handle the beauty.'

His name may now be synonymous with depictions of drug use but Irvine was initially wary of, if not downright hostile to, the drug scene. Back in 1977, when I first met him, the drug scene in Edinburgh centred on middle-class kids smoking hash endlessly, with the occasional weekend dalliance with 'blues' or other amphetamine tablets. As a special treat there was always the lottery of experimenting with LSD (either 'microdot' or 'blotting paper'). Using heroin was pretty much unheard of; I can still recall the shock of meeting a bona-fide junkie living in genteel Morningside, known as 'Dicanol Mike', who took great pride in showing off the track-marks that covered pretty much his entire body. He was the exception. Out on the schemes where Irvine Welsh roamed, it was still primarily a drinking culture. Drug-taking was frowned upon, drug users were treated with contempt, and Irvine was no different from the rest of the schemies he drank with, viewing drugs as the preserve of the middle classes who attended the fee-paying schools in Scotland's capital.

However, from this standing start of being a booze-only, anti-drug teenager, Irvine soon took a liking to getting well and truly wasted. I read in a post-*Trainspotting* interview that he said he did not like hash. That may be true now, but back in the late 1970s and early 1980s he was a serious hash head. His days at Essex University were marked by all-day drinking sessions in local pubs, topped off by getting trashed with fellow students in dorm rooms or at parties. A flatmate in the St Monance Way house where Irvine lived could get hold of every conceivable type of draw, and the flatmates also often enjoyed the exotic natural high of magic mushrooms, which were popular around that time. One particularly memorable mushroom trip for Irvine was soundtracked by 'Catholic Girls', off Frank Zappa's *Joe's Garage* album, and John Cooper Clarke's 'Beasley Street' from *Snap, Crackle And Bop*. The experience obviously left a lasting impression on Welsh, and he later made use of it in *Trainspotting*. In 'Strolling Through the Meadows' Spud, while tripping on White Dove ecstasy tablets, thinks 'aboot Frank Zappa wi Joe's Garage n yellow snow n Jewish princesses n Catholic girls'.

Irvine's preparations for his final exams in 1981 included heavy-rotation dope-smoking and a couple of weeks on a motley mix of speed and antihistamine tablets, the latter being prescribed to him by a friendly local doctor. One Saturday night session saw Irvine down eighteen of the tablets along with four pints of lager – a concoction which, the textbooks say, would have led to a sensation akin to 'dreaming while being awake'. A few more of the pills would have meant an overdose, heart attack, coma and likely death.

Eventually the novelty of smoking hash wore off, but it

probably took seven or eight years of cannabis consumption
before Irvine realised that hashish was a nasty time-waster of
a drug that killed ambition. As early as 1983, he was tiring
of it; in one letter to me he confided: 'Hash – a boring middle-
class habit but hard to give up.' By the time *Trainspotting*
had taken off, he despised the stuff and the people who used
it. In the infamous interview with *Rebel Inc.*, Irvine said: 'I've
gone right off dope. I used to smoke loads of blow ... I
found I was getting fucking stupid on blow, you know what
I mean? The smirking culture gets on my nerves too. There's
something really fucking offensive about the hippie with the
spliff, smirking fucking piously, thinking they've got it
sussed.'

But if the idiotic giggling and the soporific sessions of the
hash scene weren't for Irvine, he found other drugs much
more appealing, declaring boldly, 'I'm a chemicals man!' The
adrenaline shot of amphetamines was the perfect accompaniment for the punk scene he loved so much in the late 1970s.
He first took speed at the age of seventeen and continued to
experiment with sulphate and blues for years to come. By the
early 1980s he was dabbling with heroin, the particular
poison that would, through his later writing, lead him to
fame and fortune. In a couple of letters he sent to me back
then he wrote openly about how and why he first got involved
with the drug. Unfortunately, Irvine rarely included a date at
the top of his letters to me, but cross-referencing the concerts
and football games he mentions in these letters gives a fairly
accurate guess of when they were written.

So, in the autumn of 1982, he wrote: 'The reason I've been
quiet on the mail front recently is because I've been going
through a very dodgy period (self-inflicted) which I think (I
hope) I've emerged from. I got into snortin' smack (oh
shit . . .) for a bit and almost lost more than a few buddies . . .
Anyway I nipped the habit before it became too dangerous

and although I got thinner than thou for a while (9½ stone at 6 foot 2 inches is not a pretty sight) I've blown out all drugs and cut down drink as well.

'I've had my relapses in the last few months mind you. I scored the gold medal for wastedness on alcohol and acid at the Wakefield Festival. I can't remember any of the bands over the two days, although I understand Tull, Lindisfarne and the Blues Band went down well.'

In December 1982, recently returned from a holiday in the US and living with his mum, he wrote to me again, by now apparently off the skag and lucid enough to evaluate why he tried the drug and why he decided to call a halt to his experimentation. He started, though, by acknowledging my own sanctimonious criticism of his heroin use in an earlier letter I had sent him. 'The trite little "smack" on the wrist was appreciated too, but I can assure you the flirtation was brief and ended almost as soon as it began. I just felt I had to give it a go, but witnessing the numerous social casualties around the Wester Hailes area (the new Bronx) persuaded me that the whole exercise is pointless, futile and pathetic.'

These quotes finally nail the whispers from some critics, post-*Trainspotting*, that Welsh was in some way inventing his past as a heroin user to profit from it through his writing. If he really did fabricate his own heroin history, why would he do so in letters to me, years before he became famous? Indeed, although he has spoken sparingly of his junkie days since becoming a literary success, what Welsh has said matches pretty closely what he told me in those letters. Speaking to reporters at the Cannes Film Festival while there to promote the *Trainspotting* film, he said: 'I tried heroin when I was twenty-two or twenty-three years old . . . I was on the outside of addiction for just one summer. I did it out of stupidity and because it was there. That's why most people do it.' He did have a brief flirtation with it again in 1983, and in other interviews he has talked about using heroin for over a year, so he may have relapsed after I lost contact with him in 1984. But I think it would be unlikely, as he was by then happily married and working full-time. He told me: 'There was a lot of shame around that time in my life, I felt a bit of a failure for responding inappropriately to the situation I was in. I probably downplayed the extent to which I was using heroin, and I was banging up regularly at one stage. Most of all, it distanced me from a lot of good people, and I've spent a fair bit of time over the years mending fences, not so much for being a bad fucker, as just absenting myself without providing any reason.'

The anti-drug brigade's warning that using heroin was effectively slow suicide didn't seem to worry Welsh. These same people had told him that smoking dope or snorting speed would kill him, but it hadn't, so why should their warnings about smack be any more convincing? In any case, lots of those pious critics who were once warning him off drugs were now users themselves. He loved the initial rush of the drug flooding through his body, elevating him away from the boredom and hassles of everyday life. (As the great Charlie Mingus supposedly said: 'If God made anything better than heroin, he kept it to himself.') But, over time, he found that the drug cocooned him in a dozy state of wellbeing. Eventually he decided that heroin was not for him, and he kicked the habit, locking himself away (like Renton) and going cold turkey. There was no clinic he could go to, so he just toughed it out and watched videos instead. Irvine's never really been a fan of organisations like Narcotics Anonymous or Alcoholics Anonymous. He believes it's up to the individual to have the sense and the courage to quit on their own. He actually found it fairly easy to quit, which again tends to suggest his heroin usage was relatively brief and recreational. 'When you go down to a certain level you have to decide if you're going to resurrect or if that's it. So I decided to resurrect. And it's basically been uphill all the way from there on in.'

However short his spell as a heroin user was, it did have one unlikely side-effect: using the drug seemed to encourage him compulsively to keep a diary. Prior to his junkie days, and indeed after coming off the skag, he struggled to find the time and motivation to write down his thoughts on a daily basis. While he was using heroin, though, that task was easier. He has described his heroin diaries as rambling nonsense, full of tangents and vague, unflattering sketches of people. But years later, after returning from a rave in Edinburgh, he found those old diaries and was astonished how strong some of the writing was. It gave him the confidence to start reading extracts from the diaries to other punters at open-mic readings he would go to while coming down off ecstasy.

However good or bad they were, these writings became the basis of *Trainspotting*, and he would later say how thankful he was that use of the drug encouraged him to take down these notes religiously. But he also admitted that if he had stayed on the junk, it would have destroyed his writing career by killing the discipline needed to take the step up and write a novel with all the necessary interlinking plot lines. As he wrote in *The Times*: 'whatever benefits directly or indirectly accrued to imagination or experience, those are more than wiped out with the attendant diminishing of the will'.

For a while in the 1990s he was evangelical in his praise for ecstasy. His interview with Kevin Williamson, when both men were flying on the drug, is an interesting read. Ecstasy appealed to Irvine because, despite the intense rushes that threatened to put him over the edge, he always felt he was in control of the high, certainly in comparison to his experiences with LSD and alcohol (which by then he thought destroyed the body, the mind and the will to achieve anything in life). In that sense, he argued, ecstasy was a superior drug which made him thoughtful and appreciative, giving him insights into people that were impossible to ascertain when straight. He added, rather pompously, 'I don't see any point in anybody doing opiates now', and told how he would never have written so much if he hadn't been doing ecstasy for the previous three years. Of course, he was well aware that others could mess up while taking the drug, but argued that plenty of people mess up on alcohol too. His missionary work on behalf of the drug knew no limits; when he eventually got to meet his hero Iggy Pop, the two men tripped on E. Iggy, a renowned druggie in his day, was nervous about the prospect of trying out this new designer drug, and Irvine had to persuade him, whispering, 'Just take the pill, Iggy. Take the pill.'

Welsh's ecstasy years coincided with the rave scene, which he also embraced enthusiastically, though he initially found it hard to keep up with the constant dancing. His previous dance-floor experimenting had been restricted to pogoing at punk concerts and falling around drunk to David Bowie songs, so the rave dance scene just about finished him off. He was amazed how hard men he knew now preferred to sit around in pubs hugging each other rather than fighting with rival gangs, telling *The List*: 'I have seen a lot of people who were quite fucked up and violent, who weren't in touch with their feelings. They have taken to ecstasy and they are interacting with people in a totally different way.'

As to whether taking drugs helped him write, Irvine found that – like William Burroughs before him – it was the withdrawals rather than the actual drug high that acted as a creative spur. The time when the drug was effective was never particularly creative for Irvine, but the ugly consequences of the junkie's lifestyle, with its attendant agonies for the body and mind, the cramps and hallucinations, fuelled his imagination and forced him to write.

Writing in *The Times*, Welsh noted: 'The sad, prosaic old truth is that discipline may be creativity's ugly sister, but you'll never finish that book/album/film/script/play without both. Anything that stimulates one while eroding the other will inevitably result in frustration. Burroughs thus stands out as an exceptional figure, a writer who was, even in the extremes of addiction, often able to produce substantial, publishable output.'

Welsh is far too clever a man ever to think that drugs are anything more than a very dangerous, temporary balm for the pain and boredom of modern life. As he told the *Herald*, drugs eventually compound rather than solve those problems. 'We're all going to feel pain in our lives. We're all going to lose loved ones. We're all going to have relationship break-downs. We're all going to lose our jobs. But the pain is finite. It does go. But if you're on drugs all the time, you're not actually dealing with it . . . the actual drugs become the source of the pain . . . Now, if my wife left me or all the books got remaindered, the last thing I would do would be to go out drinking or take drugs. But at the time you don't have the emotional vocabulary and I didn't behave appropriately.'

These days Irvine says he's too old to do drugs seriously, but in the 1990s his drug-taking experiences were the natural choice for subject matter for his first book.* *Trainspotting*'s contents, though, were always going to be controversial. Writing about drug addiction wasn't new, of course; Irvine was only the latest in a long line of writers who had detailed

---

* Since he became famous, Irvine often has people offering him drugs at readings or in clubs, slipping coke or dope into his hands. These people needn't bother, because Welsh says he always flushes such unwanted gifts down the nearest toilet once the benefactor is out of sight.

their experimentation with drugs. Like those before him, Welsh was always going to get criticism from predictable sources for writing about junkies. He batted away those critics with ease, pointing out how western culture's attitude towards intoxication in general and drugs in particular has been marked by hypocrisy, arguing that in Britain the legal status of a drug has nothing to do with its addictive qualities or the harm it can do. It's to do with social, political and economic factors. Welsh no doubt found common ground with the arguments put forward by another literary junkie who lived for a number of years – and died – in Edinburgh, – Thomas de Quincey, who wrote in his 1821 book *Confessions of an English Opium Eater*, 'what a man may lawfully seek in wine surely he may lawfully find in opium; and much more so in those many cases (of which mine happens to be one) where opium deranges the animal economy less by a great deal than an equivalent quantity of alcohol.'

For Welsh, the existing drug laws are brainless and indefensible. He pointed out the hypocrisy of alcohol and tobacco barons receiving knighthoods while selling a product that ruins more lives and kills many more people than illegal drugs do. Yet it's the drug users and dealers who feel the brute force of the law. After *Trainspotting* was published, some of the press anointed him the spokesman for the chemical generation (the droves of kids who rejected the prevailing middle-class culture and instead went to acid house clubs and raves). Welsh was certainly an eloquent advocate for ecstasy, always seemingly prepared with a quotable soundbite. But he was a bit mystified by such a description, calling it simplistic and unrealistic to assume that he ever set out to be a spokesman for a generation. All he ever really wanted to do was write his truth about drugs.

In the end, Welsh more or less gave up on the chance of a

reasoned debate on reforming drug laws, realising that the system is loaded against there ever being meaningful change. Instead, he concentrated on writing accurately about his own working-class community and shining some light on the oft-ignored junkie. Writing in the *Big Issue* in 1993, he explained: 'The drug user has always been portrayed in Scottish literature as a dehumanised figure, [the message being that] decent couthy working-class traditions have been sabotaged by the drug menace. It's an easy thing to do; if people are perceived as a social problem, then strip them of their humanity and put that little box around them that says junkie or homeless. People have the same needs and drives and the same network of relationships as anyone else. They don't become somehow different or alien because they have certain drug or personality problems as a result of the drug.' He also wanted to write about these people from a different perspective to the one adopted by writers like William Burroughs and the Scottish Beat writer Alexander Trocchi, noting that their junkie characters were by and large culturally middle-class figures.

6

The Muirhouse connection

In Edinburgh in the eighties you're talking about people who wouldn't normally be involved in the heroin scene, people who didn't have that Trocchi-esque attitude of setting them-selves up in opposition to society. It was just people who really didn't have a fucking clue as to what was going on.

If he hadn't been so spaced out on smack at the time, Irvine, as an old social sciences student, would probably have appreciated that the heroin problem in Edinburgh during the early 1980s was a classic case of supply-and-demand economics. The problem really came to public prominence in the summer of 1982. While most of us were watching the World Cup from Spain, growing numbers of disaffected youths in the capital – including Irvine – were injecting heroin. The gradual impact of Margaret Thatcher's economic policies was seeing rising levels of de-industrialisation and unemployment. Irvine, a university graduate working in a bingo hall, was slightly more qualified than most of the new wave of heroin users in the city. The majority were youngsters who were signing on or getting by on casual labour, living in communities where there were few social or recreational amenities. The deterioration in housing quality which had continued since the estate boom of the 1960s had reached a critically low point. Later studies showed that many people who turned to intravenous drug use came from broken homes; some had experienced physical and sexual abuse during childhood and were in care or in trouble with the law. The typical heroin consumer was no longer of the hippie, student or dissident classes, but was a member of the socially deprived groups of teenagers living on inner-city housing estates who, despite being new to the drug scene, rapidly adopted a lifestyle of reckless drug-taking. These new users – vulnerable individuals – didn't see drugs as a way of social rebellion; with little hope for the future, they just wanted to get out of it as quickly and as cheaply as possible.

If they provided the demand side of the equation, major upheavals far away from Edinburgh provided the supply. Political change in Afghanistan and Iran led to an increase in high-grade heroin from both countries finding its way on to the city streets of the UK. But it was the emergence of Pakistan as a major producer of cheap heroin that really changed the game plan. The opium poppy grown by tribesmen in remote valleys of the north-west frontier province was then processed and smuggled into India and then on to Britain. Soon there was so much Pakistani heroin flooding into the UK that the street price plummeted. As the relative cost of alcohol and tobacco soared, more and more people started experimenting. Pretty soon, the death certificates of many victims gave 'narcotic morphine poisoning' as cause of death.

In 1983, Sir John Orr, the former chief constable of Lothian and Borders Police, told the *Scotsman*: 'Within a short period of three years there has been a dramatic swing from the abuse of soft drugs like cannabis to the hard drugs like heroin. Evidence points to there being a continuous supply of heroin at street level, with massive profits for those involved in its supply and distribution.' Orr said the heroin trade was attracting so many major criminals that it was 'impossible to stamp out', and added that drug use had become commonplace in schools. He said the scourge was impacting throughout the city, though he made specific mention of West Pilton, West Granton, Royston, Leith, Wester Hailes and Muirhouse. When the supply of cheap Pakistani smack died away, users began to inject ground-up pills and share needles, leading to health issues like abscesses and endocarditis. Then the real problems began with the spread of hepatitis B, hepatitis C and HIV. By the late 1980s, Muirhouse was said to be the heroin capital of Europe.

It's always been an intriguing question as to why Edinburgh, generally perceived by outsiders as a prosperous city best known for its thriving arts festival, was worst hit. To try to find the answer I visited Dr Roy Robertson, who has been a GP in the Muirhouse area since 1979, when the local West Granton practice had about 18,000 patients on its caseload. Dr Robertson, a graduate of the University of Edinburgh, says there were about 250 heroin users in Edinburgh in the late 1970s, but by the end of 1980 the number had risen to 4,000. He first came across injecting drug users while working in the late 1970s as a senior house officer at the now demolished Northern General Hospital on Ferry Road.

'I worked there for a year, and during that time I saw quite a few heroin addicts – people with hepatitis B, respiratory problems or behavioural problems being admitted to hospital as an emergency, and others coming into the respiratory unit with pneumonia. In that ward we normally got old guys with lung cancer or chronic bronchitis, but I remember very clearly treating this young woman who had acute pneumonia. She confided in me that she used heroin. I had never come across this before and I thought it was my duty to "rescue" this person, who was roughly the same age as me. I spoke to the consultant, but he said, "Just give her some heroin and get her out of the ward. We don't want her in here; she is just going to start trouble as she is withdrawing." I was pretty shocked that we would consider giving her some injectable heroin, but we did, and that did cure her withdrawal symptoms. The second thing that shocked me was his complete lack of interest – he thought looking after her was not our job. He was right in a way, we weren't kitted out to do it.'

After a brief spell working in Kirkcaldy, Dr Robertson started work in North Edinburgh, where he was to witness the early stirrings of the heroin and illness epidemics among a large number of his patients, usually young men from the Muirhouse, West Granton, Drylaw and Pilton areas. Most of them had just left local schools and were unemployed or in casual employment on building sites. Invariably, they were young, healthy and fit prior to getting drawn into the heroin scene. 'In that year of 1979–80 I saw dozens of people who were using heroin. All of a sudden, because I was taking an interest in them, people were coming to the surgery in droves.

'My partners were saying, "Get rid of these people, they are bad news and it's not our job to look after them." Again, they were right; it wasn't our job to look after them. But when they started coming in jaundiced with hepatitis B (and as we found out later, hepatitis C), they became a medical problem. One day in 1981 this guy came in; he was jaundiced and needed some opiates, some painkillers. I asked him what this was all about and he said, "Oh, it's just the 'hep'. Everybody's got it, haven't they?" And I said, "What do you mean, everyone's got it?" He was a young man working as a labourer on a building site, so I said to him, "You inject heroin. How many of your friends inject heroin?" And he said, "Everybody, everybody I know."'

Dr Robertson told me he still treats the man to this day,

though he is now a chronic alcoholic with HIV and multiple other health problems. The patient's partner later died from HIV/Aids, and his son was murdered. It's an all too familiar tale, which Dr Robertson, through his interest in the medical consequences of illegal drug use, has documented over the past 30 years in a succession of influential papers detailing the human tragedy suffered by injecters and their families.

Dr Robertson believes that the closure of a surgical supply shop on Spittal Street in the city centre had a direct negative impact on the problem and led to the sharing of needles becoming routine. The supply store provided equipment to the medical profession, but it became increasingly popular with drug users who went there to buy clean needles and syringes. This trade escalated alarmingly to the point where the shop was selling boxes of needles to drug injecters – some users would even travel from as far away as Glasgow to get clean works. The owner came in for criticism and was threatened with prosecution, and eventually went bankrupt. Dr Robertson recalls how 'the shop went out of business in September 1981, and from then on you can almost map the steep growth curve over the next couple of years in the hepatitis B epidemic and, later on, hepatitis C and HIV.* But the visible manifestation of it back then was cases of hepatitis B; we had a test for it then. There were no tests at the time for hepatitis C and HIV. We didn't, of course, know at the time that HIV was there.'

Along with Dr Ken Roberts, another partner at the Muirhouse Medical Group, Dr Robertson supplied clean needles and syringes to a small number of patients, but the

---

* A study of Edinburgh drug users in the *Archives of Internal Medicine* shows that the principal cause of death in the early years was overdose; later it was HIV/Aids and hepatitis C. Death totals peaked in 1994, the year after *Trainspotting* was published, though this reflects the long incubation period of Aids. Death rates then begin to fall, reflecting the introduction of effective antiviral drugs and treatment.

majority of addicts turned to crime in their efforts to avoid dirty works, breaking into hospitals and doctors' surgeries. Dr Robertson admits: 'When you think about it, it's not great to supply a small number of needles into a large population of drug users; it just leads to them sharing. You really need a large number of needles so everyone has a clean needle every time.'

The shortage of clean needles led to the rise in the notorious shooting galleries where up to twenty addicts would gather and borrow or rent injecting equipment from other users. At best, the equipment they used was rinsed with tap water between injections. There was no serious attempt at sterilisation, despite the commonplace practice of 'washout' (drawing blood back into the syringe after injecting to flush out any remaining heroin). There was no viable needle exchange scheme back in the early 1980s, and the inevitable outcome was the spread of diseases associated with injecting.

There was, according to Dr Robertson, another reason why the problem was so much worse in Edinburgh in comparison to other urban centres in the UK. 'There was actually more heroin in Glasgow. The sociologist Jason Ditton wrote a famous paper about the rapid rise in heroin use in Glasgow in the late 1970s and early 1980s, but the people he came into contact with there were mainly smoking it. It was a similar story in cities like Liverpool and London, where there was also a large heroin subculture. In Edinburgh there seemed to be an injecting culture; most of our patients had never smoked it. I put it down to the fact that it was a new drug-using subculture; there was no previous caseload. In London you were introduced to heroin by a bunch of old guys who showed you what to do and what to avoid, like sharing needles. Here in Edinburgh, they were straight into injecting.'

The government treated the problem as a law enforcement issue for a long time, concentrating on criminalising users rather than viewing them as a medical health emergency and providing a more compassionate response. The local community was largely left to fend for itself. One addict in Muirhouse, Morag McLean, set up the Support, Help and Advice on Drug Addiction (Shada) group in October 1981, backed by local GPs and social workers. Until then, addicts had to wait three to four months before gaining entry into the Andrew Duncan Clinic of the Royal Edinburgh Hospital, where they were given gradual reduction quantities of the heroin substitute methadone.

But with the exception of a farm run by the Cyrenians charity on the outskirts of the city, which temporarily housed recovering addicts, there was nowhere for the users to go once they left hospital. They had to return to their community, where many of their friends were still injecting and the temptation to lapse back into using again was strong. Morag McLean told the *Glasgow Herald* in the summer of 1982 how she knew of four pushers living within ten minutes' walk of her home. With addicts needing up to £100 a day to feed their habit, crime and in particular housebreaking levels soared. GPs' practices soon had scores of heroin users on their books.

The Scottish Office response was slow, with long bureaucratic delays in reply to requests for adequate funding. For a couple of years Shada had to operate from a scruffy wee hut in Muirhouse called The Villa. Eventually, in 1984, a £40,000 grant from the government allowed Shada to employ four staff, including two much-needed full-time counsellors. But reading back issues of the local community newspapers shows that funding problems persisted throughout the 1980s. Eventually, in 1989, the situation got so bad that Shada staff were forced to strike before Lothian Health Board finally agreed to demands for increased funding.

Early on, there were no needle exchange schemes or effective antiretroviral drugs to combat the spread of infection

– and as a result death rates from Aids soared. The first Aids cases were reported in Muirhouse as early as 1983, but the government's response to the growing crisis was niggardly and drew criticism from Dr Robertson, who thought that the national campaign was years behind the local addicts' experience. Scare stories in the media, such as the one about teachers at Muirhouse Primary being advised to wear gloves if treating kids who got cut in a fight, did not help. In January 1986, readers of the *North Edinburgh News* (formerly *Commune*) were told that 'in the Muirhouse and West Pilton area where there are many [intravenous] drug users it has been found that up to 60 per cent are infected with the virus (they do not have Aids). The virus is spread amongst this group by injection of blood (by sharing needles).'

Slowly, the authorities began to adopt a more compassionate, harm-reduction-based response to the problem. Dr Robertson says the findings of a 1986 conference in Newark, New Jersey, which made it plain that it wasn't just the homosexual and drug-using communities that were at risk from Aids, led to the issue being taken seriously in political circles. The following year saw a nationwide advertising campaign warning: 'Aids. Don't die of ignorance. Anyone can get it, gay or straight, male or female'.

The same year saw a change of attitude at a local level in North Edinburgh with the setting-up of a needle exchange scheme at Leith Hospital, along with an Aids counselling and screening clinic. Indeed, Scotland was leading the way when it came to needle exchange, ahead even of Amsterdam. Dr Robertson also believes strongly that the increased use of methadone as a prescribed substitute for heroin 'effectively switched off the HIV epidemic' in the area, while it continued apace in other countries where methadone was not used.

Dr Robertson's efforts to identify how HIV was introduced to the local community are worthy of a book in their own

right. He was closely involved in a follow-up study of a
caseload of local addicts which produced interesting results.
'We particularly wanted to find out how the virus epidemic
of injecting drug users and HIV came into Edinburgh. There
were only two or three places which had these problems like
Edinburgh did at that time. Milan in northern Italy, New
York, and there was evidence that it was in Spain too. It was
seeping into other places like Amsterdam, but they did not
have an epidemic of cases; they had a slow rise in prevalence
over several years. The feature that made Edinburgh different was the rapid introduction of HIV and the spread to so
many people in the space of eighteen months or so.

'We thought it might have come through the Spanish
connection; the World Cup was in Spain in 1982, and a lot
of our patients went there and injected heroin. Then, of
course, there was always traffic to Amsterdam. People went
there to buy drugs. Then there was this intriguing character
called American Andy, who was a legendary figure back
then. People reported back to me a lot of times about this
guy. He had lived in California, come to Edinburgh and
injected in Muirhouse, and then gone away to London. I
eventually found him, through a long, complicated story, in
a seaside town in the south of England. He didn't want to be
tested for HIV, and as far as I know he has never been tested.
I don't think he's positive, because he is still alive. In order to
try to investigate this we got blood samples from HIV-infected
people and compared them to similar samples from patients
with HIV in Dublin, Amsterdam, Florida and New York. We
found that our HIV virus-type was similar to Amsterdam, so
it probably came from there.'

These days, Dr Robertson, who is also chairman of the
National Forum on Drug-Related Deaths, is kept busy trying
to help the survivors from the 'Trainspotting generation'.
While writing this book I read a front-page article in the

Herald detailing how those introduced to heroin in the 1980s and 1990s were now paying the ultimate price. An official report showed that 212 of the record number of 580 drug-related deaths in 2011 were people aged between 35 and 44 – those exposed to the first wave of widespread heroin abuse in Scotland. Years of chaotic lifestyles, with drug-related physical and mental health problems, have finally caught up with these people, their bodies unable to cope any longer with the amount of drugs they still use.

Dr Robertson told me how he met Irvine shortly after the release of *Trainspotting*. 'Radio Forth asked me to do an interview along with him. I said I had never heard of him, so I read the book, and then Irvine came along and we stood together to do an interview in the pouring rain outside the house on Muirhouse Avenue where he had grown up. This was before he became well known. He was a bit cagey, but quite happy to tell me a bit about his background. At the time I was more famous than he was, which is hard to believe! He came back into the surgery and we had a cup of tea and he signed the book. I remember him asking me about hep C, which at the time we had only just got a test for. That was the next wave, and in a way it was a bigger wave than HIV and will probably kill more people. Then he went away, and I thought I would probably never hear from him again.

'I thought the book was fantastic, just amazing, and I still do. In a way we really owe Irvine Welsh a great debt, for publicising these things in a way that was so inflammatory and caught people's imagination. Our own approach to trying to draw attention to these problems had been success-ful, but less so than it should have been. I suppose in a way someone like Irvine is much more influential than the Minister for Health in getting things into the public imagination. How many people even know who the Chief Medical Officer is in

Scotland? Someone like Irvine, who can get the story out into the public domain, is really worth their weight in gold.

'Our other great allies were the gay community. If they hadn't been there, then our drug users wouldn't have been of interest to anybody. Gay men were marginalised and stigmatised back then much more than they are now. They were considered to be a closed community and therefore less of a threat to the population. A government like Thatcher's was not in the least bit interested in our community. But all of a sudden young heterosexuals and females became important. Aids became a threat to the general population. Norman Fowler* made a trip to California and suddenly realised what the threat was. He was able to get the government to set up a cabinet committee on Aids.'

The sterling work done by the doctors at the local practice, and the later impact of Irvine's book, meant that the Muirhouse community unexpectedly became the focus of widespread attention. Edinburgh was suddenly on the international map as the centre of a potential explosion of African-style Aids transmission. Roy Robertson recalls: 'It was an amazing couple of years. Professionally, it was very exciting. Ken and I both took the view that we would do as much as we could on the medical front, but we would not get involved in anything commercial or publicise Muirhouse surgery. We felt the area should not be stigmatised too much. But we couldn't keep it out of the media; there were press, TV cameras. We even had *Playboy* magazine here. There were a lot of voyeurs, fortune-hunters and people just wanting a quick story. But we felt that this HIV thing was so important that we had a responsibility.'

---

* Secretary of State for Health and Social Security in Margaret Thatcher's government in 1986.

7

Under the influence?

Whenever somebody says, 'Oh, you write just like so-and-so', I have to go off and read some of it.

When *Trainspotting* was published, critics and academics almost immediately started to draw comparisons between Irvine and other successful novelists. The list of writers who have supposedly influenced him is long and varied and includes the likes of Louis-Ferdinand Céline, Martin Millar, Charles Bukowski, James Kelman, Alexander Trocchi and William Burroughs. The question is an intriguing one and is made slightly confusing by the man himself issuing contradictory statements. Occasionally he will mention having read and enjoyed some of the above writers prior to writing *Trainspotting*. More often, he will say that the influence on him of these authors is mostly in the minds of critics. During the research for this book, he told me: 'The influences thing is a strange one. Often it's books that you don't like in some way that influence you – you think, "I could do better than this shite." Sometimes you like a book or music, but it doesn't influence you at all, or at least you don't think it has until later. The truth about it is that this is the most mystical part of it. I really don't know. I just make up stuff in the interviews, usually based on what I've been reading, but how much they've influenced me – well, your guess is as good as mine.'

During his E-fuelled discourse in *Rebel Inc.*, Irvine actually said he never read novels. 'I've never been a particularly well-read punter. I've always preferred sort of books that dealt with the sort of real-life kind of ideas, physical and natural and social sciences, and that sort of stuff. I'm quite sceptical about what real insight any novelist or creative writer could have. I don't think there's been one significant fucking novel that's ever advanced the human condition.' While it's certainly true that his pre-*Trainspotting* heroes were musical rather than literary, the idea that he was some sort of illiterate brute roaming the streets of Edinburgh is way off the mark. As Sandy Macnair told me: 'We were both fairly voracious readers, and William Burroughs was always one of Irvine's favourites. I recall one night in the Diggers [the Athletic Arms] when some biker guy was canvassing folks' choices for their top ten books. Everyone else's lists were what you would expect – writers like Hunter S. Thompson and Carlos Castaneda. But when Irvine submitted his selection, they were all by Burroughs!'

Dave Todd concurs that Burroughs was one of Welsh's favourites back in the mid-1980s. 'We used to discuss our favourite books, and Irvine never ever mentioned any of the books he cites as his favourite books now. Back then, he was a fan of Burroughs's *Naked Lunch* and Iain Banks's *The Wasp Factory,* which was fairly new at the time. I do think that *The Wasp Factory* had an influence on Irvine. He pooh-poohed Sandy for his choice of *Lord of the Rings*, and often said that he wasn't going to read it in case he liked it!'

Whatever latent abilities Irvine had as a writer back in the mid-1980s, they would be worthless unless he had the confidence to put them down on paper and to find the route to 'becoming' a writer – not an easy thing to do for a lad from a culture where reading great literature, let alone writing it, was not considered normal or important. His schoolboy interest in reading had been reinvigorated by his uncle Jack, who worked as a fireman but studied English Literature through the Open University in his spare time. Jack had passed on some Evelyn Waugh books to the Welsh family, and Irvine was soon engrossed in the *Sword of Honour* trilogy. Reading through the entire 664-page epic of aristocrat Guy Crouchback's Second World War travails, it's difficult to find any direct link between Waugh's beautifully nuanced satire and Welsh's often brutal style. Still, Welsh would later say that reading Waugh's work was a life-changing event for him, the real starting-point of his interest in literature and an unlikely source of inspiration for *Trainspotting*. Even though he wrote about people and places far removed from urban Scotland, Waugh remains one of Welsh's favourite writers to this day: 'I loved his prose and his way of setting out relationships between his characters. That odd mixture of respect and rivalry, love and contempt, was to be a huge influence on my own writing. I recognised the people around me in the type of relationships he mapped out.'

However much he admired Waugh's work, and could find unlikely connections between the worlds of privilege and poverty, the fact that Waugh was a public-school boy who had later attended Oxford University merely reinforced Irvine's belief that writing was something done by a well-heeled cultural elite. Working-class boys from a grimy Edinburgh housing estate weren't meant to write books. He began to think the idea of being a writer would end up as another failure, just like his sporting and musical dreams. He now realises this to be 'self-defeating nonsense', but back in the mid-1980s failure was Welsh's 'culture of expectation'. In fact, he was merely looking for reasons *not* to write and looking for reasons to fail, but for a while he gave up on the idea of writing a book. Then he discovered the work of William McIlvanney.

Reading the Kilmarnock-born novelist and poet's 1977 novel, *Laidlaw* removed the final invisible barrier blocking Irvine from achieving his ambition. The book tells the story of Detective Jack Laidlaw's attempt to track down the man who has killed a teenage Glasgow girl in a brutal sexual attack. McIlvanney is generally considered to be a great influence on the current generation of Scottish crime writers, but the link to Welsh is less obvious until one actually takes the time to read *Laidlaw*. Then you can tell why Welsh found the book to be a revelation. 'McIlvanney wrote about people I could identify with, and they were central characters, the stars of the show, not token villains or comedians.' McIlvanney may inadvertently have kicked off the whole 'there's been a murder' genre (the phrase is actually used three times in *Laidlaw*), but here was a fellow working-class Scot (the son of a miner) who could write forensically and beautifully about actual pubs Irvine had drunk in, who wasn't scared to write about the poverty, bigotry, gangsters and graffiti Irvine knew too well. You can almost hear Irvine saying to himself, if he can do it, why can't I?

McIlvanney also allowed characters like the murder victim's dad, Bud Lawson, to speak in the vernacular. Lawson was 'a mobile quarrel with the world', a phrase that could quite easily be applied to some of the characters on whom *Trainspotting*'s Begbie was based. Irvine knew plenty of guys just like Bud Lawson. Although the different nuances between the Scottish west-coast dialect and the language used in Muirhouse are apparent, the message was clear: a Scottish writer didn't have to stick to the Queen's English to produce a powerful – and award-winning – work. I'm sure reading McIlvanney subliminally influenced Irvine's own writing style. *Laidlaw*'s psychopathic hard man John Rhodes dispenses violent retribution in a manner Begbie would have been proud of. Both Welsh and McIlvanney are great at crisp, funny dialogue and brief, acidic pay-off lines. One of the best lines in *Trainspotting* comes very early on when Renton describes Sick Boy, who is desperately in need of a hit, as having 'nothing in his eyes but need'. You can almost imagine McIlvanney, in his lilting west-coast accent, speaking those words. It's a lovely line, compassionate and telling. Reading McIlvanney helped Irvine to bridge the gap between what he wanted to do and what he felt capable of doing.

Irvine quickly read and enjoyed the work of two other stellar west-coast writers, James Kelman's *The Busconductor Hines* and Alasdair Gray's *Lanark*. Kelman's book in particular, with its even more authentic use of the vernacular in prose, was a particularly liberating find for Irvine. It helped convince him that regional dialect could be used as the main language in powerful works of literature and didn't have to be restricted to comedic works or pulp fiction. Irvine first became aware of Kelman after reading a great review of his debut novel in the *NME*. According to Welsh, discovering these great contemporary authors led him to rediscover Scottish historical literary greats like Hogg, Stevenson (whom he considers to be Scotland's greatest writer), Grassic Gibbon and Burns. Irvine then went through a phase when he became almost as obsessed with literature as he was/is with music and football. He read voraciously and eclectically – Russian classics, Salman Rushdie, Sir Walter Scott, de Quincey, Coleridge, Huxley, Martin Millar, Trocchi's *Cain's Book* – always trying to find 'a voice and a set of social circumstances that chimed'.

When *Trainspotting* became a massive hit, one of its most

talked-about and controversial features was the use of Leith vernacular. Although he would probably dismiss the debate as elitist nonsense, Welsh became synonymous with this style of writing, so it's interesting to learn that his first stab at his debut novel was actually done in Standard English. He soon gave up on that idea, feeling unhappy writing in a way he considered to be unnatural and pretentious. Writing in the vernacular just felt more natural, and he also no doubt took some pride in its use. He remembers as a schoolboy feeling angry about being chastised for using the Scots word for yes – 'aye' – in class. One could hardly call it cultural oppression, but little things like that did have an effect on Irvine's take on the world. So most of *Trainspotting* was proudly written in streetwise dialogue through interior monologues.

Welsh would later explain to Ladislav Nagy in the *Guardian* why he chooses to write in the vernacular. 'I write my column in Standard English. For journalism it's a great language: exact, precise, a little anal, a little dull, but great for conveying information and instruction in service of the empire! For novels, for looking at social groups and cultures, it has more limited application; it's just not funky enough. People don't use it in films, television or in real life. Why do they persist with it in books? Writing should reflect the myriad of contemporary different cultures. Language is living and evolving. Writers shouldn't be fucking curators.'

Irvine once said that he never thought anyone outwith the narrow confines of Edinburgh and its environs would even understand the book, let alone buy it in any great numbers. I think he was being a bit disingenuous here, especially having seen how the likes of Kelman and McIlvanney had gained strong reviews and no little commercial success. Sandy Macnair, who proofread the rough copy of *Trainspotting* prior to publication, told me: 'I did suggest he include a glossary at the back to explain the slang terms to the uninitiated, but Irvine's view was that readers would understand the context, at least, if not the actual specific meanings.' The whole controversy about using vernacular language is a bit of a red herring, anyway. As the writer John Mullen has pointed out, most of what appears to be unfamiliar in *Trainspotting* is just standard vocabulary spelled differently and delivered with a strong Edinburgh dialect. So, 'were' becomes 'wir', 'to' becomes 'tae' and 'and' becomes 'n'. What did set it apart was the inclusion of choice Edinburgh phrases like 'biscuit-ersed', 'barry', and 'likesays'. But, really, even the densest of readers could soon figure out what they meant.

Irvine's next major inspiration was the polar opposite of Waugh. He came across Chicago writer Iceberg Slim's autobiography, *Pimp: The Story of My Life* – a graphic, cruelly misogynistic and violent tale – in a second-hand bookshop in Soho. He was soon raving about the book's 'wit, verve, rage and humour', and the influence on his own writing style is obvious. *Pimp* and *Trainspotting* work along similar lines, with occasional flashes of humour and beautiful prose helping to take one's mind away from the violence and gore. Slim's honest depiction of his hatred for his whores and the violence he metes out to them also made it easier for Welsh to portray Begbie's own viciousness and hatred of women. There's a scene in *Pimp* where Slim, coked out of his head, picks up Melody – 'a beautiful white bitch' – in a bar, and later recoils in rage when he discovers that she is in fact a he. Again there's a link here to the scene in the *Trainspotting* film when the unfortunate homophobe Begbie has an almost identical experience with a transvestite.

When you read the following passage from *Pimp*, it – with the addition of some Leith-style bad language – could almost have come from the pages of *Trainspotting*. 'He pulled my belt from my trousers on a chair. He tightened the belt around my arm above the elbow. My veins stood out like blue rope.

He stabbed the needle into a vein in the hollow. The glass tube turned red. I lay there freezing to death waiting for the smack to slug the sickness and pain out of me.'

Welsh soon tracked down the 1967 follow-up, *Trick Baby*, and was equally impressed by it and by the rest of Slim's catalogue. He became such a devotee that he wrote the introduction to Canongate's 2009 reissue of *Pimp*. There he explained that 'one of Slim's most endearing features was that he never made any excuses for the life he led. His writing is characterised by a scrupulous honesty about the social reality and the hyper-real theatricality of street life . . . Iceberg Slim did for the pimp what Jean Genet did for the homosexual thief and William Burroughs did for the junky: he articulated the thoughts and feelings of someone who had been there.' I don't think it is stretching things too far to suggest that Welsh did the same for the disenfranchised Edinburgh druggies.

Reading Iceberg Slim was enormously empowering for Welsh and gave him the confidence to write honestly in his own voice, and without embarrassment and excuses for his own people, the schemies of Leith and Muirhouse. He wanted to highlight what was going wrong in these communities. 'What I was concerned about was the social landscape we'd be left with after this: baldly, the substitution of drugs for jobs in the poorest parts of Britain.' Irvine blamed the state for creating social conditions that marginalised many Scots communities, turning people to crime and drugs. He says he wanted to highlight how gifted, intelligent people from the schemes underestimated their own talents and self-destructed. Welsh would write about these people who didn't have any access to power and were living on the edge of society, but not impose his moral authority on their actions. He would just 'capture them on paper'.

8

Banging on the word processor

Once I decided this is what I'm gonna do, this is what I'm gonna write about, in this way, I was very confident. There was no doubt about it that it would work out and get published.

When Irvine sat down to write *Trainspotting* he gathered all the notes, the doodling and the diaries that he had kept from way back to the time of his first trip to the US. Initially, though, he couldn't see how they would amount to a book. He felt he didn't yet have the ability to write genre fiction, and in any case he considered that particular option to be not much better than the drudgery of real work. Instead, he decided to try to make sense of his own life by writing about people who, like himself, had struggled with recurring drink and drug problems throughout their lives, people who were generally considered to be losers and failures through repeatedly messing up. All the major characters in the book have their own debilitating addiction/compulsion. Sick Boy is hooked on sex and junk. Begbie gets his kicks through casual violence. Second Prize is a failed footballer turned alcoholic.

Spud can't stop stealing and has a drug problem of his own. And, of course, Renton – the novel's anti-hero – is a junkie, as are Alison, Tommy and Johnny Swan. The persuasive effects of the subsequent play and of Ewan McGregor's dominant performance in the film have elevated Mark Renton to the position of the major character in *Trainspotting*. However, that's more a tribute to the talents of the writers who adapted the book for stage and screen than an accurate reflection of Irvine's original intention.

Once he began writing, Welsh worked very hard to see it through. 'The real story of how I wrote the book was getting up early in the morning, using my imagination and banging on the word processor. Some of the inferences and associations I've read and heard from different sources of what this meant, where this came from, who this character was influenced by, have been pretty ludicrous.'

Of course, for anyone who knew Irvine the whole issue of whom a character was based on is endlessly fascinating, as you look for elements of yourself or mutual friends in each person he wrote about. On our pub crawls back in the late 1970s we would often meet an angry small-time crook called Jimmy, whom I've always thought bore at least a passing resemblance to the character of Begbie. Now sadly deceased, Jimmy was christened 'the man of violence' by Irvine and was a sinister presence on many an all-day drinking session. Like Begbie, he had a penchant for carrying a sharpened knitting needle on his person for use during bar brawls, although Jimmy had a bit more class and humour about him than Begbie would ever have. I recall Jimmy being asked once why he had dished out a fearful beating to some poor guy and him replying: 'The cunt wisnae a man of style.' Jimmy never really warmed to me, and I suspect he thought I was leading the young Irvine astray. Irvine used to tell me how Jimmy – who, like Begbie, was virulently anti-drugs – would enquire as to my whereabouts with the quaint enquiry, 'Where's yer fuckin' junkie mate these days, Welshie?'

But although there are similarities between Jimmy and Begbie, it's far too simplistic to say that they are one and the same. In fact, all the characters in *Trainspotting* are composites, constructs drawn from Irvine's own life experience and the working-class culture he grew up in. Irvine usually picked their names by leafing through the Edinburgh phonebook and selecting at random. To help develop the characters and to define their personas, he would make out an imaginary playlist of songs they would listen to, where they stayed and whom they slept with. Similarly, some of the scenes that ended up in the book actually happened. The horrific incident where Begbie glasses some poor sap in a bar was based on an incident witnessed by Welsh in the old Cottar's Howff bar on Edinburgh's Rose Street.

Of all the book's characters, Renton is probably the one whose life's trajectory – especially the road travelled from council scheme to university and the subsequent descent into drug addiction – most closely resembles Irvine's. Renton is aggressively witty and sarcastic and uses his sophisticated (in comparison to his junkie friends) patter to talk his way out of many a tight corner. Both author and character are equally at home in academia or in the gutter. There is also the passage in *Skagboys* where Renton, while in rehab, starts writing a diary, making a conscious decision to use vernacular language as 'That is more like I sound in my heid ... why try tae sound different?' This mirrors exactly the decision Irvine took when he started to write *Trainspotting*. There is also a more straightforward link in that Renton's brother is a Hearts fan, as is Irvine's. But again, it's far too reductive to take that argument any further and say that the book is some sort of coded record or prism of Irvine's own life. Welsh would later dismiss this suggestion, telling *Dazed and Confused*

magazine that it 'comes from a kind of middle-class belief
that fiction and empathetic imagination is the preserve of the
bourgeoisie and that someone from a different background
cannot possibly have those tools . . . Obviously, there's a bit
of me in the character, but I created it. It's like – where does
it stop? Does that mean I'm a football thug and a rapist like
the character in *Marabou Stork*?'

It's a sad comment on Scottish society that characters like
the psychotic Begbie are instantly recognisable. Irvine told
me: 'It's even sadder that he is recognised all over the world.
Russians, South Africans, they all tell me about their Begbie-
esque pals.' It does genuinely worry him that characters he
created, like Renton, might be seen as role models. He thinks
this response of readers tells you all you need to know about
the society we live in. In Begbie, Welsh created a character
that he despised, but interestingly he later said that he had
very little control in the process. Echoes of voices and violence
he had experienced in real life came to him 'arguing and
shouting' as he wrote and immediately found their way into
the book. The upshot was the terrifying character of Francis
Begbie, whom the *Guardian*'s John Mullan succinctly
described as 'a character next to whom all others seem
hampered by scruples. We know that he is entirely without
compunction or sympathy because he tells us so in the
portions of narration allotted to him.'

Welsh would later explain: 'I want to create characters
who speak for themselves, in their own conflict. I don't want
them to prove my ideas. So, if the characters come to me as
racist or sexist, or violent or psychopathic or whatever, so be
it. I'm not going to set myself up as this great liberal who
approves or disapproves of the characters in the book. To me
they only exist as a culmination of behaviour.'

As for the subject matter of *Trainspotting* – that was an
easy choice. It's ironic that it took the explosion in heroin

abuse and the subsequent horrors of HIV and Aids on the schemes to give writers like Irvine a legitimacy and a way to write about their native city. Irvine was interested in people living on the margins of experience and how those vulnerable, fucked-up individuals interacted, not only with fellow victims, but also with the rest of 'normal' society. But rather than take the standard bleeding-heart-liberal approach of blaming the state for forcing people into a corner where they have to behave badly, Welsh liked to put his characters in situations where they do things that are clearly beyond the pale morally. The reader has to question how that can be defensible or even comprehensible.

Irvine would later write in the *Guardian*: 'What I've always been able to do is put people in extreme situations. I like to see how, when people are in a bad position, they can just make it worse. That's been my overwhelming interest . . . I wasn't really interested in telling the story of one or two people with drug problems so much as showing that such behaviour always takes place within a context. It's not isolated. Such behaviour has repercussions for the individual and for the people surrounding the individual. I didn't want to present the junkie as isolated and cut off. I wanted to focus on the relationships and cultural pressures surrounding these characters. Obviously, there are extremes of behaviour people can get into, extremes of antisocial and fucked-up behaviour, and I didn't want to spare that.'

Unlike some 'middle-class voyeurs who wrote exploitatively about other people's misery', Welsh was writing from experience, and he certainly wasn't wilfully trying to shock people. He told the writer Sue Wilson that he personally was not shocked by the stories he told. 'I think shock is largely a middle-class reaction to it, imagining all these dirty working-class people doing these violent things to each other. If it's somebody doing it in a drawing-room it seems to be a lot

more acceptable; the violence is in the environment. There
are bits in it that are ugly, there's behaviour in it that's really
ugly, but that's the reason for showing them.'

The novel's title came to Irvine after he saw a painting by
his old friend Dave Todd, which depicted a luxury train full
of partying yuppies whizzing through the now derelict Leith
railway station, which is full of skeletons. It was like a ghost
train in reverse, with the skeletal 'trainspotters' outside looking in. Irvine thought the train represented Edinburgh city
centre, with its culture, affluence and festivals. The station
represented the peripheral housing estates. In an interview in
the *Big Issue* in 1993 he explained: 'I wanted to do a book
about Edinburgh and attack the perception of it as this bourgeois city where everything cultural happens, a playground
for the *Guardian*/Hampstead middle classes. There is another
reality that runs parallel with that, and that's why there are
none of the discernible traditional Edinburgh landmarks in
it.' The title makes the gentle, often derided as meaningless
activity of trainspotting an analogy for the pointlessness of
trying to nullify your life with smack.

Stylistically, Irvine opted to construct the book in a frag-
mentary way, and unkind critics would later belittle
Trainspotting as just a collection of (admittedly brilliantly
realised) pub yarns thrown together. There's an element of
truth to this, perhaps demonstrated in the mercifully brief 'The
Elusive Mr Hunt', which adds little to the story and is no more
than the retelling of a tale that used to do the rounds in pubs
back in the day. That's not to belittle the short story, of course,
and there have certainly been times in his career when Welsh
has favoured the collection of stories over the full-length novel.
Perhaps the initial excitement and glowing reviews meant that
the book's disjointedness was overlooked.

The book also allowed Irvine to get on his soapbox about
politics, especially in Renton's famous 'colonised by

wankers' speech, which neatly summed up the powerlessness and the anti-Thatcher sentiment felt by Scots in the wake of the 1979 referendum, which had destroyed any immediate hope of devolution. This passage was sometimes misread as an attack on the English; in fact, it was more a verbal assault on the Scots, who cannot even find a decent culture to be colonised by. Irvine has always had a great fascination and affection for the English, having studied there, lived there for many years and married an English girl. He would later vent his frustrations about the Scots in his *Rebel Inc.* article. 'You measure yourself on the fucking ability to fucking produce eleven football players to somehow get a result against this colonial power and then you can forget about everything else. Just sit in your fucking wee hovels and fucking bevvy for the rest of your life. It's just really fucking sad, man.' He saw the book as a working-class voice rather than a Scottish voice, and was delighted when his friends in Newcastle and London later told him they recognised individuals from their own social background in its characters.

9

A truer voice

I was delighted, and I think it's probably the biggest high I had as a writer.

Irvine Welsh on the publication of his first
short story in *New Writing Scotland 9*

The Scottish literary scene of the early 1990s sparkled with a new wave of young writers embracing a fresh approach to the craft. Throughout the country, but most notably in Welsh's native city, aspiring novelists and poets were bypassing the orthodox, somewhat safe and conservative publishing system and instead adopting a do-it-yourself approach to getting their work into print. Inspired by the success of Glaswegian writers such as James Kelman and Alasdair Gray, fanzine-style literary publications like *Clocktower Press* and *Rebel Inc.* began to spring up, offering a new platform for those eager to write in their own voice about the disempowered ordinary folk in their own, invariably working-class, communities. It was a movement which would radically alter what was deemed acceptable to write about, and what was perceived as commercially appealing, both in Scotland and further afield.

Though he was to become included in this new wave of young Scottish writers (indeed, some critics saw Irvine as the movement's figurehead), Irvine didn't really consider himself as part of the group prior to the publication of *Trainspotting*. He admired the vitality and talent of many of the new writers and had met a couple of them, including Alan Warner, in pubs and clubs. Later he would become a fully-paid-up member of the 'Scottish Beats', but the notion that he was part of some group of fellow-minded scribes when he was actually writing *Trainspotting* is fanciful. Writing his debut novel was a solitary pursuit for Irvine. Very few people knew he was doing it. Sandy Macnair – who socialised a great deal with Irvine around then – told me: 'I can't say I was really aware of it – until one day he casually mentioned that *Trainspotting* was going to be published.'

Irvine's mention of meeting fellow writers in pubs and clubs reflects the fact that, whatever alternative illegal stimulants were on offer, good old boozing played an important role in bonding the writers together. Pubs like Black Bo's, the St James Oyster Bar and the Antiquary in Stockbridge (where Monday-night readings were held) were popular with most of the city's writers back then. Alan Warner, who wrote arguably the best book to come out of this new wave, *Morvern Callar*, told me how important the pub environment was back then. 'Nothing could be closer to the truth, and that exactly describes the writers – male and female – from around that 1990–96 period and beyond. My entire generation of writers – and an older one such as James Kelman and Tom Leonard's – came unashamedly from "bars and pubs" in Edinburgh and Glasgow. My recollection is that virtually everyone drank a great deal and attempted to remain in the pub as long as humanly possible; there was a heavy party intent and we all gravitated around certain bars. We were all readers, and liked music of all sorts and books of all sorts.

The pub remained absolutely central to that writing culture.'

Alan is keen to point out that the pubs were not the preserve of male writers. 'I don't know where this idea comes from that women don't go to the pub. I don't know any women who don't go to the pub. Our drinking groups actually included many of the type known as "female human beings", including the editor Charlotte Ross, who was involved in the feminist magazine *Harpies and Quines*, the painter Rosie Savin, and the novelist and short story writer Laura Hird.' Warner hails from Connel, near Oban, but has an impressive memory when it comes to recalling the popular bars among the Edinburgh writers. 'Rose Street was too touristy and the prices too hiked, so it was more downmarket pubs. I was often in the Talisman Bar in Waverley Station, the Malt Shovel with the railway crew or the Hebrides Bar with highlanders. I liked McGuffie's downstairs from the Doric till they poshed it up. You could get a pie and pickled egg in there. Now it's like caviar: a pie and fucking pickled egg in a pub. Though none of us were students, student happy hours were taken full advantage of.' The poet Roddy Lumsden was such a regular at the St James Oyster Bar that mail was occasionally sent to him there. Roddy – who wrote a fine poem called 'St James Infirmly' – told me: 'If anyone didn't have my address in the early 1990s, they could be assured that a letter would reach me there, as it was like my second home.'

Although he soon became synonymous with the alternative fanzine scene, Welsh's first published extract from *Trainspotting* appeared in the more mainstream academic annual anthology, *New Writing Scotland 9 (NWS 9)*, which was produced by the Association for Scottish Literary Studies (ASLS). Irvine later explained how he had sent the typescript to *NWS* after reading an earlier edition of the journal and deciding that he could do better than 99 per cent of the published stories and poems.

So it was that in the summer of 1991 a scruffy A4 type-script arrived at the home of one of the journal's editors, the novelist Janice Galloway. She and her co-editor, Giffnock-born poet Hamish Whyte, were used to receiving speculative chapters from hopeful writers, but even they were taken aback by Welsh's short story 'The First Day of the Edinburgh Festival'. Sitting in the kitchen of Janice's Pollokshields apartment, sipping coffee and sifting through the submitted work, as Hamish recalls, they were soon scratching their heads in disbelief. 'I remember asking Janice, "What on earth do we have here?" We were really fussy that submissions should be nicely presented, and Irvine had sent us a real dog's breakfast of a typescript, badly typed on crumpled paper. It almost got rejected for that alone. Then there was the subject matter. We read it again and again and concluded that it definitely had something; it was exciting and different.'

In terms of the language he used, Irvine submitted a toned-down version of the story that eventually appeared in *Trainspotting*. In the first paragraph alone there are fourteen minor spelling differences. The *NWS 9* piece has 'was' instead of 'wis', 'of' replaces 'ay' and 'arm' is used for 'airm'. Even so, the subject matter and the coarseness of the language used set it apart from the rest of the anthology, which is full of elliptical short stories and poems by writers including Duncan McLean, A.L. Kennedy and Ron Butlin (who went on to become Edinburgh's Makar, or poet laureate). The introduction revealed that a couple of ASLS members were not keen on the journal surviving, but the editors argued that 'Scot Lit' as a cosy study of the past was not enough: 'We must still support the vital and volatile brat that is literature in the making (whatever the trauchle involved).'

Eager to find out more about the author, Galloway and Whyte decided to include Irvine's story in the ninth volume of *NWS*, which was published in October 1991. Hamish recalls, with a nice touch of understatement: 'We thought it might shock the more staid echelons of Scots Literature, and in our introduction we described the story as "Edinburgh dirty realism".' In the notes on contributors at the back of the journal, Welsh wrote: 'Irvine Welsh, who lives in Leith, is currently completing a brightly optimistic novel full of sympathetic, generously spirited characters.' He received a payment of £10 per page for the short story and was genuinely enthused that someone would even consider publishing his work; years later he described it as the biggest high he ever had as a writer.

Galloway and Whyte invited Welsh to read the chapter at one of the launches for the new edition of the journal. Hamish remembers that 'some people were predicting that he would be some hopped-up Leith junkie out of his mind on smack. But then when we met him he was quite the opposite – pleasant, funny and a perfectly reasonable guy.' Janice, who just two years previously had released her stunning debut novel *The Trick Is to Keep Breathing*, was equally impressed and charmed by the new star on the literary scene. In particular she was wowed by how confident and connected this unheard-of writer who hailed from one of Edinburgh's most notorious housing schemes was when it came to reading his work to the public for the first time.

'I also recall how particular and how dramatically polite he was. He was really pleased to meet everyone and was a bit of a charmer really. He had lovely eyes – and I suspect he knew he did. The main thing for me was how much the story assumed from his reading it out loud. He wellied it, refusing to read like he was slightly embarrassed by the whole thing – and that was a treat. His confidence that the work was worth a listen showed, and Irvine was a genuinely terrific reader, as were some of the other new writers such as Alan

Warner, Duncan McLean and Jane Harris. I was proud of him after that first reading, proud to have been allowed to see and select his work.'*

Irvine Welsh always insists that getting *Trainspotting* published was a surprise for him, and that he had no game plan to become a famous writer. Janice Galloway confirms that, for most if not all her contemporaries, the primary aim was just to write about people and places they knew, rather than harbour dreams of writing a bestseller.

'Those kind of ambitions were just not an issue. We were trying to shift ground from the rather staid creature literature had become. We were almost "trying out" writing in those magazines to see what happened. Publication of a novel beyond that was a possible next step, but not something to base any notion of a career on. Most of us had other jobs unrelated to writing to support us and did not see this as abnormal, or some kind of status to rise above. It wasn't a status game. While politics and the whole "greed is good" social ambition seemed to be running riot down south, this putative rise of new writing in Scotland from so many seemed a thing unrelated to that. Writing a Jeffrey Archer

---

* Shortly after *Trainspotting* was released I went to see Irvine give a reading at Paisley Town Hall. I remember being quite nervous for him, when he stood up to start speaking, thinking he might be overawed by the large crowd. I needn't have worried. Straight away he won over the audience with a brilliant reading that a stand-up comic would have been proud of. It was almost like listening to him tell a story to a crowd of mates in an Edinburgh pub back in 1977. No matter the audience, Irvine was a born entertainer. He thanks Duncan McLean for improving his reading techniques, telling the *Guardian* how he tried to emulate McLean: 'He was a stand-up comedian and he told me that it wasn't enough to go to a reading and just read the story; instead you have to give it big licks, put on voices and get the pacing and intonation right, hold people's attention.'

million-seller was not what we were aiming at. We were aiming at finding a truer voice.'

Within days of the publication of *NWS 9*, the literary grapevine in Scotland's capital was buzzing with rumour and conjecture as to who exactly Irvine Welsh was. And the question wasn't just being asked in Edinburgh. Out in South Queensferry, ten miles north-west of the city, a young village-hall janitor and talented writer called Duncan McLean sensed that he had found a kindred spirit when he read 'The First Day of the Edinburgh Festival'.

'I just loved that story for its drama, its language, its shock value and for the perfect jab of the ending. Like my story in *NWS 9*, Irvine's chapter was set in Leith, which was a radical move at the time. Also, I knew the betting shop in Muirhouse where the infamous suppositories-down-the-bog scene took place. I was amazed and over-joyed that somebody other than me had decided to put this obscure but to me immediately recognisable place into fiction. At a reading in a Waterstones store in Glasgow I asked Janice about Irvine, but she said she had no idea who he was. His story had just arrived unheralded like everyone else's.'

Fraserburgh-born McLean had cut his teeth writing sketches and songs for the theatre until James Kelman's 1984 debut novel *The Busconductor Hines* grabbed his attention. Kelman's brilliantly offbeat writing skills and his emphasis on writing about the real life of working-class Scots inspired Duncan to turn to prose fiction. By 1992 London publishing house Secker & Warburg had signed up McLean as the leading light of the Scottish new wave. His own calling card, *Bucket of Tongues*, published in March 1992, was highly impressive; like Kelman before him and Welsh to come, Duncan was a master storyteller who had a pleasing capacity to shock with his chosen subject matter.* But McLean wasn't just a talented writer; he was also – through his own literary magazine – determined to champion the other new talents that were emerging in the early 1990s. The man who signed Irvine to Secker & Warburg, Robin Robertson, told me: 'The real hero of this story is Duncan McLean, who selflessly promoted other writers through his Clocktower Press.' Robertson recalls going to Birmingham to see Kelman and Janice Galloway on an Arts Council reading tour promoting story collections published by Secker & Warburg in early 1991. He was extremely impressed by McLean's own reading that night. 'I was just blown away by this young man from my neck of the woods, reading short pieces from what was to become *Bucket of Tongues*. I went up to Duncan after his reading and asked him to send me a manuscript.'

Like Galloway, McLean had no time for the conventional ideal of literary stardom. His idea of writers who had 'made it' was Iain Crichton Smith, Norman MacCaig and George Mackay Brown. '*Clocktower* writers were trying to write new stories, written in the language of the day, about the ideas and problems that confronted us here and now. It was always about seeking out the new, the exploratory, the unsafe. We thought that, probably, nobody much would want to read such stuff. But if you write with honesty and integrity about the world around you, that was all that mattered. Popular success was irrelevant.'

A few weeks after reading the *NWS 9* piece, Duncan saw

---

* *Bucket of Tongues* is difficult to find these days, but it's well worth a read. Alan Warner rates it highly. 'I have to be honest and say at the time I kept comparing *Trainspotting* to *Bucket of Tongues*, which I believe was a mistake on my part. Both consist of short, scabrous Scottish prose sketches. I thought *Bucket of Tongues* was the better book, but I really enjoyed *Trainspotting*. It made me laugh so much and it moved me emotionally.'

a letter in the *Scotsman* of 18 October 1991 from an Irvine
Welsh of 2 Wellington Place, Leith, complaining about audience members walking out of a matinee performance of the
Royal Lyceum Theatre's production of Trevor Griffiths' play
Comedians. According to the letter-writer, the sensitive souls
going to the play should have expected a bit of strong
language and shouldn't have spoiled the evening for the rest
of the audience by marching out. 'While I accept that some
narrow-minded types will be upset by explicit language, it is
unfortunate that such people cannot suspend their prejudices
for a few hours. Their behaviour was unsettling to other
members of the audience, and an insult to the highly gifted
actors on stage.' Duncan's attention was also drawn to
another letter underneath Irvine's which appeared to be from
one of the narrow-minded types – a Mrs E.M. Bogie of
Ravelston Dykes. She complained in true Mary Whitehouse
style about the play's foul language, concluding: 'Surely an
ordinary audience could only have a feeling of shame that
such a degrading play could be produced and supported by
so many illustrious bodies representing Edinburgh.' Duncan
immediately guessed that the two letters were the work of the
same person and that Irvine had managed to dupe the newspaper's letters editor. Irvine and Sandy Macnair had written
the letters as a mischievous wind-up, not dissimilar to those
the playwright Joe Orton used to send to the press under the
name of Edna Welthorpe, a guardian of public morals.
(Curiously, Welsh was not dissimilar to Orton in looks and
in his sardonic, bitchy take on life back then.)

   Duncan immediately wrote to Welsh asking him if he
would like to contribute to McLean's own literary venture –
the fledgling *Clocktower Press*. Irvine was genuinely over-
whelmed that a well-respected, up-and-coming writer like
McLean was taking an interest in his work. He agreed to get
involved, saying he had a novel ready for publication, though

secretly his reaction was 'Fuck, I better write this now!' Welsh's letter in reply offers an insight into his writing process and his ambitions in the days just prior to his elevation to literary fame and fortune. 'Many thanks for your note and the generous comments about the story in *NWS 9*. It's encouraging to get such positive feedback (and unsolicited!) particularly from someone whose stuff I admire. The story in *NWS 9* was really my first ever completed – let alone published – piece of work. I've been scribbling away for ages on the creative side, but have lacked the discipline to sit down and put my drafts into a presentable format. (A common story, I'd expect.) So I've reached the difficult stage of this novel, the part where I've got to sit down and hack the bastard out. What I've effectively done is strategically withdrawn and started to re-edit some old short stories, including the one in *NWS*. The short stories are interwoven, and it gives me encouragement to see the editing process completed for each individual story. Hopefully completion of these short stories will give me the bottle to get stuck into the unwieldy manuscript of the novel.' Welsh would later describe how he bashed out a draft of 250,000 words based on his old notes and diaries, then lopped off the beginning and end and wrote a new 'heist' ending.

Welsh and McLean were soon collaborating through the Clocktower Press, which issued a series of influential booklets, or 'cultural interventions', between 1990 and 1996. The two writers became friends, offering advice and support and editing each other's work. Welsh would later pay tribute to the role McLean played in getting *Trainspotting* off the ground. In a letter to Duncan in April 1993 Irvine wrote: 'Thanks again for your encouragement, without which it [*Trainspotting*] would probably still be lying on my shelf gathering dust.'

Along with an old friend from the University of Edinburgh,

Scotsman reporter James Meek, McLean had brought out the first issue of *Clocktower* – a modest sixteen pages featuring short stories by himself and James – in December 1990. *Clocktower*, which took its name from the prominent feature of the village hall in South Queensferry where Duncan worked, was modelled on the punk and football fanzines which had emerged in the late 1970s. Both men had been frustrated in their attempts to get their work into print through the mainstream publishing industry. Rejection slips were upsetting enough, but what was even more annoying was the delay between having their work accepted and publication – in extreme cases it could mean waiting around for up to two years before their work saw the light of day.

Ever since university days, McLean and Meek would meet and swap typescripts, ideas and criticism. Duncan told me how those 'intense, fresh and exciting' days with Meek differed from the friendship and working relationship which gradually evolved with Welsh. 'By the time Irvine and I met, we were both adults, late-twenties in my case, mid-thirties in his, so there wasn't the same youthful exploration. He certainly sent typescripts to me, and I think I sent him one or two things as well. We were both relatively serious about what we were doing, and relatively sure of ourselves as individuals (if not always as writers) so there was a more measured approach. We certainly discussed ideas about writing during preparations to get his pieces into the *Clocktower* booklets, and I no doubt gave my criticisms or suggestions as editor too. But in those days, none of us really knew what was likely to work. I remember telling him I thought *Trainspotting* was a terrible name for the book. No one – not me, not Robin Robertson, not even Irvine – predicted the book's huge success.'

Duncan remembers that, early on, Irvine – though very sociable in every other way – was not really part of the whole literary gang that was revitalising Scottish literature in the early 1990s. 'As far as I am aware he was solitary in his writing, though I do recall meeting him on a couple of occasions in the Blue Blazer pub at Tollcross. He had a suit and tie on; he looked like an office worker. He claimed to be unsure of the worth of what he had written. On the other hand, he thought very carefully and argued hard about any small changes to the text. This led me to believe he knew exactly what he was doing. Another time we met in the bar of the Filmhouse. We would meet after work and talk for an hour or two at most. I also met him once in a tiny office in the Council Chambers; he was sitting there telling me this was where he had written half of *Trainspotting* while he should have been working.

'We met for the specific reason of getting the *Clocktower* booklet prepared, so that's what we concentrated on. No doubt we talked about what I was writing, about personal things, about other new folk *Clocktower* was going to publish (Irvine was always interested in, and supportive of, folk like Alan Warner and Alison Kermack), but mostly we just talked about which bits of what would become *Trainspotting* to publish first, about my editorial comments, about the cover, etc.' During one such conversation, McLean suggested to Welsh that he send the *Trainspotting* typescript to Robin Robertson at Secker.* It was a piece of advice that would radically change the course of Irvine Welsh's life.

* Robertson became aware of Welsh's work when he read and thoroughly enjoyed the stories in *NWS* and the *Clocktower* pamphlets. He then asked Duncan to help persuade Irvine to send a typescript to Secker.

10

Past tense

I don't think he knows how I feel about him because we're Scottish and not very good at talking about feelings. I'm sure I've tried and he's just brushed me off. But he has been a great inspiration to me.

Irvine Welsh talking about Duncan McLean

Publication of his first short story in *NWS 9* wasn't a wholly positive experience for Irvine. Formerly his writing had been a hobby, seldom shared even with close friends. Now the word was out that a new talent was on the scene and people wanted to get a hold of his debut novel. The only problem was that it was far from complete. In a letter to Duncan McLean dated 25 November 1991 he mentioned how publishers now had unrealistic expectations of him and how he was now experiencing the 'pain of rejection'. Partly, though, he admitted, this was due to his own naivety. 'Most of it was retrospectively inevitable, as I've been sending material to magazines who wouldn't publish my sort of stuff in a proverbial month of Sundays. Now I'm actually looking at the magazines first before I punt the stuff to them.'

One such magazine, *DOG*, run by the poet David Crystal, published a short story destined for *Trainspotting* – 'Traditional Sunday Breakfast' – in December 1991. The Glasgow-based *West Coast Magazine* also agreed to run another *Trainspotting* short story, 'It Goes Without Saying'. Irvine told McLean how the harrowing tale of the death of Lesley's infant child was 'from the same clutch of progressive (in the sequential rather than qualitative sense!) short stories I'm working on in my current collection. You'll notice it's written much more phonetically than the story in *NWS 9*. That's because the story was originally in that form, but I rather cowardly compromised by sanitising it for publication.'

A couple of weeks later he wrote to McLean again, enthused to have discovered that so many of his own acquaintances were also writing great prose and poetry in their spare time. For a while Welsh toyed with the idea of bringing out a booklet of his own, which would have featured the work of those friends. He asked McLean for advice on the costs involved and dealing with printers and distribution, though the idea never came to fruition.

It's difficult to overestimate the influence Duncan had on Irvine in the year prior to the publication of *Trainspotting*. When, years later, Irvine was asked by the *Guardian** who his key mentor was in those early days, he chose McLean. 'He was very encouraging and pushed me to finish it . . . He helped me a lot with my work. He told me mundane things about how to use dialect in my stories. I also learned a lot from how he uses dialogue to move the narrative along and I've tried to use that in my writing.'

After a traditional festive season of over-indulging on the

---

* Welsh also cited Janice Galloway, Jeff Torrington and Kevin Williamson for endorsing him and giving encouragement in those early days.

grog, Irvine got down to work again in 1992, writing to
McLean and offering him support after he had received an
unfavourable review. Although *Trainspotting* eventually
received ecstatic reviews from just about everyone who
mattered, Welsh's subsequent novels have on occasion been
dismissed in vicious critiques. Back in 1992, Irvine had
already adopted his own defiant response to negative criticism of his work. When it came to reviews, Welsh opined
that one critic's 'lack of a common voice' is another critic's
'evidence of great versatility'. 'Either people like it or they
don't. If they don't, fuck them, there's plenty who do.'
Refreshed by a holiday hammering the Guinness, he
completed work on the short stories that eventually appeared
in the Clocktower publication *Past Tense*.

Irvine suggested the title for the booklet and also offered
advice on the order in which the works should appear: 'Her
Man', 'Memories of Matty', and 'Winter in West Granton',
followed by 'The Elusive Mr Hunt'. According to Welsh, the
majority of the works submitted were like 'real' short stories,
'though "Memories" is a bit more of a link story, where a funeral
is used for character and plot (in so far as one exists) development. It may work in the context of extracts from a novel'.

In April 1992, Welsh's *Past Tense: Four Stories from a
Novel* was issued by Clocktower. With an eye-catching cover
and graphics by the illustrator Peter Govan, the sixteen-page
booklet packed a powerful punch, though strangely sales
were sluggish, and the only reviewer who offered it perceptive positive criticism was Douglas Gifford in the *Books in
Scotland* quarterly. Duncan sent a copy of *Past Tense* to
Robin Robertson at Secker & Warburg. Robin was already
aware of Welsh's writing, having read the story in *NWS 9*
and had contacted Duncan urging him to get Irvine to make
contact with Secker.

Duncan told me: 'I have the distinct memory that the

reception from folk who had bought or read the earlier *Clocktower* booklets was a bit cool – or uncomprehending. Irvine's booklet was definitely slower to sell or even to give away. But it wasn't a problem – nothing about *Clocktower* was ever a problem, because nobody ever had any expectations, and everyone was simply happy to have a story or two in print, even if only 300 copies were printed and even if no one – and that includes me – was getting paid.

'Our commercial aspirations never went further than earning enough to print the next booklet. I tried to circulate them to other writers who I thought would enjoy them, or indeed be creatively annoyed by them; and to libraries, so that if anyone was crazy enough to look for Irvine's work, or Alan Warner's, at least they would find their *Clocktower* stuff. I also sent quite a few around the world to magazines in the hope of getting a listing or review. Listings in excellent US publications like *Factsheet Five* were actually better than reviews. All of these avenues did bring in a few sales, and very occasionally there would be a reading by me or some other contributor where we could sell five or ten copies.

'And, before you knew it, all 300 copies were gone . . . except in Irvine's case. The reaction from people who'd bought the first few booklets was a bit lukewarm. So his sales were slower. I had copies lying around even after Irvine started to be successful, when they started cropping up in dealer's catalogues at inflated prices.' (Eventually, in the summer of 1994, a shrewd Oban book dealer, Bill Cowan, paid £5 – the normal price was £1 – each for the remaining 60 booklets.) Duncan sent the last two to Welsh. In his accompanying letter he spelled out to Welsh how slow sales had been. 'I've been getting orders of one or two a week from various parts of the country (England mostly) for the past six months, gradually whittling away the backlog.' Despite the slow sales, Clocktower published another short story by

Welsh, 'Trainspotting at Leith Central Station' in the *Parcel of Rogues* issue of June 1992.

When *Trainspotting* became a global phenomenon, some cynics rounded on Welsh, accusing him of writing sensationally about topics that were bound to sell. In fact, writing in the early 1990s about junkies on a peripheral Edinburgh estate was about as far from a successful commercial game plan as one could imagine. Duncan remembers that very few people shared his enthusiasm for Irvine's writing style or his subject matter in those early days.

As to why the initial response to Irvine Welsh's booklet was so lukewarm, Duncan offers a few suggestions. Early on in his writing career, Irvine seemed reluctant to take part in the fringe literary scene, to do readings or to socialise with many other writers. 'Irvine had football friends, rave friends, work colleagues, family, some of which crossed over, some of which were entirely separate – but not literary friends, aside from Paul Reekie and a couple of other Edinburgh acid house-type folk. Also, outwith the context of the whole novel, the stories in *Past Tense* are good, but they lose much of their emotional impact, simply because you don't know the characters. So it was great to publish the booklet, but judged of itself, it wasn't the most satisfying literary work. I remember Kevin Williamson (who founded the equally important *Rebel Inc.* literary fanzine) quite liking the booklet, but then he read the whole of *Trainspotting* while on holiday at my house in Stromness – he stayed up all night reading it and was completely bowled over by the book. I think that was the experience for a lot of folk who quite liked the booklet, but didn't love Irvine until they read *Trainspotting* as a whole.

'Irvine's phonetic representation of speech was a real novelty back then, except for the small number of really keen folk who had read Tom Leonard. I know, of course, that people all over the world had experimented with phonetic representation for years – not least Scott, Hogg and various less worthy Scottish writers. But no one had done it for Edinburgh speech, and no one had done it at length in Scotland at all for decades.

'Irvine came along and did it in a fresh way, and at length, and, I mean this as a compliment, unselfconsciously. He wasn't hung up, as I was, about arguments about apostrophe use in the novels of John Galt, he just felt he wanted to convey the sound of his characters' voices and thoughts, and used orthography to do it . . . no problem. Except it was such a novelty that lots of people didn't get it initially. One of the great things that Irvine's success has made possible is the complete openness to phonetic representation in narrative – in any of a thousand different ways.'

Comparing the four stories that appeared in *Past Tense* with the four chapters as they appeared in *Trainspotting* is instructive, and shows that, as mentioned earlier, Irvine was not going to make the mistake of sanitising his work again. The first short story, 'Her Man', sees Secks (Second Prize) and Tommy gallantly trying to intervene in a particularly ugly and violent falling-out between a man and his woman, only to have the bruised and bloody female turn on them. Welsh did make lots of changes here, but mostly minor ones: he replaced the vernacular 'eh' and 'ehs' with the standard 'he' and 'he's' throughout, but this is balanced by changing the phrase 'he says' to 'he sais'. Elsewhere he just tinkered with the spelling of vernacular words, changing 'thaire' to 'thair' and 'mibye' to 'mibbe'. It's a similar tale in 'After the Burning', which would become part two of 'Memories of Matty' in the book, and in 'Winter in West Granton' and 'The Elusive Mr Hunt'.

Back then, Welsh was primarily writing for his own people on the council estates; if others latched on and enjoyed it, all well and good, but the author was not going to compromise to keep them happy. When, soon after its release, one hapless journalist suggested that *Trainspotting* should have a glossary of translations of Leithspeak, Welsh responded in caustic style, taking aim at the middle classes in Edinburgh's New Town. 'The last thing I want is those fuckers up in Charlotte Square putting on all the vernacular as a stage-managed thing. It's nothing to do with them.'

Welsh would no doubt find common ground with one of his contemporaries, Alan Warner, who argues that there exists in Britain 'a sly, unspoken literary prejudice' against authors writing about their own community. Warner believes there is a 'reluctance in a certain readership to accept that profundity can be found in working-class as well as middle-class experience . . . When I started to write I was fired up to prove – to myself at least – that a novel or novels could be forged out of the community I knew. It really was very important to me to try to force the social reality I knew into the novel form.' His own stunning debut *Morvern Callar* was the antithesis of the Oxbridge novel, which he felt had an unhealthy dominance on the shelves of our local bookstores. Like Kelman, Torrington and Welsh, Alan Warner proved that Scots could write about their own communities and sell lots of copies too, not to mention win awards. *Morvern Callar* collected the Somerset Maugham Award in 1995.

Alan told me how he first became aware of Irvine's writing through reading *Clocktower*. 'I was in correspondence – and in pub contact – with Duncan, who had just moved from Edinburgh up to Orkney with Alison Kermack, but he was publishing some of my own work in *Clocktower*. And it was round then that Kevin [Williamson] was publishing my story "Real Pure Poseur Thing" in *Rebel Inc*. I clearly remember in the summer of 1992 buying *Parcel of Rogues* with the green cover in East End Waterstone's [now gone]. It contained "Trainspotting at Leith Central Station", which must be

Irvine with two American tourists at the Scott Monument, Edinburgh, 1978.

Irvine poses with a draught excluder, Sighthill, Edinburgh, 1979.

The author, photographed by Irvine Welsh sometime in 1977.

Sandy Macnair enjoys a quiet drink with the author in Robbie's Bar, Leith, 2011.

Ready for demolition in the summer of 2011, one of the last remaining maisonette buildings on Muirhouse Avenue, Edinburgh, where Irvine grew up.

The Gunner bar, Muirhouse, Edinburgh, summer 2011.

Irvine (second row from front, far left) with staff at Telford College, Edinburgh c. 1975.
The News, Telford College magazine, 25 August 1995.

personnel matters

Best wishes go to the latest batch of early retirees who are *Alasdair James, Tom Lugton, Maureen Malcomson, Annie Paul, Janet Tulloch and Maureen Yates*.

The photograph shows a group of General Education staff c1975, and appropriately, Alasdair is front left. *(The person who said he is still wearing the same jacket should be ashamed of himself.)* You should be able to spot six other staff who are still with us - presumably **Anne McKillop** was going through an Abba phase at the time.

Another point of interest concerns the dark-haired young man standing behind Alasdair. He is best-selling author **Irvine Welsh**, who in 1975 was carving out a reputation for himself as the world's worst AV Technician.

The first ever advert for *Trainspotting* appeared in the *Hibbie Hippy* fanzine, spring 1993.
Illustration by Dave Todd and text by Sandy Macnair.

QUESTION TIME:- What do Gordon Hunter,Alex Miller,Wallace Mercer, Jimmy Savile,Keith Chegwin,Sean Connery,Yoko Ono,Jimmy Sandison,Gordon Durie,Anne Diamond and IGGY Pop all have in common?

ANSWER TIME:- They all make appearances in "Trainspotting",a novel written by one-time Hibs Monthly scribe and effervescent eight-tentacled East Terracing E-head OCTOPUS,these days sporting the somewhat unlikely literary handle of "IRVINE WELSH."

This 343 page jambo-bashing tone will be published by Secker & Warburg in mid-August 1993,and the advice from this humble proof-reader is to shoplift this shock-horror sensation on sight. (Or as it's a bit bulky some of you may even consider paying hard cash for it.)

No Sunshine on Leith in these grim pages,as the action follows a bunch of lowlifes around familiar boozers,dole offices and other Edinburgh locations..with some of the lowlifes in question bearing alarming likenesses to acquaintances of the author.

The aforementioned Mr Mercer should certainly read it,as one glance at his depiction therein could well precipitate a cardiac arrest, before he has time to call up his lawyers.

Is it slanderous?

Are Hearts crap???

"TRAINSPOTTING"

"William Burroughs' "Naked Lunch" meets Hubert Selby Jr's "Last Exit To Brooklyn" in a style which makes James Kelman read like William Wordsworth." - Hibbie Hippie (and you can quote me on that)

NB to Octopus: It's not every day you get four writers names dropped in the one quote - that's at least one autographed copy you're due me.

(37)

TRAIN SPOTTING

A Novel by Irvine Welsh

Martin Secker & Warburg

Michelin House, 81 Fulham Road, London SW3 6RB
Telephone 071-581 9393   Telex 920191   fax 071-589 8421

Irvine Welsh
2 Wellington Place
Edinburgh   EH6 7EQ

6 October 1992

Dear Irvine Welsh

I've tried to reach you a few times by telephone, but without luck. I wanted to tell you that I think your novel is extremely good and would like to publish it as a Secker Paperback Original - in the same series as Duncan McLean. I can offer an advance of £1,000 against a royalty of 10%, for world rights.

I look forward to hearing from you.

Yours sincerely

PP   Robin Robertson
Editorial Director
(signed in his absence)

Registered Office: Michelin House 81 Fulham Road London SW3 6RB Registered no. 311333
Part of Reed International Books

Martin Secker & Warburg's contract offer to Irvine for *Trainspotting*, 6 October 1992.

After spotting it through a restaurant window while having lunch with the photographer, Irvine poses under an appropriate Intercity billboard, East Fountainbridge, Edinburgh, summer 1993.

Irvine Welsh in his natural habitat – The Blue Blazer bar, Spittal Street, Edinburgh, summer 1993.

Oil painting, by David Todd, of Irvine with the backdrop of the old Leith Central Station.
The painting was done in 2005 as a wedding present for Irvine and Beth.

Duncan McLean and Irvine at the Edinburgh Book Festival, 1993.

Alan Warner in O'Donoghires Bar, Dublin, September 2001.

Robin Robertson.

Irvine with Robin (right) and friends in Sofia, Bulgaria, 2001.

irvine
Welsh

'Ah wis tempted tae swally the suppositories, but ah rejected this notion almost as soon as it crossed ma mind. They were designed for anal intake, and there wis still enough ay that waxy stuff oan them tae suggest that ah'd no doubt huv a hard time keeping them doon. As ah'd shot everything oot ay ma bowels ma boys were probably safer back thair. Home they went.'

Trainspotting

The original jacket artwork for *Trainspotting*.

This photograph of the *Trainspotting* film cast was shot by Lorenzio Agius for Stylorouge's poster campaign but was never used.

Muirhouse 1, Rest of the World 0. *Trainspotting* tops a 1997 poll of the greatest books of the twentieth century.

TOP 30 BOOKS

IRVINE WELSH: Platform for new talent

1 TRAINSPOTTING
Irvine Welsh

2 LORD OF THE RINGS
J R R Tolkien

3 1984
George Orwell

4 CATCHER IN THE RYE
J D Salinger

5 HIGH FIDELITY
Nick Hornby

6 ANIMAL FARM
George Orwell

7 CATCH 22
Joseph Heller

8 HITCHHIKER'S GUIDE TO THE GALAXY
Douglas Adams

9 TO KILL A MOCKINGBIRD
Harper Lee

10 THE HOBBIT
J R R Tolkien

11 JURASSIC PARK
Michael Crichton

12 IT
Stephen King

13 FEVER PITCH
Nick Hornby

14 THE WASP FACTORY
Iain Banks

15 ON THE ROAD
Jack Kerouac

CONTINUED

16 STAND
Stephen King

17 THE LOST WORLD
Michael Crichton

18 A CLOCKWORK ORANGE
Anthony Burgess

19 BRAVE NEW WORLD
Aldous Huxley

20 BRAVO TWO ZERO
Andy McNab

21 AMERICAN PSYCHO
Brett Easton Ellis

22 2001: A SPACE ODYSSEY
Arthur C. Clarke

23 PRIDE AND PREJUDICE
Jane Austen

24 LORD OF THE FLIES
William Golding

25 MISERY
Stephen King

26 FEAR AND LOATHING IN LAS VEGAS
Hunter S. Thompson

27 THE FIRM
John Grisham

28 THE CROW ROAD
Iain Banks

29 ACID HOUSE
Irvine Welsh

30 INTERVIEW WITH A VAMPIRE
Anne Rice

JOHN GRISHAM: A Firm favourite

PolyGram Filmed Entertainment
INVITE YOU TO THE

Trainspotting 18

PREMIERE PARTY

THURSDAY	FEBRUARY
EXPECTED TIME OF ARRIVAL: **22:00** DEPARTING AT: **02:00**	**15**

AT THE BRIGGATE CENTRE
72 CLYDE STREET, GLASGOW G1

WORLD CHARITY PREMIERE
IN AID OF CALTON ATHLETIC RECOVERY GROUP

ADMIT ONE

TICKET NO.
013

PolyGram
Filmed Entertainment

A VALID TICKET ON THE DAY
WILL BE REQUIRED

Invitation to the *Trainspotting* world charity premiere party in Glasgow.

Blur's Damon Albarn and Irvine – in a T-shirt for the striking Liverpool dockers – accept the Brit Award for Best Soundtrack, 1997.

'It's back . . . the play that shocked the nineties!' Flyer for the tenth anniversary tour of the *Trainspotting* play in 2006.

where I first read Irvine. In dialogue, Irvine really nailed that glorious, rich seam of misanthropy which certain phlegmatic, working-class Edinburgh personalities inhabit. "That cunt is just a fucking cunt and he fucking needs tae ken I ken he's a cunt. Cunt." If you show that sentence to someone who went to one of Edinburgh's private schools – and possibly has no Scottish accent at all, despite having spent their entire life in Edinburgh (yet will still insist there is no such thing as English colonialism of Scotland, or even class difference) – they will be likely to tell you that it's an exaggerated sentence. But that is an absolutely realistic sentence of spoken dialogue. You can hear sentences like that on the bus or in the pub every day in Edinburgh.

'The next thing I heard was a letter from Duncan McLean in 1993, shortly after he had read an early draft of *Morvern Callar*, encouraging me to submit it, as "Irvine has had his novel called *Trainspotting* accepted by Secker & Warburg – the title is meant to be a symbol of the pointless monotony of heroin addiction." I still have that letter. *Morvern Callar* was accepted for publication by Jonathan Cape on 22 November 1993, though not published until February 1995. I am always late to any party. By that time, I must say, a sort of negative reaction to new Scottish writers had already started. Irvine was very supportive in giving the book a blurb on the back cover in early 1995. And later, when I was totally fucking skint, he kindly offered to lend me money to keep me going – but luckily I got a book deal to see me through, and I know he was deeply generous to other folk – which is not forgotten by me.'

With *Past Tense* published and his typescript of *Trainspotting* sent to Secker & Warburg on 5 June 1992, Welsh departed for a couple of weeks of 'space cake and Heineken abuse' in Amsterdam, enjoying life in one of his favourite cities while working away on his writing in his spare time. He took up an invitation from a friend, Pete Gillick, to do a reading in a bar in the Jordaan district, an area he described to Duncan McLean as 'a sort of Amsterdam Stockbridge ... I think it was well received, even if punterspeak is a wee bit lost on the impeccably RP-English-speaking Dutch.'

But while Irvine and Anne partied in Holland, Robin Robertson, editorial director at Secker & Warburg, was trying to contact him to offer him a contract. When Irvine eventually returned to Leith and heard Robin's voice on his answering machine, his initial thought was that one of his friends, using a laconic, posh Scots accent, was trying to wind him up. Also waiting for Irvine was a letter from Robertson describing the *Trainspotting* manuscript as 'extremely good' and offering to publish it as a Secker Paperback Original in the same series as *Bucket of Tongues*. Irvine apparently took some persuading before he accepted the letter was genuine. The financial bait – an advance of £1,000 against a royalty of 10% against world rights – was modest, but pretty much the going rate at the time for a debut work by an unknown writer. Duncan McLean's view is: 'He got paid a tiny advance by Secker before it came out, and there was a small print run: it was really due to the success of the play version, and then the film, that the book became such a hit around the world. The film encouraged thousands of people to read the book who otherwise would never have dreamed of doing so, and when they did they found out that it was fantastic.

'I remember thinking Irvine was a bit daft, because he accepted a smaller advance than I had got a year earlier for *Bucket of Tongues*. If he'd told me that he was sending it to Secker I would have told him what advance I'd got, and he could have held out for at least the same. I got £1,500 for *Bucket* and Irvine told me he got £1,000 for *Trainspotting*, and I have no reason to disbelieve him.' McLean would later persuade Secker to pay an advance of £8,000 for his follow-up work, the novel *Blackden*.

As for most first-time writers, the thrill of actually finding out that – against the odds – his book was going to see the light of day outweighed any worries Irvine had about the modest advance. In his letter to McLean of 8 October 1992, Welsh wrote about the prospect of becoming a published author and revealed how he had obviously caught the writing bug. Work was well under way on his new project: 'Obviously, I'm chuffed to bits to get the novel published – although unfortunately it'll fuck up the slow sales of *Past Tense* further – or will it? I'll try to promote it at the *NWS* reading in Glasgow next week. I must admit though, that my main feeling is relief that I can forget about the bastard and get on with something else ... I've already started my next novel. It's a historical romance (well, sort of) with explicit sex scenes every tenth page, some of which may come out but are included to maintain my interest. It features soccer casuals, phalidomide [sic] victims, ecstasy dealers, transsexuals, right-wing psychologists and schitzophrenic [sic] nurses as central characters and I've only written forty pages so far! Still, I'm enjoying myself thoroughly with it. My working title is *The Blue Gene Babes*.'

Robin went up to Edinburgh in the autumn of 1992 to meet Irvine, and a few months later, in early 1993, Welsh travelled down to London to talk again to Robin and to Lesley Bryce, who would do most of the copy-editing on the book. He was relieved to find out over a few beers that they were two people he could get on with. Robin told him that *Trainspotting* would be released by Secker at the same time as *Red Tides*, the second collection of short stories by the Edinburgh poet and fiction writer Dilys Rose. Irvine thought the simultaneous launch was 'a clash of styles if ever there was one'. Work was continuing on *Blue Gene Babes** and he was trying, without success, to 'keep drugs out of it' (letter to McLean, 27 November 1992). Even in the early stages of his writing career he was aware of the danger of being pigeon-holed as 'that drug writer'. In the same letter he showed a touch of irritation at not yet having received payment from *NWS* and complimented McLean on his ability to write bad sex. 'I like the idea of writing bad sex (as you'll see when the novel comes out).'

* *Blue Gene Babes* never saw the light of day after Robin turned it down in late 1993. Here's Irvine's explanation to me of exactly why the idea was binned. 'This was an abortion of a manuscript that was written on cocaine, where I thought I could write an artsy post-modern novel and photocopy my gas bill thirty times (I kid you not). One of the best things Robin ever did was to tell me it was a pile of crap and to write a proper book I wanted to write. I wrote *Marabou Stork Nightmares* right after – I think this was a way of clearing the crap out my head to find a way into that book.'

11

All things Scottish

I honestly thought the whole thing was an elaborate wind-up by my mates.

When Irvine signed his one-book contract with Secker & Warburg on 26 June 1992, his name joined a roster of some of the greatest writers of the twentieth century. Since its foundation in 1936, the London-based company had published the work of writers as diverse and influential as Günter Grass, Jean-Paul Sartre, Tom Sharpe, Umberto Eco and George Orwell (publishing in 1945 the first edition of Orwell's seminal work *Animal Farm*). Robin Robertson joined the firm in 1985 as senior editor and compares working for Secker in the mid-1980s as akin to the last days of empire. Back then, Secker was based in Poland Street, Soho,* in

---

* By the time Irvine arrived on the scene, Dan Franklin had taken control at Secker, and the denizens of the Poland Street HQ had moved to the more sterile and corporate Michelin House on Fulham Road. But if Irvine felt a little nervous about following in the footsteps of Orwell and Grass, he needn't have worried. As Robin remembers, Secker & Warburg was 'muddling along in a haze of cigarettes and booze'. The one-time regular at the Gunner in Muirhouse no doubt felt right at home.

a tall, narrow Georgian townhouse which had a warren of little rooms, each overflowing with books and typescripts. According to Robin, Secker was a firm with 'a distinguished past but a rather haphazard present', staffed by charming and eccentric work colleagues who seemed to have emerged from 'the pages of *Gormenghast* rather than *Bleak House*'.

Robin remembers London publishing in the 1980s as still very clubby and conservative, with publishing houses, magazines and newspapers all in each other's pockets. There was a palpable sense – even that late – that publishing was the preserve of men with an Oxbridge degree and a private income. Deals were done over lunches that lasted into the early evening, with boozy launches to add to the mix. Robin might be a son of the manse – his father was a Presbyterian minister in rural Perthshire before becoming chaplain at Aberdeen University – but he recalls having no problems fitting in with the drink-sodden environs of Soho.

'On my first morning, I was nervously sitting at my desk on the top floor waiting for things to begin. It was nine o'clock. About an hour later, I heard the post-boy labouring up the stairs, making a strange clinking sound. He reached the editorial landing with a case of wine, which he opened up and started feeding into the fridge. Ten minutes later he was back with the beer. He nodded at me and asked if there was anything I needed. "Ah . . . a bottle of whisky?" I said. "I'll bring it up with the mail," he replied.

'In that first week I went looking for some office supplies and found what looked like a stationery cupboard under the stairs. It did have some paper and pens, but it was really a walk-in liquor store with crates of vodka and enough wine and beer to get us all through Armageddon. As I went back up to my editorial eyrie, I wondered idly why there were piles of used Jiffy bags at every landing. The answer came after only a few days, when I was working late and heard a terrible crashing from the stairwell, followed by silence. I went through and saw one of our illustrious authors sprawled among the Jiffy bags on the landing below, his slightly wobbly editor gazing down at him. "It breaks their fall, you see?" he said.'

Despite the boozy culture, Secker & Warburg was still capable of producing the goods. Two years prior to Robin joining they had won the Booker prize with J.M. Coetzee's *Life & Times of Michael K*. Robin quickly came to the fore within the company and was delighted soon to have two of his favourite authors – Coetzee and John Banville – under his wing. After a rather messy purge of the poetry department, which saw the editor fired and several of the existing poets' contracts cancelled, Robin was put in charge of the poetry list. It was a powerful position where he effectively had carte blanche to enlist the type of authors and poets he admired. He recalls that 'the ensuing fuss acted as a call to arms, announcing a new line of attack, and it helped – I can now see – to encourage a sense of a new order. From that point, I started to take on writers whose work I felt was not reaching enough readers: John Burnside, Anne Enright, Janice Galloway, James Kelman, Aidan Higgins, A.L. Kennedy, James Lasdun, Michael Longley, Aidan Matthews, Eugene McCabe, Duncan McLean, Ben Okri, Peter Redgrove, Adam Thorpe, Jeff Torrington, Alan Warner – and Irvine Welsh.'

In Robertson Irvine found an ally and a friend who would champion his work for years to come (Welsh's 2012 novel *Skagboys* comes with a message of thanks to Robin for sticking by him over the years). However, it was definitely a case of opposites attracting. Robin, an accomplished poet in his own right, came from a genteel, middle-class background and had been educated at a leading fee-paying school, Robert Gordon's, in Aberdeen. He may once have been described by a journalist as someone with a 'sleepy, seemingly permanently stoned smile', but former colleagues I spoke to remember Robertson as a shrewd editor and risk-taker who expected high standards from them and from his authors. As one fellow editor commented to me: 'Robin has no time for the dull or the mediocre.' During the research for this book, I met Robin in the Coach and Horses pub in London's Soho and found him to be friendly and helpful, with a nice wry sense of humour. We met to talk about Irvine on the day of the opening ceremony of the 2012 Olympics. The fact that the stunning ceremony was put together by Danny Boyle – one of the many individuals who did well out of the *Trainspotting* story – did not go unnoticed.

It's undeniable that Secker seemed to have the knack of signing up writers who could deliver beautiful prose and poetry as well as sell large numbers of books, with Irvine being perhaps the finest example of this. But Secker was undoubtedly helped by the spirit of comradeship among many of the Scottish authors who were used to helping one another and would point their friends in the direction of the London publishing house. Duncan McLean in particular urged Irvine and Alan Warner to send manuscripts to Secker. In some cases it was the author rather than the publisher who made the initial approach. From way back in the 1970s, the Scots had shown a healthy spirit of camaraderie, with Tom McGrath's Midnight Press and the writers' co-operative attached to the Print Studio Press in Glasgow helping to nurture the writing talents of the likes of James Kelman, Alasdair Gray, Jeff Torrington and Liz Lochhead. Polygon Books, under the editorial stewardship of Peter Kravitz, also helped bring Scots writers to a wider public with a commitment to new Caledonian fiction at a time when it was much less fashionable in London.

By the time they had moved to Secker, James Kelman and Jeff Torrington had been around for so long they could almost be considered the old guard, but Irvine told me that he has a healthy respect for both writers: 'Jeff and Jim were brilliant to me. Two kinder-hearted, more generous men you'd be hard pushed to find. There was often the idea that the Edinburgh-based Rebel Inc. mob was hostile to the Glasgow writers, but this was a myth. We loved and admired them, and they were incredibly generous and supportive of us. Jim, and to a lesser extent, Alasdair Gray and Tom Leonard, fought a lot of battles with the upper-crust literary establishment to validate different voices. It allowed the rest of us to have fun. I was determined not to get drawn into this; the point had been made as far as I was concerned. I never realised that, sadly, this hegemony is entrenched, and each generation of new writers will fight the same battle – like painting the Forth Bridge.'

The publication of Gorbals-born Jeff Torrington's debut novel *Swing Hammer Swing!* by Secker in the summer of 1992 was the culmination of the ultimate literary slow-burner success story. After taking thirty years to write it, Torrington found immediate acclaim and won the Whitbread Book of the Year prize in 1992. His success was made all the more poignant as by then he was in the grip of Parkinson's disease, but he remained a generous and supportive friend to new writers, including Irvine. When *Trainspotting* eventually emerged, it came with a stirring recommendation on the front cover from the Glaswegian writer. Following Torrington's death in 2008, Irvine paid tribute to his 'humane and coura-geous friend', adding that 'it might have taken him a long time to find his literary voice, but it was well worth the wait: *Swing Hammer Swing!* was so vivid it was almost hallucinogenic.'

Torrington had been recommended to Secker & Warburg by James Kelman, and the latter also had a profound influ-ence on the new east-coast school. Perhaps the greatest of the

clutch of Scottish authors to come on to the literary scene in
the 1980s and 1990s, Kelman's insistence on his right to
communicate uncompromisingly in his own native tongue
and not to kowtow to the London bourgeoisie made him a
hero and mentor to the younger generation of Scottish writers, encouraging them to write about their own lives and
their own people in their own language. Duncan McLean
says: 'When *The Busconductor Hines* [Kelman's debut novel]
came out in 1984 it just blew my mind. For the first time I
was reading a book about the world I lived in. I didn't know
literature could do that.' It would be another ten years before
Kelman won the Booker prize. The sheer power and beauty
of his writing in *How Late it Was, How Late* won over even
the doubters in the south of England, though Alan Taylor,
the Edinburgh critic and journalist, was also one of the judges
that year. Although the novel was commissioned and edited
by Robin Robertson, he had left Secker by the time of the
1994 Booker prize and was not invited to the ceremony.

James Kelman's acceptance speech on his night of triumph
at the Booker was a stirring defence of the literary tradition
he belonged to, championing the validity of indigenous
culture and the right to defend it in the face of attack. 'I see
it as part of a much wider process, or movement, towards
decolonisation and self-determination: it is a tradition that
assumes two things. 1) The validity of indigenous culture
and 2) the right to defend it in the face of attack. It is a tradition premised on a rejection of the cultural values of imperial
or colonial authority, offering a defence against cultural
assimilation, in particular an imposed assimilation.
Unfortunately, when people assert their right to cultural or
linguistic freedom they are accused of being ungracious,
parochial, insular, xenophobic, racist.

'As I see it, it's an argument based solely on behalf of validity, that my culture and my language have the right to exist,

and no one has the authority to dismiss that right. They may have the power to dismiss that right, but the authority lies in the power and I demand the right to resist it.'

Kelman's triumph was a vindication of everything the new wave of Scottish literature stood for, but his career trajectory showed that even a writer as defiantly Scottish as he was had to head south to get the financial rewards his work deserved. He got a tiny £200 advance from Polygon for his first book, *An Old Pub near the Angel* and they could not meet the modest demand for £1,000 for his 1987 collection of short stories *Greyhound for Breakfast*. Secker & Warburg could, and after Kelman approached Robin they eventually released the book, which went on to win the Cheltenham Prize.

So, economic necessity and the cash constraints on the Scottish publishing sector were key reasons why Scottish writers gravitated south of the border. Irvine was fortunate in emerging on to the literary scene at a time when London publishers were beginning to take an interest in things Scottish. Besides Kelman and Torrington, Alasdair Gray won the Whitbread Novel Award and the Guardian Fiction Prize for his 1992 novel, *Poor Things*.

Robin Robertson will tell you that it was the excellence and the variety of the writing rather than some patriotic mission to bring Scots to the attention of the nation that persuaded him to sign up so many fellow Scots to Secker and his next employer, Jonathan Cape. From Alan Warner to Janice Galloway and A.L. Kennedy, what these writers had in common was their rejection of the notion that London was the sole cultural and linguistic centre in Britain.

'I remember being vaguely concerned about the number of Scots I was signing up for Secker and Cape, but I justified it by pointing out that I wasn't doing it just because they were Scottish. Au contraire, as Beckett said, I was doing it because each of them was a writer of excellence – and not only that, they were all strikingly different from one another. That efflorescence in the late 1980s and early 1990s was an extraordinary flowering of great Scottish writing that, sadly, has not been repeated. It's worth remembering that, at this time, almost none of these writers were represented by agents. I was picking them up from reading magazines and anthologies, and by word of mouth. I think I was simply reacting – as any editor would – to the sudden discovery of wonderful new work.'

Looking back, Robin takes some delight in remembering the effect the influx of Caledonian writers had on the more narrow-minded literary elite in London. 'I didn't encounter much personal hostility as a Scot, but was distinctly aware of cultural resistance to many of the books I was publishing – particularly those that presented non-Standard English. I knew that Jim Kelman was a thorn in the side of the English establishment, and I was delighted to let their representatives expose their bigotry in public. Within Secker, Dan Franklin was always very supportive of everything we did. But the people higher up, the sales directors and the marketing people, as far as they were concerned it was just another incomprehensible Scottish book, which I seemed to be making a bit of a habit with.'

When Irvine sent his typescript to Secker, he seemed to have learned little about the importance of presentation. As with his initial approach to NWS, its appearance left a lot to be desired. After reading the script and accepting it for publication, Robin passed it on to a junior editor, Lesley Bryce, who remembers that the typescript was printed, single-spaced, on a dot-matrix printer. 'I think the paper still had those little perforations down the sides. It was a nightmare to read, but it was immediately exciting. It was like nothing else; gritty wasn't the word, it was filthy, funny and bleak – the side of Edinburgh you don't see on a tin of shortbread.'

Lesley had started work with Secker in 1986 as an editorial secretary, working for Robertson. Both were graduates of Aberdeen University, a connection that Lesley believes helped her get the job. It doubtless helped her case that – unlike some of the workers in the Poland Street office – she was an enthusiastic supporter of James Kelman's work. 'I loved working there. Robin was putting together this great list of writers, so it was a really exciting time. I never had to make coffee, though I did have to restock the editorial fridge – there was a lot of partying! When Robin read *Trainspotting* he was immediately hooked and made Irvine an offer. It's easy to forget just how bold it was for Robin to publish *Trainspotting* – many in the London literary world still struggled with the brilliant James Kelman, and *Trainspotting* seemed certain to be even more offensive to them.'

Lesley and Robin considered cutting a strand of *Trainspotting* which they thought did not work, but eventually decided against any major changes. Early in 1993 Lesley travelled north to Edinburgh, her native city, to meet Irvine in his Leith Links flat. 'I spent a day with him going through the editorial changes: the phonetic language had to be made consistent and there were numerous small bits of rewriting, cutting, strengthening etc. At no point did we consider toning anything down or attempt to make it less controversial. Occasionally there would be a joke I did not get, and Irvine would tease me for being from the wrong side of town – or knowing nothing about football! The joke would be left unexplained and intact. I did point out that all the female characters in the novel bleed, for one reason or another, which Irvine thought was pretty funny – and said (at least partly in jest) that it was probably a reflection of his own sick mind. Irvine was fantastic to work with, great sense of humour, very open to suggestions, but also very clear about what he wanted and didn't want. We went for a curry at lunchtime, and I think he also took me to his local. Weirdly, it turned out that his flat was directly behind the block where some good friends lived – we could see the Hibs flag in his window from their kitchen.'

Once the editing was done, Lesley moved on to other work, but was always aware of the publishing phenomenon that took place over the next few years. 'I do vaguely remember a few afternoons in the pub with Robin and Irvine. I think we all hoped it would become a cult classic among those drawn to the dark and seedy side, Irvine as a Scottish Bukowski, but we did not expect such a wildly positive response from the literary press. Everyone was astonished at its success, including those convinced of its genius. I left Secker not long after it was published, and Dan and Robin moved to Jonathan Cape soon after that. Robin asked me to copy-edit *The Acid House* and *Marabou Stork Nightmares* as a freelancer, and I did abridge *Trainspotting* for audio, but when *Filth* arrived, I'd just had a baby and didn't have the time or energy for another trip to the dark side. These days I live just off Portobello Road in London, and it still makes me smile to see all those 'Choose Life' T-shirts, nearly twenty years on.'

Often overlooked in all the fuss made about the film and the play, the audiobook, which was released to tie in with Danny Boyle's film, is a little gem of an adaptation. Lesley Bryce had the difficult task of cutting Irvine's sprawling epic of a novel into dialogue that would fit into three hours of cassette tape. Lesley recalls: 'I discussed it with Irvine, and we agreed that the easiest way to shorten the novel would be to take out the secondary strands, leaving the central narrative with Renton and co. more or less intact. He told me to just go for it. Then it was a case of pruning carefully. Irvine

wasn't anxious about it, didn't want to be closely involved
and was happy to just let me snip away. So, farewell to quite
a few bleeding women!' Lesley did a grand job of excising a
lot of the weaker parts of the book that add little to the overall narrative. The omission of – for me – the stand-out story
in the book, 'Her Man' and the drug-deal section of 'Station
To Station', is regrettable, but overall the audio version
moves along impressively and has little in the way of filler.
The selection of stories and characters is similar to that made
by John Hodge for the film, with the likes of Stella, Stevie
and Nina and their tales consigned to history. The listener
instead gets hit by a succession of Irvine's best and most
memorable stories. But even within these stories, Lesley made
changes, like omitting some of the dialogue in the verbal
power struggle between Renton and the odious drug dealer
Mikey Forrester. The only parts of the book that are repli-
cated virtually word for word on to tape are 'Trainspotting
at Leith Central Station' and 'Winter in West Granton'.
Elsewhere, the sequence of the stories, like 'A Leg-Over
Situation', is altered from that of the paperback version. The
only new text on the audiobook comes in the quaintly named
'Cock Problems', where a whole new passage is included,
perhaps suggesting that Irvine was unhappy with the original
version.

The actual reading of the work was shared by Irvine and
his friend Tam Dean Burn, and was done in one day at 6T4K
Studios on Broughton Street in Edinburgh. There are some
basic sound-effects to add to the mix, like footsteps, background chat while Renton travels on the number 32 bus to
Muirhouse, and the weird sound of an accordion version of
'We Are Hibernian FC' in the background as Renton suffers
withdrawal hell in 'House Arrest'. But mostly it's just Welsh
and Burn, and they do a fine job of the readings. Irvine is less
to the fore, but his low-key, mumbling, panicked voice is just

right, especially for the desperate 'Junk Dilemmas'. The real
star of the show, though, is Tam Dean Burn, who went on to
play a wide range of roles on stage and screen and to collabo-
rate with Irvine on many stage and film adaptations. Here he
delivers a real tour de force, notably when reading the
thoughts of Leith's number 1 psychotic hard man, Begbie.
Burn captures all the menace and madness of the character
perfectly, and, whisper it, he might even have made a better
Begbie than Robert Carlyle. Finding a copy of the audiobook
cassettes is not easy these days. Last time I looked, the only
new tape version of the audiobook was selling for £354 on
Amazon! Luckily, Tam Dean Burn is now working on a
complete and unabridged version of *Trainspotting* and
Skagboys, which runs to twenty compact discs.

During his visit on business to Edinburgh the previous
autumn, Robin took time to meet Irvine in a Goth bar on the
Bridges and discuss with him all aspects of the publishing
process, including Robin's editorial suggestions. 'He was very
quiet and slightly suspicious, friendly but guarded; perhaps he
still thought it was a wind-up. I don't think he had ever come
across a member of the species of the publisher before,' says
Robin. It was decided that *Trainspotting* would be released as
part of an imprint of white-flapped paperbacks which also
included *Bucket of Tongues, Swing Hammer Swing!* and A.L.
Kennedy's *Looking for the Possible Dance*. Robin explains:
'The imprint was partly a reaction to the increasingly grim
owners of Secker, who were very anti-art. I had always wanted
us to end up being like Picador had been in the 1970s or
Penguin in the 1940s. These books we were doing sometimes
sold better than we expected, but it was pretty unusual stuff
with small print runs.' It may seem odd now, but, as with
most of the other imprint series, there was no official launch
for *Trainspotting* – launches were reserved for name authors

only. The initial print run was 3,000 copies, with a small number of hardback copies sent out to libraries.

Although the front cover for the first edition was designed by Peter Dyer, Irvine was given a free hand by Secker & Warburg to think up a good illustration. He was lucky in that two of his friends were talented artists/photographers. First he approached Dave Todd, who had been painting for years and had already been commissioned to do a couple of book covers. Dave eventually did three excellent illustrations, but although Irvine loved them all they were not used on the cover. One version was used to illustrate Irvine's first interview in the *Big Issue* magazine. Dave Todd would later do a full painting of Irvine in Leith Central Station, unmasking from behind a skull, as a wedding present in 2005.

In the event, it was another of Welsh's old pals, Dave Harrold, who took the iconic 'skull mask' photo that was used on the front cover of the first edition of *Trainspotting*. Dave had known Irvine from way back in the early 1980s, when they had met on a night out at the Burke and Hare pub in Edinburgh's Grassmarket. Fast-forward ten years and Dave was working successfully as a full-time photographer when he got a call from Irvine asking him to take some photos. He told me how he got involved in the project.

'When Irvine moved back to Edinburgh from London with Anne, I used to see him every now and then, sometimes at the football, sometimes in the pub. I knew that he and Sandy Macnair were contributing to literary magazines and to writers' groups. And I used to hear people say that Irvine was building up his little bits and pieces of writing into a bigger work. Back then he had his own full-time job and he was writing in all his spare time – even very early in the morning before going in to work. Irvine was someone who liked a shandy or two and wasn't known as an early riser, so I could tell, if he was getting up at six in the morning to write, that he was really serious about what he was doing.

'I took the photos on a Friday lunchtime. Irvine was working that day at the council offices, so it was essentially done on his lunch-hour. He asked me to meet him at the joke shop at the foot of Victoria Street, not far from his workplace. I thought, what the hell does he want to meet there for? Does he have something corny planned for the photo? As I arrived there Irvine was coming out with a bag and he pulled out these two skull masks, and I thought, hmm, interesting!

'I had this idea that I wanted movement and people blurring in the background in the shot, so I suggested we go down to Waverley Station. I wanted to take a photo of Irvine with the 12.18 train from Glasgow just arrived in the background, with all the doors open and the passengers emerging. But on the way to Waverley it started raining very heavily. When we got there it was really, really grey and dark in the station, so I was a bit concerned. I knew then I had to up-rate the film, so I used a 400 ASA film but I pushed it to 1600 – what is known as "push processing". I was using my favourite Nikon FM2 camera, which is all manual with no electronics, and I used my favourite lenses – a 105mm Nikon lens which was slightly telephoto and great for portraits, and a very wide 20mm lens which gave great impact, distortion and depth of field.

'The photo that was used on the cover was taken with the 105mm Nikon lens, open very wide, because you can see the front face is just out of focus and the second head is in focus.* There's hardly any depth of field in the photo – the only thing that is sharp is the face of the second man right in the middle of the picture. I think I just shot one roll of film – 36

* The second man, in the photo has asked not to be identified in this book.

pictures. I always tried to work quickly, and the whole shoot was done in about 30 minutes. We did that shot first, then as we were walking back through the concourse I saw the departure sign by the cluster of public phones, and we took a picture there that I really liked. On the book cover, they used the first shot just as I had taken it – horizontally, small and with the two trains, quite eerie, with their lights on in the background to balance the offset where the eyes are looking down at you.

'Later, I printed off the seven that were my favourites and showed them to Irvine. He really liked them and sent them off to Secker & Warburg. I was a working photographer back then and did quite a lot of work for publishers like Canongate and Mainstream, but when I heard it was Secker & Warburg I knew this was a different league. A couple of weeks later Irvine got back in touch and said they were keen to use one of the photos, and that I would get paid. Later he sent me a card with the first print of the cover of the first edition. I really liked the eerie feel, the minimal design with lots of white and using the picture whole-frame with the trains in the background. I just thought, wow!

'After we took the photos we went for some Mexican food. Around that time we always met up for a Mexican meal, so when the first copies came through, Irvine gave me the Secker & Warburg card cover and signed it inside: "Cheers Dave, thanks for the Mexican scran!" My partner's dad recently came across an article where a distinguished journalist said the two greatest book covers of modern times were *Trainspotting* and *A Clockwork Orange*. But I cannot say that taking that photo really boosted my career as a photographer. Looking back, maybe I should have shown that image around and told people, "See this multi-million selling book – I did the cover!" But I never did.'

12

Fear and Lothian

I'm not saying that the reviews should not be taken seriously. But sales are important too, and sales in a way allow you to get beyond the critics. It's nice to have critical acclaim, but there is something tangible about sales that removes the element of a single, subjective opinion.

Soon after signing up with Secker, Irvine learned that things were not well at his new publisher. During the winter of 1992 their parent company, Reed International, made two editors, including Lesley Bryce who had just finished editing *Trainspotting*, redundant. This left the firm worryingly short of staff to read scripts and commission books. Welsh was concerned at the idea of a pool of inexperienced copy-editors and feared a decline in standards at Secker, with the publisher playing safe and not taking risks signing up new writers who dared not to write in Standard English. Irvine encouraged other Scottish writers to sign a letter of protest to Secker's parent company. But it was all to no avail, and Secker muddled along in a way that would eventually see Robertson leave for Jonathan Cape and take most of his writers – including Irvine – with him.

Despite the problems at Secker, Irvine signed another book deal with them on 21 July 1993, and *The Acid House* came out just seven months after the release of *Trainspotting*. (The deal also led to the later novel *Marabou Stork Nightmares*.) Irvine was, by then, starting to really enjoy writing, and he was churning out work at a prodigious rate. Robin bought the second book but paid a similar advance to the £1,000 dished out for *Trainspotting*; at that time there was nothing to suggest that Welsh's sales figures would suddenly take off. In his letter to Duncan McLean on 13 April 1993 Irvine wrote about some of the short stories that would eventually appear in *The Acid House*. 'I feel quite positive about it, although I suspect as you alluded to in your letter that most literary types will find it a bit of a head-fuck. Still, that's the way the cookie crumbles . . . I'm seeing Robin from Secker about the short stories and novella I've been working on, tentatively entitled *A Smart Cunt and other stories*. I thought of that title as I don't think Secker wouldn't [sic] go for something called *A Smart Cunt*. It's a novella and a collection of other stories, most of which are 15–20 pages long, so too long for the mags. I've completed most of them, and have a few more to rewrite. I've also taken the second draft of my new novel from the word processor. I'm hoping for a final draft for August, but the raving season has started . . . It should be quite different from *Trainspotting* although to be honest I haven't a fucking clue what it's actually about.'

Prior to the Secker publicity machine rolling into action for *Trainspotting*, Irvine's old friends played their part in promoting the upcoming novel. The first adverts for *Trainspotting* appeared in Sandy Macnair's Hibs fanzine booklet *Hibbie Hippie* and took the form of two cartoons by Dave Todd. The first one, showing the Hibbie Hippie and Fox (Dave's nickname) hurtling on a train towards a petrified Octopus, appeared in the 'Hibees History – League Cup

Glory 1972' edition. The second one, showing Octopus being smashed by a locomotive, appeared in 'Grumpy Gibby's Mightiest Moans'. Sandy wrote some praise which appeared by the latter cartoon, warning readers that the upcoming book made 'your average William Burroughs novel look like *The Tale of the Flopsy Bunnies!*'

The imminent publication of his debut novel meant that Irvine was – for the first time in his fledgling literary career – about to come up against that most intimidating of creatures, the literary critic. As mentioned earlier, Irvine had decided that he would try to bypass the 'liberal bourgeois critics' and write for his own people, working-class clubbers and schemies. He thought most broadsheet critics just didn't understand working-class culture, and were most at ease reading traditional prose in which working people were gently ridiculed. He would later explain to the *Big Issue*: 'For most people I know, the book, play and film have provided them with a sense of affirmation that a life they know, or know of, is being portrayed without the accompaniment of a bleating, middle-class . . . voice telling everyone how horrible or what victims the characters are.' He was genuinely delighted when told later that he was the most-read author at one of Scotland's most notorious prisons. Given the choice of praise from an inmate at Saughton Prison or an *Observer* critic, Irvine would take the former every time. But, for all his protestations, Irvine wouldn't have been human if he hadn't been just a tad apprehensive when the first reviews came out. He need not have worried. Even if his mum and all his aunties had taken turns to write the columns, they couldn't have been much kinder.

The media buzz really began with the 'Fear and Lothian' pre-publication review in the *Herald* of 31 July 1993. The reviewer, 'A.C.', told readers: 'Critics, prize-giving juries, and readers alike are hereby served notice *Trainspotting* marks the arrival of a major new talent ...' That same month, *GQ* magazine got on the bandwagon with a storming review, and the *Literary Review* called *Trainspotting* a 'wonderfully sordid depiction of how the other half dies and why it matters'.

By the time Kenny Farquharson of *Scotland on Sunday* sat down with Irvine in early August, the press office at Secker had woken up to the fact that they might be on to something a bit special here, and were, according to Kenny, waging a campaign of hype unprecedented for a debut Scottish author, enthusing breathlessly that the book would be huge and that Irvine was 'just a lovely man'. Farquharson, a lovely man himself but not one to be fooled by hype, agreed that the book was something special. '*Trainspotting* turns out to be a genuine wonder ... the *Sunday Post* reader's worst nightmare ... it is revolting, funny, scary, and deeply affecting.' He added that Irvine's book destroyed the myth that only west-coast writers could write urban working-class literature.

Another stellar review came from Lucy Hughes-Hallett in *The Sunday Times*, who wrote the classic line which would be much repeated in the future: '*Trainspotting* is the voice of punk grown up, grown wiser and grown eloquent.' Hughes-Hallett added: 'This is a book that gives pause to anyone who might be tempted to try heroin – one which describes vividly, authoritatively and non-judgementally, junkies' intense, ephemeral pleasures and their long-drawn-out pain. It gives a voice to the silent, swaying figure at the back of the late-night bus, the one nobody wants to sit next to. It describes the lower depths from the viewpoint of the people who live down there. And despite the wretchedness of its subject matter, it is full of energy, the negative energy of anger but also the positive energy of youth and recklessness and of the author's vigorous intelligence ... Welsh's prose is dazzlingly self-assured. He can pour out torrents of obscene, abusive, almost meaningless dialogue – the kind of ritual exchanges whereby young males mark out their territory – and then turn the current with a nicely waspish witticism . . . This is a novel about hopelessness . . . But the impression it makes, thanks to Welsh's humour and his virtuoso way with language, is one of unstoppable vitality.'

Equally if not more important in raising the book's profile down south was the work done by Elizabeth Young, a Scot in exile in London. A freelancer most closely associated with the *Guardian*, Young was the first literary journalist to secure an interview with Welsh. To do so she had to overcome a fair degree of reluctance at the *Guardian*, where, perhaps understandably, they were unwilling to give much in the way of column inches to a then unknown Scots writer. Young had already written a glowing review in the paper, telling readers how 'Irvine Welsh's first novel smashes into the neat shop front of contemporary literature like a runaway car on a ram-raid'. Though perceptive enough to recognise and detail the book's flaws, Young nonetheless concluded her review with a stirring recommendation. 'Welsh's considerable achievement lies in the documentation of a way of life that has become an enduring necessity for huge numbers of people and which has been minimally represented in fiction: a life of poor accommodation, indifferent health, scams, deals and fantasies of escape, provisional sexual arrangements, long days with the curtains drawn in hard-to-let flats and the video on, with the dope and the lager and the speed or the smack. Welsh evokes this landscape with considerable vitality and humour and also manages to suggest the massive contempt and indifference with which so many people regard the societal structures as presented through government, courts and media.'

You would think, given the splendid review, that the

ensuing interview in London, where Young met Irvine and
Anne, would have been an easy one. However, Young recalls
in her posthumous collection *Pandora's Handbag: Adventures
in the Book World* that Irvine was wound up very tight and
very suspicious. 'He seemed to radiate distrust of the media
and to be determined to dislike me and everything he assumed
I stood for.' Obviously still uncomfortable in the media glare,
Welsh told Young that he did not see himself as a writer, or
have any ambitions to be one. It was a line he repeated in a
number of interviews around the time of the book launch,
and I think he genuinely meant it, though within a couple of
years he would become deadly serious about his craft. Irvine,
incidentally, does not recognise Young's recollection of that
London meeting. 'I did like Elizabeth; she was a strong advocate, and a decent person. But she had anxiety issues and was
very, very nervous during this interview. I had picked that up
during numerous pre-interview calls she had made to me.
The reason I brought my wife along (I'd *never* normally do
that) was solely because I felt that another woman being
present might have put her at ease. But she was very nervous,
to the extent she found it hard to frame questions and continually apologised to me for the state she was in. But I liked her
a lot and admired her writing, and I was very sad to hear of
her passing.' Young, who died, aged just fifty, in the spring of
2001 after battling the hepatitis C virus, continued to champion Irvine's work right up until the end, convinced of his
worth as the most gifted of the young writers who emerged
in Britain during the 1990s.

Ian Bell of the *Observer* was a tad more restrained in his
praise, noting how the shadow of James Kelman lies over
Trainspotting. Bell pointed out that there is nothing new in
writers noting how working-class Edinburgh is invisible to
New Town professionals. (Irvine would probably counter
this argument by saying he was writing for a new audience

who usually read only football programmes and the racing pages of the *Daily Record*.) Bell concluded that 'it sounds grim, and it is. Yet the novel manages to draw great wit and energy from its wasted souls. Welsh is strong on the rhythms of speech, on the sub-poetry of slang and obscenity which renders characters real. If he ever remembers that the author is just another character he will be a considerable novelist.' When I reminded him of this review, Irvine's response was: 'I got a lot of advice on how to write a successful novel back in those days – almost always from people who never had.'

By the time the 1993 Edinburgh Book Festival came around, the buzz about *Trainspotting* was becoming deafening. On the day of the book's release, 30 August, Duncan McLean and Irvine did a reading at the Festival in Charlotte Square which sold out fast. Irvine apparently was keen on persuading everyone in the audience to take ecstasy so as to appreciate his reading properly, though it's not certain how many took him up on the challenge. The writer Bella Bathurst recalls that both men provocatively read out the filthiest sections of their books, resulting in at least half the audience walking out. But Duncan told me: 'I hate to spoil a good story, but I don't remember people walking out at all. It's possible that some did and I just wasn't aware of it, but my memories of the event are entirely positive – both my stuff and Irvine's went down well as far as I can recall, both with friends and with unknown audience members just vaguely interested in youngish Scottish writers. I have a strong memory of Irvine reading the "Traditional Sunday Breakfast" chapter, which would have turned a few stomachs, right enough. He went down very well, not least because he had a significant posse with him giving vocal and moral support. I remember Paul Reekie was there, wearing a Cossack-style fur hat. Kevin Williamson, Gordon Legge and Robin Robertson must have been there, and of the older generation of writers, Andrew Greig was definitely there. We went for a drink or two afterwards and then went our separate ways.'

On sale at the event was *Folk*, the newly released Clocktower pamphlet, which contained four pieces by Irvine that would eventually emerge in *The Acid House* as the 'Sexual Disaster Quartet'. Duncan recalls how he sold twenty of the booklets after the reading . . . which was exactly twenty more than the number of his own books he managed to sell. Irvine received ten gratis copies of *Folk* as token payment for his contribution.

Alan Warner remembers meeting Irvine and Kevin Williamson in the bar at the Book Festival. 'Robin Robertson was very interested in *Morvern Callar* so we met briefly. Duncan introduced us all. I remember that although I was a huge reader, I didn't really understand what a "book festival" was, nor what possibly went on there. It was a bit like an Ann Summers or a fondue party. I never really have got over that. Also I think I was probably in a sort of typical jealous/defensive writer mode then: "Irvine has got his novel published, so how do I get mine published?" I do remember at that book festival I was stoned and wearing this scarlet brightly reflective jacket,* and I get the feeling Kevin and Irvine might have been up on something, and they were most fascinated by my jacket – kept reaching out and touching it – but also, I felt a sudden movement of my sleeve could upset the entire social balance and tip things into a new place. Such were the times.

'I have always got on with Irvine, from that shiny-jacket day. He's just one of those interesting blokes. Of course, before he was a published writer he would have been like that. A pub philosopher. What the English call "hail-fellow-well-met". I don't agree with everything Irvine says, but I've never heard

---

* Robin remembers this jacket as being 'an orange hi-vis railway jacket'. Either way, it's safe to say it was bright.

him say something that wasn't amusing, insightful or interesting. He was one of those been-around-the-block blokes – naebody's fool, into music and good times – who you meet in every Edinburgh pub, often in the afternoon when suckers are at work. But I think in the early years Irvine and I were brought closer with a sort of forensic amazement at what was happening to us (especially happening to him, of course) due to both our sudden entrances into the book world. I think we felt we were looking out for one another, and I know he was for me in a world we had been thrust into (at our own doing), and we were sort of kids in a sweetie shop. And of course we shared the same publisher, so there was much to gossip about that.

'Shortly after that, I think we did a reading together in Broughton Street at the Unemployed Workers' Centre. I remember both of us reading there, with Paul Reekie as MC and lots of drinking. That was the reading where you got a raffle ticket with each bottle of Beck's, so I was bound to win something, though thankfully I missed the first prize. The first prize was a holiday for two: two tabs of LSD. I won a porn video, got home wasted at 4 a.m., and when my girlfriend saw me, very drunk with a porn video, and asked where I had been, I explained, "Just at a poetry reading."

'I wasn't too sure of how *Trainspotting* was edited and organised. I felt some of the pieces felt non-connected to the main soul of the book – but at the same time I liked that digressive nature which opened the book up into a big capillary system of connections through Edinburgh – an Edinburgh which was essentially an inner world, very like Céline's Paris in *Journey to the End of the Night*. Real and not real – often hellish. Yet very knowing and confident about its own community and culture, though the community was disintegrating. But to me a story like "Bad Blood" seemed to dilute the rhythm of the central Renton narrative a bit. At the same time, I was bowled over by many moments in the book – even still, that great sequence when yon peripheral character, Stevie, is stuck with Renton and the boys and they are all singing the republican songs at Hogmanay, then he gets the phone call from the girlfriend. I really identified with that and found it very moving. For a first novel, Irvine really knew how to form a dramatic situation again and again; he had an absolute natural talent for that, and I guess the episodic nature also gave it the rough, haphazard edge which made it more realistic. And people should remember, Irvine never arrived with that "Look at me. I am a remarkable literary figure." He never had that attitude, never thought of himself as a writer. Irvine was just "Here you go. I've written this." He was nothing to do with the literary scene and, of course, a lot of establishment figures fucking hated that.'

The glowing early reviews for *Trainspotting* meant that by the time the judges for the 1993 Booker prize gathered to deliberate on that year's short list, there was growing demand for Irvine's debut novel to be included. The chair of the judges that year was former Conservative arts minister Lord 'Grey' Gowrie, soon to become chairman of the Arts Council. The panel also included Professor Dame Gillian Beer, Anne Chisholm, Nicholas Clee and the French novelist Olivier Todd. In the event, after six months of reading and discussions, *Trainspotting* never quite made it to the final list of six books – Tibor Fischer's *Under the Frog*, Michael Ignatieff's *Scar Tissue*, David Malouf's *Remembering Babylon*, Caryl Phillips's *Crossing the River*, *The Stone Diaries* by Carol Shields, and the eventual winner, Roddy Doyle's *Paddy Clarke Ha Ha Ha*. Robin Robertson was hardly surprised by *Trainspotting*'s omission, telling me: 'I never dreamt it would get anywhere near the Booker. I loved the book, but I really didn't imagine many other people taking to what was, and still is, a tough vernacular voice.'

Part of the *Trainspotting* legend is that the book caused much angst and dispute among the panel of judges. Another variation of the story that does the rounds is that it was the women on the panel who objected most strongly to the book, and were particularly offended by the occasional brutality meted out to women and the misogynist attitude of characters like Begbie. Yet when I put that story to Gillian Beer, she replied: 'No, I have absolutely no recollection of any judge having threatened to resign over *Trainspotting*. I remember long debates over *Trainspotting,* which did indeed come close to the short list (if Booker had then had a long list, it would of course have had more prominence). The arguments included how fully realistic the book was and how successfully, or not, women were portrayed in it. As I remember, there was quite a tussle, but of a thoughtful and not ill-tempered kind. Everyone agreed on the book's power.' When I put this to Irvine, his response was: 'This does not square with Gowrie's comments on radio some years after, when he publicly said that two women judges threatened to resign from the panel if the book was considered. I'm in no position to state which is the more accurate account, nor am I particularly interested.'

Lord Gowrie wanted the judges to select a winner that 'had radioactivity' – that would be remembered for years to come and not fade away. Of the six books shortlisted, perhaps only Roddy Doyle's winning entry fulfilled that criterion, but even its impact pales in comparison to *Trainspotting* when it comes to long-term influence. The slight on *Trainspotting* didn't bother Irvine one jot. Robin cannot even remember discussing the issue with Welsh, who was never a fan of the award and still dislikes it to this day, telling me: 'I think prize-winning authors tend to work towards some kind of consensus. I knew that I was never that guy, so it wasn't on my radar.' At the 2012 Edinburgh

Book Festival he took aim with both barrels and decried the Booker as 'highly imperialist-orientated, which alternated prizes between largely English upper-middle-class writers and citizens of the former colonies'. He concluded that 'the Booker prize's contention to be an inclusive, non-discriminatory award could be demolished by anybody with even a rudimentary grasp of sixth-form sociology'.

13

On the back of a tiger

The good thing is it happened when I was in my thirties. If it had happened when I was in my twenties it would have been River Phoenix or something.

Irvine likened dealing with the initial burst of fame as similar to riding 'on the back of a tiger'. Once the hype started to grow it seemed like everyone wanted to meet him, take him to lunch, buy him a pint or give him some dope. The hangers-on moved in, and people who wouldn't have given Welsh the time of day when he was a nobody suddenly flocked to his side in the pub. But he gradually managed to come to terms with the major changes in his life that fame had brought. He had enough savvy to play the fame game on his own terms and avoid being sucked into the celebrity circle. It also helped that, prior to the release of the film, the success grew incrementally, which at least allowed him to get used to it. While naturally suspicious of celebrity culture, he wasn't totally immune to its attractions – turning up at award ceremonies on occasion, writing a monthly column for lads' magazine *Loaded* and becoming a bit of a media floozie for a time. So, yes, there was much Welshian excess and 'drinking for Scotland' done over the first few years after publication.

And there was his continued involvement in the rave scene, with all its psychotropic sideshows. One of the first things he did with his book earnings was invest in top-quality turntables, a mixer and acid house records and set himself up as a DJ. Cue synchronised eye-rolling among his old mates. I have to admit the whole rave scene passed me by, so it's a bit unfair for me to judge it or the people involved. I'm sure you really had to be there. Anyway, Irvine was happy enough immersing himself in that culture for a number of years. As the author of the hippest book around, the fact that he was older than most of the clubbers was overlooked, and he recalls being offered drugs in just about every club he attended.

The rave scene was important to Irvine in another way, as he increasingly did readings at club nights. Rather than restrict his public appearances to staid venues like Waterstone's where everyone quietly sipped the complimentary warm plonk, Irvine wanted to attract an audience who wouldn't usually come to readings. The first reading/rave was the 'Invisible Insurrection', held at Edinburgh's La Belle Angèle club in 1993, where writers read their poetry or prose, accompanied by slides or other visuals, before giving way to live bands or DJs. It was started by Welsh and Kevin Williamson, a Hibs fan from Thurso who had previously edited the community newspaper *Tollcross Times*, though Irvine admits, 'I just suggested the name and Kev did all the work.' Chill-out club readings were also popular, where clubbers sat around listening to readings while coming down off their particular drug of choice. Irvine also continued to contribute to literary magazines like *Rebel Inc.*, which had been started in 1992 by Kevin Williamson.

Fame was never going to be a wholly positive experience

for Irvine, though, and it didn't take long for the backlash to begin. Despite the book giving an accurate and honest portrayal of the reasons why people took heroin, Irvine soon came in for caustic criticism from those who thought he was mythologising and prettifying the drug-taking experience and turning it into entertainment, without portraying the total devastation drugs can cause. The official government body Scotland Against Drugs warned that the portrayal of addicts as some kind of anti-heroes would make drugs trendy for susceptible youngsters. For the most part, Welsh declined to debate the subject. 'I didn't really make any protestations about that at all. I think that was more irritating to people than anything, that I wouldn't get into all that. As far I was concerned, the book spoke for itself. It was only when pushed I'd reluctantly cough out some trite soundbite.'

Closer to home, Welsh was criticised for reinforcing negative stereotypes of working-class communities like Leith and Muirhouse, with accusations that he had made money out of depicting a problem that was already history. Literary critics also began to find fault in *Trainspotting* and the follow-up books, accusing Welsh of misogyny and highlighting what they perceived as his weakness in writing believable female characters. Irvine's response to me was: 'They *are* believable female characters. They might be cowering victims or abused or in the background, but the main characters are generally desperate guys going through bad times in their lives. They aren't going to be surrounded by strong, dynamic, self-actualised women. If you tried to put those sort of women into the context I'm writing about, it just wouldn't ring true.'

Mostly he enjoyed arguing his corner, but every now and then he adopted a blunter response, once telling a reporter 'I'll do what I want to do – if you like it, great, if you don't, fuck off.' He told me: 'There was maybe a bit of hostility towards me at the time, as I was in London rather than up in

Edinburgh. I was supposedly playing the big-time Charlie down there, but it wasn't the case; I probably partied harder when I came back to Edinburgh, and London was basically where I'd lived most of my adult life.'

Further down the line, there was a rather messy public falling-out between Irvine and Will Self when the English writer criticised the film's depiction of drug addiction. At the time Irvine hit back, saying he hadn't written the book for the 'Will Selfs and the public-school types of this world to pontificate over in their drawing-rooms and their broadsheet columns'. Looking back on the controversy now, Welsh regrets getting suckered into making that response. 'Will, though he didn't care for the film, was always very support-ive of the book. I think we both realised that we were being set up by journos in some kind of literary Blur–Oasis type of thing, an ex-junkie pissing contest. I felt as if I was being coerced into this thing with him and drugs, and also sensed the same line of questioning with Kelman and being work-ing-class, and with Ian Rankin in being from Edinburgh. The reality is that I get along with all of them, even though I was constantly being set up to diss them and other writers.'

Alan Warner told me an interesting tale that seems to sum up the growing antagonism directed against Irvine. On this occasion it came from the bastion of Middle England, the *Daily Mail*. 'I remember once after *Trainspotting* came out, this fucking journalist phoned up my old mum. This cunt from the *Mail*. It is a total mystery to this day how he got my mum's phone number. By chance I was in the house, so I took the call. This guy – with one of those cut-glass English public-school accents – *refused* to believe Irvine hadn't gone to a private school. He had this delusional concept that Irvine was a total construct. This journalist could not accept that a working-class guy who had not gone to a private school and a posh university like him could have sold a million books and made money, etc. It was almost fascinating to listen to him. He was quite bitter about it. A prole had been let into the annual ball. He was begging me to spill the beans on the "real Irvine". I threatened him.

'I want to make an important point here. A lot of people in the Scottish writing establishment have changed their tune today, but there was a huge, seething amount of middle-class hostility to Irvine and *Trainspotting*. The novel was slightly ignored, of course, when it was first published, in that typically insecure Scottish media way. They always heap pages and big it up on well-established authors who aren't Scottish, Updike and stuff like that, because it makes them feel "cosmopolitan" and important. So they toe-suck the fucking conservative literary line in a deeply insecure and provincial way. But, as *Trainspotting* sold more, a violent and spoiled-child reaction began from certain critics. Literary pundits were threatened by *Trainspotting*. It was a fly in the ointment of middle-class Edinburgh and the New Town globalised yuppies. Certain critics were furious they had no control over the book's success, that they had not given it their insignificant seal of approval. The ego of some critics/book reviewers never ceases to astonish and delight me. Many have since changed their tune about Irvine because it is advantageous to their careers. They can appropriate Irvine into their gentrification concepts of literature. Now some of them take a certain delight in being "ironic" about how much they like Irvine's novels. But they were hostile bastards in the early years. Believe me. I know their names.

'The book had been a huge bestseller even before the film was released, which was just an incredible phenomenon and a wonderful thing for Scottish literature. Nothing had happened like that in Scottish bookselling or fiction since Walter Scott, and even then *Trainspotting* was much more worldwide and quicker. So a lot of middle-class sensibilities were trodden on, and there was a reaction. There is a prejudice against writers who are writing from within their own communities. This is a prejudice of the middle class and it comes from them, because the middle class don't have communities, so they don't understand it. That was what was so great about *Trainspotting*. It was written by someone from inside the junkie community, not some bohemian or middle-class journalist looking in on it.

'Now, I am not saying everyone has to like *Trainspotting*. People are entitled not to like it. But it was the success of the book, and the middle-class impotence to do anything about it which angered them. They had to swallow a lot of bile . . . I believe that's why there was a bourgeois reaction against the book, and very quickly a safer and more palatable type of Edinburgh writing had to be established. This happened.'

As the hype grew, feature writers flocked to Muirhouse to get the views of bewildered local junkies. In general, their response was 'Who the hell is Irvine Welsh?' Hardly surprising, given that he left the area twenty years previously and was writing about a scene that was already history. *Vox* magazine even went as far as to case out the 'notorious' Montgomery Street, where Renton lived in the book, imagining they would find some cross between the Bronx and Amsterdam's red-light district. Anyone who has ever lived there would have told them the most exciting thing to be found on Montgomery Street was the chicken supper in the Montgomery Fish Bar.

Politicians weren't slow in getting in on the act either. Rumour had it that Donald Dewar, who went on to be Scotland's First Minister, would not even consider reading the book. Irvine actually thought more of Dewar for *not* reading *Trainspotting*. 'I did admire that. People shouldn't feel compelled to read something just because it's supposedly vogue. A lot of people pretended to like and get *Trainspotting*.

I just wanted to write a little fucking book about where I came from, and what I was up to, what everyone was up to.'

To a certain extent the backlash from within Scotland was an example of the infamous 'Him, Ah kent his faither' attitude by which successful Scots are brought down a peg or two. As Irvine recalled when *Trainspotting* sold 10,000 copies, 'I was like a hero. "You're fuckin' tellin' our story, good on yer, telling it as it is. Go on son." But when it sold 100,000 copies they said, "What the fuck?" About the same book!'

The tabloid press began to take more of an interest in Irvine as it slowly dawned on them that a cultural phenomenon was unfolding in front of them. When he was arrested in January 1996 at a Partick Thistle–Hibs game he ended up spending the night in the cells at Maryhill police station. The police later erroneously gave his age as 44 rather than 38. He recalls: 'It was my own fault. I was so out of it I just shouted different numbers at random.' The *Scotsman* called him 'the oldest swinger in town'. For a while, Irvine took to carrying his passport around with him just to prove that he was born in 1958. But the age issue refused to go away, and *Q* magazine dubbed him 'Uncle Irvine', accusing him of suffering from delayed adolescence. Irvine sportingly agreed, even arguing that he actually suffered from prolonged adolescence, having 'never really grown up beyond a certain point'. Gradually, *Trainspotting* also became subsumed into the whole Cool Britannia/Britpop movement of the mid-1990s. Kylie Minogue, at the time the hottest act on the UK pop scene, endorsed Irvine's writing in an interview with *The Face* magazine in May 1994. In January 1996 things took an even more bizarre turn when 'Britain's number 1 pop pin-up', Damon Albarn of Blur, met Irvine in Mather's bar in Edinburgh before the pair embarked on a mini-pub-crawl. To add to the confusion, one reporter, who described Welsh as Albarn's 'hero', even described Mather's as 'trendy'.

Irvine was confused and a bit fearful about what becoming a literary success, and being suddenly elevated to the status of cultural agenda-setter, would do to him. So it came as a welcome surprise to find out that so many of the successful new wave of Scottish writers – dubbed the 'Rebel Inc. Beats' – remained grounded despite their success. I've read in some features people claiming that Welsh was 'discovered' by *Rebel Inc.* Not quite. His work had already appeared in *NWS 9* and *Clocktower*, and he was already on Robin Robertson's radar if not under contract to Secker & Warburg. That said, the camaraderie among the Rebel Inc. crew played a crucial role in keeping Welsh sane when *Trainspotting* took off in such a spectacular way. Irvine recalls: 'Kevin Williamson was very important to me at this time, and even more important to the scene in general. He was the first to see something socially interesting was happening. When editor of the *Tollcross Times* he ran a short-story competition, expecting a handful of entries. He got almost 2,000. He picked up that there was a massive dissatisfaction in Scotland, and that people were writing about it, expressing this in fiction. He unified the scene under the Rebel Inc. banner and, although he would hate the term, brand. This was important because we all had our distinct acolytes. Sometimes there was crossover, sometimes not. But Kev united everybody under a common banner and, with my help here, stylised the scene by giving it a contemporary, ravey, clubby sensibility and thus drawing more people in.

'Kev knew how to get publicity and work the media, putting on events and publicising them with attention-grabbing shock tactics, often involving drug "prizes" for best poem, story etc. He was greatly influenced by Situationism and was a Malcolm McLarenesque character at the time, and a self-confessed media whore. Now he's the opposite: wild horses wouldn't drag him anywhere near a journo with a microphone and notebook.'* Williamson and Welsh co-wrote the 1993 spoof *A Visitor's Guide to Edinburgh*, which had the charming front cover showing Greyfriars Bobby holding a hypodermic needle in his paw.

Gordon Legge, the Falkirk-born author who by 1991 had already published two acclaimed books – *The Shoe* and *In Between Talking About the Football* – was also a steadying influence. Irvine told me: 'I'd always equated literary success with becoming an arsehole for some reason, and I think this fear of success was a big thing for me. Gordon Legge was a great influence on me. I used to meet him at gigs and think, wow, this cunt has written a couple of fucking brilliant books, and he's still a nice guy.'

Two other writers on the Edinburgh scene at the time who helped Irvine a lot were Rodney Relax and Barry Graham. 'Rodney was another guy cut from the same cloth. He was an Edinburgh punk face, and having somebody like him involved in the burgeoning literary scene made it easier for me to feel comfortable there. Barry Graham was also massively important to me, because he was another guy you couldn't put in a box. He was a Buddhist ex-professional boxer who loved Guinness; he was fabulously well-read and outrageously opinionated. In an environment where support-iveness could turn incestuous, he was spiky and confronta-tional, and just what the scene needed. As he was a near-neighbour in Leith, we became close friends. Barry had already been through the course, with three novels published by Bloomsbury in London, and was an enormously support-ive friend.'

Another, more left-field influence on Welsh was the maver-ick writer Paul Reekie, who was raised in Fife before moving

---

* Williamson didn't respond to several requests to contribute to this book.

to the capital aged sixteen. Variously described as poet, iconoclast and outsider, Reekie, who took his own life in June
2010, had a profound influence on Irvine, the pair tearing
through the mid-1990s together on a frenetic trip through
raves, police cells and football stadiums. Irvine believes that
Reekie was perhaps the greatest talent of all the writers on
the Edinburgh scene. He was certainly one of the least well-
known, and not a man who took the publishing process too
seriously – only a couple of pieces of his writing were
published during his lifetime. His poem 'When Caesar's
Mushroom Is in Season' took pride of place as the epigraph
to *The Acid House*. Irvine explains that 'Reekie was the key
man for me in enabling me to realise that you didn't need to
be one-dimensional to be part of the local literary scene. I
knew him as a face in the Leith pubs, the clubs, and at Easter
Road. He was an astonishing guy, a total one-off. We would
go to Easter Road and pull some of the hoolie element into
discussions on art and literature, and then head for readings
or art shows and talk football and aggro to the artsy
cognoscenti.

'Paul hated, or maybe feared, the idea of success. He was
good at everything: could have been a pro football player, as
he had trials for several major clubs; should have been a rock
star, had a great voice and stage presence; was an amazing
poet, but hated to publish. I think he was a true punk; he was
anti-success. He was the most well-read person I've met. We
got ripped at clubs and followed the bass with Anne and
Rosie,* and had a whale of a time. His death a couple of
years back was a massive blow to me.'

For a while Irvine struggled to feel at ease in the London
publishing world and to manage people's expectations of
him. It took him a while to break down those barriers and

---

* Rosie Savin, Reekie's partner at the time.

realise that he was in there on merit. 'This sounds incredibly arrogant, but it generally wasn't my merit I was questioning. Sometimes – not always, but sometimes – I would think, who the fuck is this person, and what do they have to do with books and literature? There were a lot of talented and committed people on that scene, but a lot of parasites too; they brought little to the table.'

Irvine pays special tribute to two people for helping him navigate through the celebrity jungle. He recalls watching Duncan McLean handling being thrust into the limelight after the release of *Bucket of Tongues*, managing to maintain a space but still having time for people. 'He got the balance just right, which isn't easy to do when lots of people want you to do all sorts of things.'

A more unlikely influence was the Salford-born boss of Factory Records, Tony Wilson. When Irvine's books started to sell in big numbers Wilson took him under his wing, well aware that going from zero to hero was not an easy thing to do. Irvine wrote: 'He's seen it happen with bands, and he knew what would happen to me before I did.' Irvine had first met Tony when he used to visit Manchester's Hacienda club during the acid-house days of the early 1990s. Irvine was an admirer of Wilson and of the Factory bands, and believes the fact that Wilson was older than him helped him to feel at ease in the club. Wilson organised Irvine's first tour, with the opening night being at the Hacienda. Irvine came on stage to rapturous applause. 'To go back there and be the guy who was holding the floor was a big emotional charge for me. I was surrounded by young girls snogging me and guys slapping me on the back. It was a foretaste of the madness to come, and Tony was always looking out for me, and I'm eternally grateful. He guided and protected me.

'People like Tony and Jeff Barrett from [record label] Heavenly were the first people to say to me, "You're not going to be like a writer, you're going to be like a pop star. This sort of writing and the sensibility behind it isn't literature, it's rock'n'roll. There are no real precedents for this sort of book." I thought this was a bit fanciful, but they were absolutely right. I was treated in a very different way to most writers. I would have loved this kind of fame in my twenties, but I was actually, in some ways, looking forward to easing into a more crusty, literary type of fame. It never really happened. Tony loved Manchester and totally believed in it. When he called you an "honorary Manc" it was the greatest compliment he could give anybody.'

On his friend and fellow writer Alan Warner, Irvine says: 'Alan and I, I felt, had much the same outlook. We knew you had to get out there and we enjoyed the support of the group, but I think we were both suspicious of the gang mentality. It wasn't that I didn't like hanging out and socialising, I liked it too much and knew I could be easily sucked into it, and I had way too many other outlets for that. I quickly realised, and I can't speak for Alan, but I think he did too, that writing a book is about being alone for large stretches of time, just sitting down and doing it. There were many writers on that scene as talented, if not more so, over short bursts than me. But I was really determined to make a go of it. And I knew it took a big time investment.'

Eventually Welsh moved on from the Edinburgh set, as did Alan Warner, who moved to Ireland in 1997. Welsh's employers at Edinburgh City Council allowed him to take a sabbatical from his work, and rather than stay in the goldfish bowl of Edinburgh, Irvine set off on a quirky trail that took him to London, Amsterdam and Dunfermline and then back to London. He had a 'therapeutic' year in Amsterdam during 1995, buying a season ticket for Ajax and signing a new two-book deal early that year. But by March 1996 Irvine was living in Dunfermline, Fife. He was still getting used to the idea of being a full-time author and had lots of time to kill every day. He likened it to being back on the dole, hanging out with wide-boys and boozers and kids who stole cars.

Interest in the new wave of Scottish writing wasn't confined to these shores. While the Scottish media always tended to downplay its significance, American publications weren't so circumspect. In the winter of 1995 the writer Lesley Downer came to Edinburgh to research an article on the Rebel Inc. gang. The resultant feature, 'The Beats of Edinburgh', appeared in the *New York Times* of 31 March 1996. And so, bizarrely, the New York elite were introduced to the pleasures of a day on the grog in Robbie's Bar, where the writer says she met with Duncan McLean, Paul Reekie, Gordon Legge and Alan Warner. She wrote about how they 'get up at noon, drink, talk and write the day away and party through the night'. This certainly bore no resemblance to the lifestyle Duncan was leading at the time; in fact, he cannot even remember being in Robbie's that day, although he did meet the author alone in a café on Waverley Bridge. Duncan says, 'It was great US coverage, but also one of the most Disneyesque versions of the writing scene at that time. I remember me and Alan at least laughing our heads off at it, but being slightly appalled too. I think the writer was just giving the Americans what she thought they wanted ... I remember laughing to myself when one of those fabled fact-checkers phoned me in Orkney from the *NYT* to check if it was all true, but all she asked me about was the names of my books and where I grew up, not whether there was any truth in the pub-crawl orgy of beer, smoke, piercings, shaved heads and literary arguments.'

Downer told readers that Welsh was the leader of the group, but added that he was an enigma even to them; none of them apparently knew anything of his background, what he did in the 1980s or even what school he attended. The man himself was, unusually for him, absent from the all-day session, which apparently continued until the early hours of the morning in the Oyster Bar near Waverley Station. Instead, Downer met Welsh, 'icon of nineties Britain', in the Ship pub in London's Soho, where our hero was drinking with members of Primal Scream. She thought he was a 'skinny, unhealthy-looking man in his thirties, with a round battered face like a dissolute cherub who has seen too many late nights'. She found him to be articulate, intellectual and intensely serious, arguing not in broad Muirhouse but in educated Scots as he dissected the English middle classes.

Looking back on the feature Welsh says: 'I recall being fucked for that interview, as I'd been on one with Innes and Bobby, and I think we'd all gone on to Oasis's party. I remember trying to hold it together for the interview – that was probably why I sounded so posh and deliberate. To me, though, that article was the high-water mark of international recognition of that scene. It's pretty much unprecedented for the *New York Times* to send a journo to Edinburgh and to have three pages in the *New York Times* magazine about Scottish writers. It made quite a splash in the English press and was snootily ignored by the Scottish press, especially the *Scotsman*, who always tried to pretend Rebel Inc. didn't exist. I think the Scottish press, especially the *Scotsman* publications, are very conservative, not just politically, but their view of Scottish society seems very much the same as it was in the 1970s. The London press are sliding to extinction, but the Scottish press seem to have embarked on a consistent strategy of sprinting towards the abyss.'

Robin Robertson told me another revealing tale of how the Scottish literary scene appealed stateside. 'I was in New York with a bunch of other people, giving a reading for the *New Yorker*. There was a buffet afterwards, and I was determined to meet up with Tina Brown, the magazine's editor. I didn't spend very long in her company, but when she found out I was in publishing she asked me, "What's hot?", and I immediately said, "Scottish writing". This was sometime in 1994, just after *Trainspotting* had come out but before it had started to get big.

'I thought what I said to her would go in one ear and out the other, but when I got back to London there was a message on my answer machine asking me to ring someone called Dick on a New York number. So, I rang this number and the person who picked up said, "This is Dick Avedon. Tina's told me I've got to come over and photograph some Scottish writers."'

Richard Avedon, one of the great fashion and portrait photographers, met up with many of the top names on the Scottish literary scene in Glasgow on 28 November 1995. Robin got together ten leading poets and writers: Alan Warner, Kathleen Jamie, Duncan McLean, Robert Crawford, Janice Galloway, Don Paterson, John Burnside, Alasdair Gray, A.L. Kennedy and Irvine. Unfortunately, James Kelman couldn't make it.

Robin recalls: 'We were all due to meet in a hotel and a mini-bus was to take us to the Clutha Vaults, but there was no sign of Irvine. For the first twenty minutes this was kind of amusing, but after about half an hour people started getting a bit pissed off. But he finally arrived in the hotel reception, wearing this big sheepskin jacket which, back then, he wore until it fell off him, grinning from ear to ear, and I took him to one side and told him he was a complete cunt. And he replied, "I don't care, I've just necked a couple of eccies." He was out of his tree but great fun.' The group moved on to the Clutha Vaults. 'Richard Avedon was tiny; he had this old Hasselblad camera, which was probably bigger than him. He asked me to help compose the shot, saying, "I don't know who these people are, who are the big names?"'

Almost twenty years on, Alan Warner still has surprisingly vivid memories of the photo-shoot and the subsequent drinks session at the Clutha Vaults, which is known as the Writers' Pub in Glasgow. 'I remember a sexy witch had just put a curse on me. She sent me great photos of herself – starkers – but she said I would feel ill and turn into a white snake due to her spell. So, if you look at that Avedon photo,* you will see that I am wearing a crucifix, which I did for about a year. My dick didn't even get bigger. I asked Avedon to make sure the crucifix stood out for personal spiritual reasons, and he wrapped it in this black plastic reflective paper. He was most impressed a witch had put a curse upon me and he asked me about it a lot. I wanted to ask *him* about Marilyn Monroe and many other things – but you don't want to seem like a nosey-parker from Oban. Irvine kept calling him "Dickie".

'It's a miracle I can remember anything, because there was a free bar at that photo-shoot; they knew that was a sure guarantee to get the Scottish writers along. A shame Jim Kelman didn't make it. The photo-shoot started around midday. Avedon had assistants. Boys and girls – all beautiful. I recall drinking Guinness with triple Rémy Martin chasers all day; the three survivors at about eight in the evening were me, Irvine and John Burnside. The geezer who owned the bar – Brendan – is a nice fellow, but he had us chucked out, and I am sure he barred us from there. I must say, I thought that was a real personal career high in my life: "Writers barred from Writers' Pub".'

Irvine's summary of the day is that he was 'a great advert for ecstasy over alcohol. I don't think I did anything more subversive than tell Janice and Alison [A.L. Kennedy] that they were beautiful.'

* Sadly, the Richard Avedon Foundation in New York were unable to provide us with this image.

14

The hottest thing in town

Most theatre is bourgeois shite.

The *Trainspotting* phenomenon was a slow-burning thing. It started as a cult book in Edinburgh, with word spreading gradually among the drug-using subcultures – the heroin users, and also the E-fuelled kids who flocked to clubs and raves. (Irvine was always happiest when it was at this level, confined to what he saw as 'working-class clubbers'.) Once the stage play debuted at the Citizens Theatre in Glasgow, though – just nine months after the book's release – *Trainspotting*'s notoriety began to spread like wildfire. Welsh was more than a little uncomfortable with the way that the play's success drew the attention of a 'middle-class vicarious element' to the book, though I'm sure he appreciated the effect their spending power had on his bank balance.

With all the furore surrounding the book and the film, it's easy to forget just how important the stage play was to the whole *Trainspotting* story. When I asked Robin Robertson to cite the moment when he began to realise that *Trainspotting* was going to be massive, his mind drifted back to the play's opening night in London. Sitting by the foyer bar prior to the play, he was approached by Jane Birkin, the Anglo-French singer and actress, who asked him for a light for her cigarette.

'She wasn't the kind of person you would expect to be going to the Bush Theatre, yet she had come over from Paris to see this play that was causing such a fuss. So that moment, even before I had seen the play, suggested that there really was something going on. By then we were reprinting, and sales were beginning to exceed everyone's highest expectations. It was the stage play, though, that started the real shift; reaction to it was just rapturous. It became the hottest thing in town to go to.'

As befits a working-class boy from Muirhouse, Irvine Welsh initially had a healthy disdain for all things theatrical. The most dramatic scenes he saw in Muirhouse were outside the Gunner at chucking-out time, and I remember him associating theatre with public-school types and the Edinburgh Festival, which he loathed with a passion. One of his most wicked impersonations, back when I worked with him, was of what he perceived to be a typical theatre-goer, who spoke in an arch, aloof manner. Even today, after the adaptation of his first novel has been translated into many languages and has earned rave plaudits around the world, Irvine is still reticent about getting too involved in theatre, though he now admits to being a 'closet theatre-lover'. He likes the idea of live performance; it's just the reality that often depresses him. He told the *Herald* in 2006: 'There's no money in it, it's hard to get things done, things are savaged when you do get them on. You're appealing to a small number of people rather than a big audience, and you think, why bother?' Yet Welsh's work, most notably the memorable characters, violent language and primitive passions of *Trainspotting*, was perfect for adaptation to the stage.

Just as the book was bought by many people

who previously had little interest in literature, so the play
encouraged a radical change in theatre, pulling in a whole
new audience not used to watching drama. Some of them
even went on to act and to write for the stage. Schemies in
the theatre occasionally made for much unintentional hilarity. At the end of the interval, ushers at the Citizens had to be
sent outside to the car park to ring the bell for the punters
who had gone outside for a blow. Some of the newcomers
didn't really know the protocol and would shout to their
mates sitting some rows away during the performance. At
one show, a member of the audience stood up midway
through Act One and told anyone who might be interested,
'I cannae stand this! I'm gaun to the pub!'

The two key players in successfully bringing the book to
the stage were Harry Gibson, who wrote the play version
and Ian Brown, who directed it at the Citizens as part of
Glasgow's Mayfest in 1994. That particular version debuted
in the 50-seat Stalls Studio, a choice of venue that was suitably cramped and claustrophobic. The audience entered
through a door that opened on to the playing area, across
which they had to walk to get to their seats. Intimacy probably isn't the right word for the experience, but the audience
could almost touch the actors. People who were in the audience recall thinking that the actors might even be shooting
up for real. The staging directions for the second production
of Gibson's script, for the larger but still compact 144-seat
Bush Theatre, read: 'a small studio theatre, no more than a
broom-cupboard with pretensions; really it looks like a very
small bar in which an audience has been seated by some kind
of architectural error.'

In 1993, Harry Gibson, whose adaptation of the book was
such a spectacular success, was working as an actor and play-
reader at the Citizens when he first came across Irvine's book.
'We had two new studio theatres, for which we were not

finding much in the way of powerful new drama,' he recalls. 'So, I went into John Smith's Bookshop in Hillhead seeking a new novel fit for dramatising. I asked Alison [Stroak], the manager, and she cried out, *"Trainspotting!* Everyone is reading it – and everyone is stealing it!" It had just sold out, but given the unusual circumstances she found one for me – which I think a member of staff had been reading in the loo.' Harry took the book on a train journey to Oxford, and recalls that by the time he had reached the end of the toilet-bowl scene (page 27 to be precise) he knew it was a work of genius. 'I thought the book was ideal for dramatising – it's a swatch of first-person speeches written in a vivid, credible style. It reeks of the streets. Irvine excels at monologues. I just fillet them nicely. I rang Giles Havergal, the artistic director at the Citizens, and said, "Get the rights!" Giles has fine instincts. At that time he was negotiating the rights to *Swing Hammer Swing!* by Jeff Torrington with the same company.'

Harry Gibson is the son of an Aberdeen shipwright who moved to Oxford to work at the car plant in Cowley. Gibson read English at Oxford University before working in various theatres as a stage manager, actor, director and writer. He joined the Citizens in 1979 as an actor. Giles Havergal told me: 'We wanted someone to read the new scripts we were getting. They had been piling up in the office because no one was reading them. We asked Harry to read each script and, if it was worth consideration at all, to give us one side of A4 on it, no more. Very occasionally, he would say, "This is a really, really good script and you should all read it", at which point David MacDonald, Philip Prowse* and I would immediately read it.

'Harry came to us with *Trainspotting* , so we all got copies and read it straight away and just told him, "Go, go, go!" I

* Havergal's two co-directors at the Citizens.

thought it was a terrific book. Of course, it's a horrific story on one level, but the writing was just so good and the characters were so alive. Harry was certainly a great enthusiast and is a really clever man. He is a very good actor and writer and has a very amusing if slightly acerbic character. His critiques of the plays he read for us were really brilliant, and extremely funny at times. It was always a bit of a pleasure when the latest batch came through, but really on the knuckle. When Harry said read it, you read it.'

Tall and thin, with fair, curly hair, Harry Gibson was 45, significantly older than Irvine, let alone the young actors used in the productions, when he took *Trainspotting* to the stage. Despite the age difference, Gibson put together a very intelligent and nuanced take on Irvine's book. The conclusion of Gibson's adaptation may be less optimistic than the film version, but for many the play was a more powerful and realistic adaptation. Gibson was influenced by Steven Berkoff's 1975 play *East*, which used local slang and verse to depict the brutal and at times comical life of London's East End. Berkoff described the play as an elegy for the area's 'energetic waste' – a phrase that could be used quite easily to describe the exploits of Welsh's miscreants.

Gibson, whom Welsh describes as 'about the most theatrical person I've ever met', now lives in Oxford, where he is 'quietly writing a novel'. He very kindly took the time to write me a seven-page letter detailing how he set about adapting Irvine's book for the stage. Rather than try to hack a great writer's prose, perhaps it's best to let him recall in his own words how he did it.

'I worked on the stage version over two months on the dining-room table. I bang on through it, marking up the great passages and building up lists of scenes and characters. I plot it all out on a big sheet of paper. I note particularly how a few key characters recur and link up: I'm seeking the jigsaw bits that can fit together as a neat theatrical story. Conventionally, a story has an axis and a keel, a lateral relationship between two people, groups or pressures, and forward development along "a journey" influenced by all of the rest. Ideally, everything draws to a common climax. Even in a complex and wayward Dickens novel, you can see him doing this.

'My axis was the friendship between Mark and a character I called Tommy – who was, in fact, a mix of Tommy and Spud. The Spud sequences at the outset provide their mateyness, which is then mishandled when Mark gives him a hit of skag and is finally destroyed with Tommy dying, leaving Mark feeling as if he's betrayed him. This relationship has its two sides: the real personal care for a friend versus the ritual carelessness of mateship. To care or not to care.

'Mark's smart, hard-boiled junky nihilist view of life is then the moral field where the decision must be made, so the play then spins through Mark's formative experiences, a subculture dominated by violence which stretches out to Northern Ireland (his brother's death) and is maintained locally by the likes of Begbie. So Begbie's life is also explored, and as the strands draw together (as they should) Begbie's roots are exposed in the play's ending as he pisses on his own bevvied-up father. The father is the one who at last speaks the word "trainspottin . . .", so tying up the whole play right back to its till-then curious title. My first version ended with all the characters reciting the "Our Father". Later, I thought this was too artful. I think I've used five different endings. My own favourite is the pisser.'

Harry sent his first draft to Giles Havergal, expecting him to pick holes in it and demand changes. Instead Giles sent it to Ian Brown, who made a few minor adjustments, and soon the play was ready for a debut at the Citizens. For the free preview, queues stretched out of the building into the car park, and the entire run sold out before it opened.

The play's director, Ian Brown, also had a refreshingly 'punk' attitude to theatre that no doubt appealed to Irvine. In publicity for the new show, Brown warned audiences that they would need a strong stomach to sit through the entire play. In 1994 Brown was artistic director at the Traverse in Edinburgh, having previously run the Citizens' youth theatre company, TAG. At the Traverse he earned a reputation as a risk-taker and for staging raw yet life-affirming work that most London theatres would have shied away from. He put on the Canadian playwright Brad Fraser's shocking work *Unidentified Human Remains and the True Nature of Love*, a comedy-drama about sexually frustrated thirty-somethings who try to learn the meaning of love as a serial killer terrorises the streets of Edmonton. Another challenging play directed by Ian was the Italian writer Michele Celeste's *Hanging the President*, set in apartheid South Africa and starring Stuart Hepburn, and which also featured the first professional appearance of Adrian Lester. The acclaimed production, which premiered at the 1989 Edinburgh Fringe, featured graphic scenes of buggery, defecation and masturbation. Ian recalls: 'It was done in a small theatre space and was quite sexually explicit and quite violent. I was definitely keen on using shock tactics in my directing style back then. I was quite fearless about it. You could feel the audience were being put through the mill a bit in all of these productions. But there was also a powerful, celebratory nature about them.'

Ian told me that, after Giles Havergal asked him to direct *Trainspotting*, he 'hadn't actually read the book by then, though I was aware of it. I had been doing a little bit of searching around for subjects to explore, and I was interested anyway in doing something about the seamier side of Edinburgh, and of Leith in particular. I had become aware that there was more to Edinburgh than most people think. I liked the book and thought it was very well written; Irvine's dialogue is good and comes off the page extremely well. I understood it and was really very gripped by it. I thought that, ultimately, it was really a moral book and quite moving, even though it showed people leading chaotic lives. It was obviously going to be a challenge, though, to distil it to some kind of stage version.'

The stage play was a graphic, violently disturbing, yet at times hilarious take on the book, a two-act work that contained an estimated 147 uses of the dreaded c-word. Act One opens with Renton telling the audience how he had once woken in an ex-girlfriend's home having soiled the bedclothes. Then it's on to Tommy's account of anal sex going disastrously wrong, before we are introduced to Begbie, who walks out on his pregnant girlfriend. The following scenes depict the vicious 'Her Man' story and Mark's 'Choose Life' speech before the final scenes, which see Renton, Sick Boy and Alison shoot up at Johnny Swan's in a 'highly eroticised ritual'. The act closes with the death of Alison's baby, Mark's retelling of the heroin-suppositories yarn and the turning on to heroin of poor old Tommy, along with Mark threatening to kill a squirrel for kicks. One would imagine the audience enjoyed their interval pint after sitting through that lot.

Act Two starts off more reflectively as Renton recalls the death of his brother Billy and the post-funeral sex with Billy's pregnant girlfriend, before moving on to Mark jacking up again and ending up hospitalised in a coma. More pub tales follow as Alison tells how she deals with offensive customers, and then there's a pub scene where Mark, Begbie and Tommy reflect on the death of Alison's baby. Tommy's descent into HIV hell leads into the final scene, where Mark and Begbie come across a drunk in the old Leith Central station. The drunk turns out to be Begbie's dad and the lads urinate on him. They then stand in the derelict building waiting for the trains that will never come.

Gibson wisely decided to use just four actors to speak for many characters, so as to be true to Irvine's feeling for the way folk tell stories. Portobello-born Ewen Bremner (Renton) and Susan Vidler (Alison), both of whom went on to star in Danny Boyle's film version, led the cast. Vidler and Bremner knew one another from way back, having both auditioned as children for a production of Alan Bleasdale's *No More Sitting on the Old School Bench* at the Brunton Theatre. Susan, who was educated at Preston Lodge High School in Prestonpans, initially dreamed of being a ballet dancer but eventually went on to study drama at Edinburgh's Telford College (where Irvine Welsh once worked) and the Welsh College of Music and Drama. Both she and Bremner later burst on to the film scene in Mike Leigh's fierce, brilliant film *Naked*. The other two actors making up the Citizens quartet were James Cunningham (Tommy) and Malcolm Shields (Begbie).

Ian Brown says: 'I already knew quite a lot of the actors who I thought would be right for it, so we didn't do a huge amount of auditions. I thought it was really important that we used actors who were actually from Edinburgh. We just gathered together this tight little group quite quickly. I think Ewen was the key bit of casting in some ways.

'We stuck pretty much to what Harry had done. It was designed to be done in a very small space – a 50-seat theatre – we never envisaged it being more large-scale. By its very nature it had to be very economic, and that was the spirit we all went into it with. Once we started to read it and work on it, Irvine came into the picture a bit. Every so often he would call in on rehearsals and see what we were doing. We had a good working relationship with him; he was very generous and helpful, and it was very inspiring for all of us to have him around. We felt very connected to him and to the book, and he was learning a lot too, enjoying the process of making it work for theatre and hearing his words spoken out loud by really good actors in the accent in which it was written. It really brought it to life for him.'

At the time of the Mayfest launch, Irvine was in Germany doing a reading tour for *The Acid House*. But he sat in on rehearsals for the subsequent production in Edinburgh and was totally won over by the adaptation, particularly by Ewen Bremner, who Welsh thought was perfect casting for the part of Renton. This was at a time when Irvine was genuinely perplexed as to why his 'scabby wee book' was causing such a fuss. His phone was constantly ringing with journalists asking for interviews and people wanting to cut film deals. It was only when he saw his words performed on stage that he began to see why others were getting so excited about his book. It was the first time he realised the real power and potential of some of the passages he had written. He says he proudly walked out of that first rehearsal convinced that he had actually done something special and knowing the play would be a great success.

Harry Gibson recalled the opening production at the Citizens: 'The play was set in a grimy white toilet and the acting was in-yer-face indeed; the audience was only a few feet away from the actors. I bet Bremner gobbed on them. Ian told me that he wasn't keen on rehearsing; he just went out and killed it.' The critics were equally rapt by the performance. Reviewing the show in the *Herald*, Keith Bruce was impressed by the show's 'thoroughly researched naturalism', but warned readers: 'If you consider yourselves unshockable (as some of the most persistent chucklers in this audience clearly thought themselves), prepare to be educated – especially if the darker side of the capital city with its smack culture, HIV epidemic and distinctive vocabulary is unfamiliar to you.'* The *Guardian*

* The Citizens production won the *Herald*'s 'Spirit of Mayfest' award. Unfortunately, the current staff at the Citizens didn't respond to emails and a letter asking if they had stills or posters that could be used in this book.

review was equally positive: 'For the most part it is a breath-lessly dynamic production full of dangerous, deranged perform-ances that articulate the fearful nihilism of the dispossessed.'

Ian Brown, who now works in London as a freelance theatrical director, says, 'I remember people really liking it in Glasgow and us realising we had a bit of a hit on our hands. It sold out pretty much straight away from when it opened, so the critical success, although it was lovely to have it, didn't really affect what we were doing at the time. By that point we had already sold the tickets, and from there it just grew and grew. Then I had the idea of taking it back through to Edinburgh to the new Traverse, which was a big scale-up from how we had done it in Glasgow.'

The rave notices continued when the production made the switch to the sell-out run at the Traverse as part of the Festival Fringe. The play then ran at the Bush Theatre in Shepherd's Bush for just over a month. Again, the box-office was kept inordinately busy and London critics loved the show. Carole Woddis thought that the play should be required viewing throughout the land. Woddis was particularly taken with Ewen Bremner's performance, saying he had 'a way of conveying vulnerability, nervous energy and rebellion all in the flick of those elongated fingers. But James Cunningham's ravaged Tommy, Susan Vidler as Alison and Malcolm Shields's terrifying portrait of bully boy and Mafioso, Franco, equally make the blood run cold.' Woddis thought the play was a 'harrowing testament to a generation' and said that – despite the 'gut-wrenching' subject matter – the audience 'loved the insipient anarchy of it, they groaned with the desperate degradation of it, and they thrilled to the dramatic energy of it.'

15

The spectacle of the wild

The play was very important in that it gave the story a dramatic life, and it showed me that there was a hungry audience out there for my stuff. The film would obviously realise that audience in a global sense, which has in turn fuelled international interest in the play. Even today, there always seems to be a production of it somewhere in the world.

Over the years the *Trainspotting* stage adaptation gained such notoriety that it ultimately was dubbed 'the play that shocked the nineties'. A more accurate if slightly less zippy description would have been 'one of the many plays that shocked the nineties'. Harry Gibson's work came to the public's attention in the middle of a decade that saw a sudden revival in the fortunes of British theatre. Not since the days of John Osborne's *Look Back in Anger* in the 1950s had so many talented young writers produced such challenging and controversial work. The movement became known as In-Yer-Face Theatre and was defined in the *New Oxford English Dictionary* as 'blatantly aggressive or provocative, impossible to ignore or avoid'. Writers like Sarah Kane, Anthony

Neilson and Mark Ravenhill broke taboos and shocked audiences with their use of language, nudity, sex, abusive behaviour and violence.

As the author Aleks Sierz notes in his excellent book on the subject, this new style has roots that go way back to the beginnings of Greek tragedy, through Jacobean theatre and right up to more modern playwrights such as Osborne, Pinter and Berkoff.

Harry Gibson's reworking of Irvine's book was one of the most important of the new plays; it helped draw attention to theatre north of the border at a time when the media tended to focus mainly on the London scene. Feeding off the hype that Danny Boyle's film had triggered, the play travelled further and reached a much larger audience than any of the other new plays. Closer to home, it also helped reinvigorate Scottish drama and the Citizens Theatre. Giles Havergal says, 'Trainspotting led to a whole series of Irvine Welsh adaptations at the Citizens; we must have done about six including Marabou Stork Nightmares and Filth, which was particularly good, a marvellous show. I liked Irvine very much; he used to turn up for all the shows. I remember thinking before I met him that he would be this sort of terrifying figure, and in reality he was not that way at all.

'Trainspotting certainly had a big impact on us at the Citizens, and it brought in a different kind of audience. We already had a young audience, but Trainspotting brought in a completely different crowd, which was great. Also, I think it was a real marker for the kind of work we would do in those new studio theatres . . . the Stalls Studio had just opened in 1992. I thought creatively they became incredibly important. I remember the girl's monologue in Trainspotting where she talks about being a waitress and the vile people she meets in the restaurant – at that close quarter when you have 50 people in a room that is so small, the impact was really impressive.'

A year after the curtain came down on the triumphant run at the Bush, Giles Havergal, eager to bring the play to a wider audience, decided to revive it, but by then Ian Brown and the original cast had moved on. Harry Gibson recalls how 'Giles asked me to direct it. Recast, we set it in a derelict underground rail siding with pools of water underfoot, so it was more "ambient" than the white-toilet version, with more shifting of light states and contemplative moments. Still, the scenes were jump-cut and several audience members said they felt as though they'd been doing a drug. One Citizens actor said it was the best show he'd ever seen.'

This version won the *Sunday Times* regional award for best new play of 1995, along with the Theatrical Management Association (TMA) award for best new play in 1995, though Harry is keen to stress that the awards could quite easily have been given to Ian Brown's production.

Ian Brown looks back on his crucial if relatively brief involvement in the *Trainspotting* success story with a sense of pride, but also some regrets. 'At the time I was very busy with my job at the Traverse. I didn't really have time to enjoy the success of the play; I had to move on to the next project. I probably made a bit of a mistake at that point because I just let them get on with it. I didn't really want to take it on the national tour; I thought taking it on tour would have stretched it beyond what we originally had envisaged. We had done the Citz, the Traverse, which was great, and then on to the Bush in London, and for me I had done really everything I wanted to do with it at that point.

'It was really great to be part of the *Trainspotting* story. I got on very well with Irvine and enjoyed the collaboration with him, and ended up commissioning him to do another

play, *You'll Have Had Your Hole*. That wasn't as great a
success as *Trainspotting*, but it did still manage to shock a
few people. The *Trainspotting* film is very different from the
stage play. I thought it was a great film, but it was a very odd
experience for me because some of my actors were in it but
were playing different parts. I suppose I was a bit jealous of
the film in some respects, but I also felt quietly proud because
we had paved the way for the film.* And I think the film did
owe just a little bit to the stage version. But they are two very
different things, and the stage version was just a great thing
in its own right. To see people who really love the book and
know it well having such a great time watching the play was
just a really satisfying experience. That combination of the
text, those actors and what happened in the rehearsal room
with me was something rather special. I cannot actually
remember rehearsals of many plays I've done, but I can still
remember the rehearsals for *Trainspotting*.'

Since the heady days of 1995 the *Trainspotting* play has
gone global, with sell-out runs and nightly standing ovations
around the world. There seems to be a never-ending fascination among theatre-goers for the bodily functions and drug-
crazed antics of these lovable Edinburgh junkies. Harry
Gibson describes it succinctly: 'Basically, the tame love the
spectacle of the wild.' Along the way it has helped the careers
of a host of actors, most notably *Lord of the Rings* lead
Hobbit Billy Boyd (Tommy in the Edinburgh Royal Lyceum
production), Paisley-born actor Gerard Butler (Renton) who
went on to conquer Hollywood, and *Green Wing* star
Michelle Gomez (Alison). Harry admitted to me that the
number of casts he has worked with on the play blurs in his
mind, but a couple of outstanding performances stick out.

---

* The film's producer and director, Andrew Macdonald and Danny
Boyle, watched one of the early stage adaptations.

An early Edinburgh Fringe production at the Assembly Rooms saw two unknown Ayrshire brothers, Peter and Paul Ireland, steal the show as Tommy and Renton. 'Paul came to us from his agent and then told me had a brother who fancied acting. Peter came in from Ardrossan, did Tommy like he owned it, stripped to the waist and nutted the wall! Fuck . . .' This version went on a UK tour, which was largely successful, although one would love to have been at the show in Oldham when a coachload of OAPs marched out en masse, having obviously taken *Trainspotting* to mean, well, trainspotting. Following the tour, it then opened in London's west end at the Ambassadors Theatre, opposite the ultra-exclusive Ivy restaurant. The cast and crew made an incongruous clientele in the posh diner, and also took up membership for the season at the Groucho Club. A later west end production was at the Whitehall Theatre, where the audience mingled post-show with the patrons emerging from *The Mousetrap* at the nearby St Martin's Theatre.

Aided by the stunning success of Danny Boyle's film, the play grew in notoriety and critical acclaim. It went on to have a successful run at the Players Theatre in Greenwich Village, off-Broadway, in a version directed by Harry Gibson and produced by Aldo Scrofani. After one show in Greenwich Village, the actor Brian Dennehy told Harry that it was the 'darkest' show he had ever seen. This New York version can be read in full in the collection *4 Play*, along with Harry's take on *Marabou Stork Nightmares* and *Filth* and Keith Wyatt's adaptation of *Ecstasy*. It's difficult to find *4 Play* these days, but it's well worth digging out. From page one of the *Trainspotting* section, it's obvious that Harry had written a fresh, daring and funny version which nonetheless remained loyal to the brilliance of the original. Gibson is obviously a fine writer in his own right, and I especially liked his description of the traditional Scottish fry-up: 'lumps of slaughtered and aborted animals lie twitching in a pool of boiling cow fat'. Delightful! The New York production also had innovative use of music by artists like the Chemical Brothers and Portishead. Pink Floyd's 'Shine On You Crazy Diamond (Part 1)', itself a tribute to one of rock music's most famous lost souls and drug casualties, Syd Barrett, is also used wisely.

Since then it's been produced all over the world by many different companies. (I still long to see what a Japanese Begbie looks and sounds like.) Along the way, there were plenty of crazy nights for Harry to enjoy. 'All directors drink with their actors. I have been physically carried down Sauchiehall Street to a nightclub. We did go a bit mad in Oz too. I dimly recall a big jar containing a dead rattlesnake steeped in mescal: one of our Begbies took a shot and then hung from the ceiling, bollock naked . . . hissing.'

Harry Gibson went on to do stage versions of *Marabou Stork Nightmares* (his and Irvine's favourite), *Filth* and *Glue*, and he also took over the writing of Irvine's musical, *Blackpool*. None of these – or, indeed, Irvine's own stage plays – has quite captured the magic and critical acclaim that *Trainspotting* did, and some critics have rather unkindly branded Welsh a one-hit wonder when it comes to the theatre. Gibson, who revived *Trainspotting* for a triumphant tour of the UK in 2006, again offers some interesting thoughts on Welsh and the theatre. 'His dramatic writing within a novel is exemplary. Outside of the saturation of novel-writing, drama is not his strong suit. Also, sometimes trying to factor Irvine's complicated plotting into a stage show is a bridge too far. Though he does now respect what theatre can do, he leaves it to the experts, which is just what we would wish.

'There are two reasons why *Trainspotting* attracts so much attention. Second, my cut of Irvine's text is a fine bit of professional dramatisation. But first, Irvine's text is a work of genius, standing out from the ocean of novels and dramas which have also explored subcultures of youth, poverty and drug use, often idealising them and demonising the main culture above and around them. This broadly "punk" perspective is age-old, already evident in the often-alleged "first novel", Petronius's *Satyricon,* which slangily reported from the lowlife subculture of wayward lads and the conspicuous consumption of the rich, 2,000 years ago. When the novel resumed after centuries of Christian piety, it picked up the same picaresque threads of poor-lad scams and ne'er-do-well thrills, gradually increasing its critique of the dominant, straight, commercial/capitalist/consumerist culture.'

Harry believes that two present-day TV shows, *Shameless* and *Skins,* are arguably *Trainspotting*'s most popular descendants. 'Both do what Irvine might have been the first to do in our time – they demonise the mainstream culture, assuming its moral rot as a given, and they idealise the folk living under its belly. On all platforms, *Trainspotting* stirs pundit-feeding frenzies. The book is a perfect storm of on-trend stuff: it's raw off the street, it's young, it's punk, it's junk, it's so anarchic that it doesn't even protest or rebel but just enjoys playing in its own shit, it's got all kinds of bodily and domestic squalor, it's got mucky language and filthy sex: it's just a great dirty book! And it's madly funny. And, darling, it's beautifully written . . . while eschewing novelish reflection, moral judgements, liberal handwringing, etc. It can be the righteous cry of a generation, a class, people or fuckin' planet, unadulterated by politicking and yet at the same time implicitly political. Why, it's even quasi-religious! A BBC radio critic said she heard its language as liturgical. Probably if you rub the first edition (must be that one) on a wart it'll cure the wart! And give you herpes.

'The truth is that Irvine is a natural writer: he can write long passages of cut-glass prose that would grace an Oxford don. He is also, like Chaucer, a fine vernacular storyteller. He has a very good ear for the lilt of gadges who cry to mates "yacuntye!". Hence that "sounds like a liturgy" comment: Irv has poetic depth. And he's been listening and writing in a time when speed, coke, acid and E have loosened many previously inarticulate tongues. This is just what dramatists have been trying to do for ever: giving fictional characters the speech their real models lack, to say for them what they'd say themselves if they had the gift o' the gab. The knack is to avoid giving characters suspiciously sophisticated opinions.

'*Trainspotting* has often filled up theatres which hadn't seen a cool, youthful audience for ages. My modest script has been translated into nine languages (they love it in Cluj [in Romania]) and trans-accented into Missourian American for a run in Chicago. I've just heard of interest from an Appalachian company to do it hillbilly-style. In Paris, Dresden and Reykjavik I've seen it done *à l'enfant terrible* in a playground, with too many blue-eyed boys engaging in unscripted bumming, and as an Icelandic saga-dream. And I've seen it badly murdered by a bunch of Oxford students.'

Harry once said that the play worked well in any country where there's an underclass and a problem with drugs, so one suspects it will remain popular for a very long time.

16

Filmspotting

The exciting part of it is that the book is going to be trans-
formed . . . the more transformation the better.

On 23 June 1994 *The List* magazine carried a diary snippet
telling readers that 'Andrew Macdonald's production
company Figment Films is bidding for the *Trainspotting* film
rights'. At the time, Macdonald and his younger brother, the
director Kevin Macdonald, were working on a low-budget
Channel 4 documentary, *The Making of an Englishman**,
about the life of their grandfather, Emeric Pressburger. *The
List*'s news item wouldn't normally have caused much of a
stir – plenty of books get optioned, but very few of those
deals actually lead to films. This, though, was different.
Macdonald just happened to be part of a trio who were being
hailed as the saviours of the British film industry. In 1994,
aged just 27, he, with director Danny Boyle and writer John

---

* Oscar-winning Hungarian screenwriter who, along with Michael
Powell, co-wrote, directed and produced some of the great British films
of the 1940s and 1950s, including *A Matter of Life and Death*, *The Red
Shoes* and *Black Narcissus*.

Hodge, had made *Shallow Grave* – a film that summed up their cinematic philosophy to make high-quality films to be seen by as large an audience as possible. A former pupil at Glenalmond public school in Perthshire who speaks with a friendly, slightly plummy accent, Macdonald seemed an unlikely candidate to make a film of *Trainspotting*, but he had been wowed by Irvine's book after reading it on a flight home to Glasgow for Christmas in 1993.

On 6 January 1995, *Shallow Grave* opened in the UK to wild critical acclaim. Made on a modest £1 million budget, it was an audacious piece of work – a sexy, sassy Scottish thriller with a coal-black sense of humour. It starred three of the hottest young actors around – Ewan McGregor, Kerry Fox and Christopher Eccleston – and was powered by an ultra-hip soundtrack featuring Leftfield, Nina Simone and, er, John Carmichael's Ceilidh Band. It became the biggest home-grown film at the UK box office that year. Unusually for a low-budget Britflick, it also made a tiny dent in the crucial American market, earning nearly $3 million, part of a worldwide box-office haul of over $20 million. It went on to win a Bafta award as Best British Film of 1995. Not bad for a wee film shot in just 30 days in Edinburgh's New Town and Glasgow.

So when the *Shallow Grave* team started looking for a follow-up project, they weren't short of offers. Hollywood movie moguls were thumping on their door with bags of cash, with industry rumours of them being offered a new thriller starring Sharon Stone. But, to everyone's surprise, Boyle, Macdonald and Hodge, who were concerned that Hollywood might try to enforce its values on their next film, had already decided to turn down the big bucks and opt instead for another contemporary, low-budget British film. Long before *Shallow Grave* even hit the screens they were working on the film version of *Trainspotting*. Drug films rarely do well commercially, but the success of *Shallow Grave* made it easier for Macdonald and co. to get finance for their new project. Eager to avoid dealing with a big backer like Miramax who might have demanded compromises, the trio went back to Channel 4 for finance. They came to an agreement whereby the film company got a share of their next project, *A Life Less Ordinary* with Cameron Diaz and Ewan McGregor. The £1.5 million budget for *Trainspotting* was still small by Hollywood standards, but Boyle told *Empire* magazine: 'You can get carried away with people offering you money and end up making a film that's out of proportion with your kind of audience. But, on the other hand, we couldn't make it for £1 million.'

David Aukin, who commissioned the *Trainspotting* film for Channel 4, told me: '*Shallow Grave* was a real turning-point for the British film industry. It was the first British film in goodness knows how long to recoup its costs out of the UK box office alone. It was very successful all over Europe too. More important than that, it was a really original film with a new voice that split the generations. Suddenly there was real excitement about what British films could do and could be. Initially, many at Channel 4 were indifferent to *Shallow Grave* and I was pretty sure my contract would not be renewed. But the success of that film was so phenomenal it changed the whole attitude of the channel towards film, to me and to the whole Film4 brand. It was to become one of the leading brands of the channel, but Film4, had gone into the doldrums a bit before *Shallow Grave*; there was a real issue over whether to continue with it or not. TV companies on the whole did not like making films then, because they had to wait three years before they could show them on TV.

'We bonded well with Andrew and John through *Shallow Grave*, and I literally asked them what they wanted to do next and they said *Trainspotting*. At the time I hadn't read the book, but of course I was aware of it and the impact it was having. It seemed a very unlikely book to adapt into a movie, but they were very excited about it and they had earned the right to choose their next project. They were, of course, being courted by other people like PolyGram, who had distributed *Shallow Grave*. I know they went to see PolyGram, who wanted to be the main financier. By this time they already had a screenplay, but whomever they spoke to wanted them to cut out the toilet scene; they thought it was too gross. I think that convinced them to leave the editorial with Film4 because we were prepared to back their concept. I never had any doubts about the subject matter back at that stage. In those days £1.5 million wasn't the lowest of budgets. But I felt that these were the type of film-makers that Film4 was invented to support and develop.

'I enjoyed working with them hugely. I don't think there was ever an occasion when we fell out or had any issues with them. It seemed to me that they complemented each other terrifically; they were very much of a generation, which is very important for certain types of film . . . they share the same cultural voices, tastes and interests. It's like when you get a wonderful singing group or band that come together and complement each other. It all starts with John Hodge, who is a remarkable writer who clearly has an original voice. I remember going to see *Shallow Grave* one night at the Gate Cinema in Notting Hill, and sitting next to me was Harold Pinter, who lived locally and whom I happened to know. Before the start of the film I said to him, "I'm really glad to see you here, as I believe John Hodge owes a lot to you." I actually do believe that; the crisp dialogue and wit of John's writing owes a lot to a writer like Pinter.'

In February 1994 Andrew Macdonald had given John Hodge a copy of Irvine's book with a view to adapting it for the cinema. Hodge was another unlikely candidate to work on a project about Edinburgh junkies. Glasgow-born, he studied medicine at the University of Edinburgh and went on to be a doctor, using his spare time to write *Shallow Grave*.* (He appears in the film as one of the detectives who investigate the disappearance of the flatmate.) Hodge thought *Trainspotting* was an incredible book, later recalling how the characters, language, narratives and tone of aggressive entertainment were like nothing he had ever read before. He, Macdonald and Boyle agreed to a 'blood pact' that their intended film would be as lean as a junkie's arm and stretch to just 90 minutes – *Shallow Grave* had been a masterclass in brevity and lasted just under 89 minutes. Doing the same with Irvine's sprawling book presented Hodge with some major problems. Some stories, such as the 'The First Day of the Edinburgh Festival' and 'Traditional Sunday Breakfast' had great potential, but the disjointed narrative, the use of internal monologue to tell the story, and the huge number of characters made the book an unlikely candidate for screen adaptation. Hodge later told the *Big Issue*: 'I couldn't make any headway for ages. I was so intimidated, then I realised it was impossible to script the whole book, so I narrowed it down, focusing on what made it so special.' Hodge delivered an incomplete draft of the script in November 1994 and then worked on the final draft over the festive period.

Irvine shared John Hodge's initial concerns that it would be difficult to make a coherent script from such an episodic book. Welsh didn't want to be involved in the

---

* I wrote twice to John Hodge via his agent but got no response. Letters to Danny Boyle and Andrew Macdonald also didn't got a response. The casting team for the film – Gail Stevens and Andy Pryor – did take the time to reply, but both declined to be interviewed. As for the actors, camera crew, stuntmen and so on, I tried many, but again got very few positive replies. In the end I gave up when I realised I was using up my entire advance on stamps.

screenplay-writing, believing he was too close to the material
to give impartial input. He also wanted to move on from
Trainspotting and work on other projects. Hodge later
praised Welsh for being a saintly model of non-intervention,
doubting whether other authors would be so relaxed about a
complete stranger filleting their book. In fact, Irvine was
keen for the film to be as different from the book as possible
as long as it caught the original vibe of the book. He knew
that the move to a different medium made a faithful interpre-
tation impossible. It's a sign of how good a job John Hodge
did that his version is now ingrained in many people's psyche
as the actual *Trainspotting* story. It's only when you revisit
the book that you remember stuff like it was Davie Mitchell
– not Spud – who had the unfortunate accident in bed.
Similarly, very few people now remember satellite characters
in the book such as Stevie, Stella, Nina and Second Prize
(living up to his nickname again), who were axed for the
cinematic version.

Knowing the film had to be commercial and play to an
audience outwith Edinburgh who didn't know a radge
from a gadge, Hodge had to make some difficult omis-
sions. Most mentions of Hibs and sectarianism were
binned, as was the most graphic and arcane use of dialect.
Replicating the uncompromising and, to many, unfathomable Leith lingo in a film would have necessitated subtitles,
which could have been commercial suicide. Hodge clev-
erly delivered a script that – although still distinctly
Scottish – would be understood away from Scotland. He
decided to make Mark Renton his central character and
dramatic focal point, the man to lead the audience on their
journey. Renton dominates the script, appearing in nearly
every scene of the film with just a couple of exceptions –
Spud's job-interview scene, the parts of the nightclub scene
where Spud, Tommy, Gail and Lizzy take centre stage,

and most notably Spud's dreadful introduction to Gail's parents at breakfast. Some of the slighter stories, such as 'In Overdrive' and 'Growing up in Public', which didn't add to the overall narrative, were obvious candidates for the chop. But some strong tales, including 'Her Man' and the haunting 'Junk Dilemmas', were also omitted. Hodge even sacrificed his own favourite chapter from the book, 'Memories of Matty', as it had too much material to condense properly into a single scene. Hodge amalgamated characters and turned minor incidents or asides, such as the mention of shoplifting, into major scenes in the film. On occasion, Hodge improvised brilliantly – who would have thought of bringing together a passionate sex scene between Renton and Diane, Archie Gemmill's wonder goal against Holland in 1978, and the doyen of Scottish sports commentators, Archie Macpherson? Hodge deservedly won a Bafta in 1996 for his *Trainspotting* screenplay and was nominated for an Oscar the following year, losing out to Billy Bob Thornton's adaptation for *Sling Blade*.

The coming together of Welsh and the three rising stars of the British film industry was fortuitous for all concerned. By 1995, *Trainspotting* had become the hippest, most controversial book around; it needed the right people to bring it to the screen in an original way. Irvine was desperate that his book would not turn into a drab morality tale where drug users are portrayed as victims, or a safe *Four Weddings and a Funeral*-style British film. He was lucky in that he got the right team at the right time to make the film; if it had been up for grabs in the 1970s, when the British film industry was not exactly known for risk-taking, it might have ended up a real dog's dinner. Early on, though, Irvine played hard to get, unconvinced even by Danny Boyle's persistent pleas to give them the rights. In one letter, Boyle apparently tried to persuade him by describing Hodge and Macdonald as the two most important

Scotsmen since Kenny Dalglish and Alex Ferguson. It wasn't until he sat down and watched *Shallow Grave* that Irvine realised Boyle and co. were the men for the job. Andrew Macdonald told the *Movie Connections* programme: 'We were terrified of meeting him, thinking we were going to have to take heroin and drink bottles of vodka and methylated spirits, and when we met him we had a bottle of water in the GFT [Glasgow Film Theatre] café.' After some delay, a deal was signed that gave Irvine's publishers two per cent (£30,000) of the proposed £1.5 million budget, plus a share in any future profits. Irvine received an initial payment of £25,000 of the £30,000, which he used to pay off his mortgage. Bigger paydays would come further down the line.

Rather than being just a 'drug film' the filmmakers wanted *Trainspotting* to be about friendship, loyalty and betrayal. Where drugs were concerned, they wanted their film to be honest; drug-taking wouldn't be condoned, but it would be depicted realistically. Boyle later told *The Economist*: 'The film was looking at two things. Drugs are always going to fuck you up. That is inevitable. But the actual point of getting involved – the actual journey – is an exhilarating ride, and that truth has to be addressed. You have to tell both these truths. I think the film does tell both these truths, and it uses a lot of cinematic techniques and pace to convey the exhilaration of the drug trip. But it also conversely shows the pain and horror of addiction.' Contradicting the simplistic 'Just Say No' brigade, nothing was straightforward in the film. Renton, the heartless addict, survives and escapes his addictions in the end. The most obnoxious character in the book, Begbie, is virulently anti-drugs. The nicest guy in the whole film, and the last to use (Tommy), is the first to die. Director Danny Boyle said reading Irvine's book was an overwhelming experience; it made him feel as though he had been asleep for years and had suddenly woken up. He loved the way that a landscape normally depicted as full of hopeless victims was written about with great imagination even as the drugs tore the group apart. Boyle compared *Trainspotting* to Primo Levi's *If This Is a Man*, saying that both were modern classics that changed your life when you read them. Of the three men behind the film, Boyle, who came from a working-class, Irish-Catholic Lancashire family, was closest in the kindred-spirit stakes to Irvine.

Pre-production started in April 1995 and lasted for seven weeks. Boyle already knew whom he wanted for the leading roles. Ewan McGregor – fresh from his success in *Shallow Grave* – was always odds-on favourite to play Renton, and he was the first to be signed up. For the film to be a commercial success, even an anti-hero like Renton had to be likeable. The audience had to care about his fate, so McGregor's easy-going looks and mischievous grin were a definite asset. The challenge of making this complex, intelligent but morally weak and nihilistic character loveable brought out the best in McGregor. He worked very hard, having only one day off during the shoot. Perhaps only his subsequent performance in David Mackenzie's 2003 sadly overlooked gem *Young Adam* comes close to rivalling his turn as Renton. But although he could play a mean junkie, in real life McGregor, who was brought up in Crieff in Perthshire, where both his parents were teachers, was never a drug user. The whole rave scene and ecstasy explosion just passed him by. He loved Irvine's book, finding it very moving, and would later describe winning the Renton role as like receiving a Christmas present. He threw himself into the part, losing two stone in weight and shaving off his hair, watching films like *Clockwork Orange*, reading books on drug abuse, and observing junkies at a railway station while on a trip to Luxembourg (to shoot Peter Greenaway's film *The Pillow Book*) to get the correct looks and mannerisms.

Choosing McGregor to play the leading role could possibly have been a slight on Ewen Bremner, who had played the part of Renton so brilliantly on stage. The worry was that Bremner might have been insulted by being offered the 'lesser' role of loveable but glaikit Spud. Fortunately, Bremner thought Spud was an excellent character to play. Having grown up in Portobello, just along the coast from Leith, he felt he knew the characters and world portrayed in *Trainspotting* only too well. He later told the *Central Times*: 'When I originally read the book, his parts were the ones I found myself laughing almost aloud at, and I have tried to take that humour into the film as much as I can.' Bremner's chilling performance as Archie, the crazed Scottish rough sleeper, jousting verbally with David Thewlis in Mike Leigh's brilliant 1993 film *Naked*, really marked him as a star in the making, an actor who was ready to try challenging roles. He would give a brilliant performance as the gentle, hapless, animal-loving Spud, stealing all the laughs, especially in the speed-fuelled job-interview scene.

Slimly built and just over five feet eight, Robert Carlyle was not the obvious choice to play the hard man Begbie, but luckily Danny Boyle subscribed to the view that 'small psychos are best'. Carlyle hails from Maryhill, a district of Glasgow deceptively close to the genteel west end, which is home to some of Glasgow's toughest characters. I'm sure Begbie would have felt right at home on the Wyndford estate and in the Viking Bar. Carlyle had known plenty of Begbie-type characters when he was growing up, and understood his mentality. He had already proved he was more than capable of playing this kind of role. In Antonia Bird's 1993 TV drama *Safe* he played Nosty, the violent, hard-drinking leader of a homeless gang. Soon after, he won a Bafta Scotland best actor award for a searing performance as Albie Kinsella, the twisted Liverpudlian football fan bent on revenge, in another TV production, *Cracker – To Be a Somebody*. His performance as Begbie was pitch-perfect, gradually evolving from your average foul-mouthed nutter to complete over-the-top psycho during the film. In a Bafta *Life in Pictures* interview, Carlyle revealed that he believes Begbie is actually gay and was intrigued by the character's reaction to finding out that the 'woman' he picked up in the London club was a transsexual. At the costume fitting he opted to wear pink Pringle sweaters instead of traditional hard-man clothes like leather jackets.

The filmmakers were fortunate that they could pick a group of young actors just coming of age at the right time. All of the leading men were young and ambitious, but each had already started making his mark on the cinema scene. Jonny Lee Miller had acting in his blood – his maternal grandfather was Bernard Lee, who played M in the first eleven James Bond films. By the time *Trainspotting* came around, Miller had just made a successful film debut, starring opposite his future wife, Angelina Jolie, in *Hackers*. Boyle said that once Miller sat in front of them at the interview, lolling about in his chair, they knew they had found the right man to play the arrogant Sick Boy. Kevin McKidd, the Elgin-born actor who had played the gang leader in Gillies MacKinnon's *Small Faces*, was another who made an instant impact on Boyle. The director thought McKidd was the picture of innocence, like meeting one of the Beach Boys at the height of their fame.

James Cosmo, who gave a fine performance as Renton's dad, told me that Danny Boyle was the ideal director to set the minds of the young actors at rest and bring the best out of them. 'Of all the directors I've worked with, Danny is the most supportive when it comes to helping young actors. He really understands the acting process. He's not a director who has ever been left behind generationally, and he was right there with these actors when they needed him. Danny's the most extraordinary, egalitarian director; he encourages other people to contribute in any way. It's a joy to work with Danny Boyle. It really is.'

The final piece of the jigsaw before filming could start was to find the right girl to play Diane. The film-makers wanted an unknown actress to play the role, to make the scene where she first appears in her school uniform believable. Cards were distributed around clubs, clothes shops and hairdressers, offering the chance to be 'the next Sharon Stone, Kate Moss or Patricia Arquette'. Hundreds turned up for an open casting at Strathclyde University, and a dozen were asked back to read a short scene with Ewan McGregor. Boyle later told *Empire* magazine of his first meeting with Kelly Macdonald. 'I knew straight away before she even sat down and opened her mouth that she was the one. There were a couple of other possibles, but you could just tell. And if you get that instinct, you know you're right.' At the time Kelly was nineteen, fresh out of Glasgow's Eastwood High School and working as a waitress. She had attended an amateur dramatics class for a few weeks and was considering applying for drama school. In an NPR [National Public Radio] interview she told how she was in a 'blind panic' doing the read with McGregor. 'He said I held the script in front of my face the whole time. He says he had no idea what I looked like.' She almost messed it up again at the third call-back. 'For some reason at my screen test I decided I was going to do super-acting . . . and as soon as I started doing that it was all wrong and Danny stopped me and said, "John Hodge has written a very good script and the words are all there. You don't have to put gaps in, just read it. Just say the words."' Fortunately, she listened to Boyle's advice, and so began a stellar career that would see her work with the Coen brothers and Robert Altman.

17

The Likely Lads on acid

I think Danny's done the best job he could have made of it.

From the opening seconds of *Trainspotting*, as Renton and Spud sprint along Princes Street to the accompaniment of Hunt Sales's thunderous drumming on Iggy's 'Lust For Life', you knew you were in for something special. What follows is a cinematic treat: jarring realism sits beside surreal invention and laugh-out-loud moments preface achingly sad scenes, all put together by a director at the top of his game using a dizzying array of cinematic devices including voice-overs, ground-level shots (to reflect the fact that junkies spend so much time on the floor), subtitles and freeze-frames. Harry Gibson got it right when he called the film '*The Likely Lads* on acid'. There's a real energy about the film that reflects a happy shoot; according to reports, everyone on the cast and crew was united in wanting to make the best film possible, with roller-skating sessions helping the young cast to bond together between shoots. The budget was low, but that just seemed to bring everyone even more together. Clothes were bought from local charity shops, and propmakers had to

improvise. In the notorious 'breakfast scene' – the bed sheets
were covered with left-over soup and washing-up liquid from
the canteen. James Cosmo believes that, despite the budget
and time constraints, *Trainspotting* is one of the greatest-
ever Scottish movies. 'The film shoot was so tight for time;
one certainly could not be indulgent. We just didn't have that
much time to waste, and sometimes that is no bad thing in a
movie. You had this wonderful range of fantastic actors all
pulling together on that film. Everyone's attitude was "let's
not fuck about, let's get the job done". You concentrate on
your work and that's it . . . boom, you get it done! The great
thing about Danny is that he is able to work that way and
everyone still feels happy and included.'

The title sequence was actually done on day nineteen of
the shoot and took most of the morning to get right. John
Hodge took time off from writing *A Life Less Ordinary* to
play one of the John Menzies security guards in hot pursuit
of the two hapless thieves; the other guard was one of the
film's sound crew. The chase continues down past the Black
Bull pub and the old St James Oyster Bar at the rear of
Waverley Station, a favourite haunt of Irvine and the Rebel
Inc. gang, where Renton runs into a car. On screen the scene
last less than five seconds, but it took two hours and twenty
takes to get right, with the on-set nurse having to patch
McGregor up during the numerous breaks.

After two weeks of rehearsals in a high-rise flat near
Buchanan Street bus station, filming began on 22 May 1995
and lasted for 35 days, including a week of unfeasibly hot
Scottish summer weather. The scene where Renton and Sick
Boy shoot a dog was filmed on a baking-hot day in Rouken
Glen Park on Glasgow's south side. David Stewart, who runs
Creature Feature, which provides trained animals for films,
played the part of the skinhead who is mauled when the dog
is shot. David told me that initially they intended to use a

pit-bull terrier, as in the book. 'Danny Boyle didn't think it looked vicious enough, so we got an English bull terrier – (aka Bill Sikes's dog) – instead. The actual scene was just me and the dog playing boisterously. The sound effects make it look worse.'

One day was taken out for a train journey on the West Highland Line to Corrour station near Fort William, one of the most remote stations in the UK, for the scene where Tommy fails to convince his pals of the benefits of healthy living. The crew also travelled to Edinburgh for a couple of days to shoot pick-ups (scene-setting, dialogue-free parts that pad out the action).

As with *Shallow Grave*, *Trainspotting* was mostly shot in Glasgow, which was home to many of the top film technicians in the UK. A production office was set up at the old Wills tobacco factory on Alexandra Parade, which had plenty of room to do interior filming of squats, London bedsits and suburban homes. The production office, where Danny Boyle kept a scrapbook full of photographic ideas of how he wanted the film to look, was at the front of the building along with the costume and art departments. There was also a large hall area where fourteen different sets were built. All the props were stored in the back of the ground floor; some of the in-house props were also made there. Boyle would use actors he trusted, such as Peter Mullan, Keith Allen, Victor Eadie and Billy Riddoch, who were all in *Shallow Grave*. On the technical side, cinematographer Brian Tufano, film editor Masahiro Hirakubo, production designer Kave Quinn and special-effects man Grant Mason would also graduate to working on the new film.

One of the great things about the film was the sense of authenticity about the whole drug-taking ritual. These actors seemed to know exactly what they were doing, and this led to rumours that some of them were taking method acting a

bit too far. However, the realism came from the actors working with addicts from the Glasgow-based Calton Athletic
Recovery Project, an organisation of recovering heroin users
who had united to play football and help each other stay
clean. Prior to the film shoot, Danny Boyle and Ewan
McGregor attended Calton Athletic group meetings at their
office, which conveniently was only a hundred yards from
the Wills Building. Boyle and Macdonald showed their
commitment by attending one meeting only hours after picking up their Bafta award for *Shallow Grave*. The two men
found the experience of listening to the addicts tell how
heroin had ruined their lives enlightening and also chasten-
ing. McGregor later told the *Big Issue* how there had been
some discussion about whether the actors should actually try
heroin prior to filming. After meeting the Calton group they
realised such a course of action would be disrespectful,
besides being downright dangerous. The *Trainspotting* pair
forged a strong bond with the Calton Athletic group, who all
loved Irvine's book and found it to be a realistic portrayal of
the life of an addict, and played football with cast and crew
members at rehearsals. Several of the ex-addicts appeared in
the film as extras (the footballers playing five-a-side against
Renton and co. in the opening credits are all from Calton
Athletic).

One of the Calton group – Eamon Doherty – visited the set
as an adviser to show the actors how to cook up a shot of
'heroin' (glucose powder) and 'inject' it. The stars were given
five needles and had to practise until they got it right, with
Eamon looking over their shoulder and telling them how to
do it. The scene resembled an old episode of *The Generation
Game*. Doyle would later say that meeting the Calton guys
was a turning point in the project for him; he knew that the
film would at the very least depict drug-taking responsibly
and accurately. The mutual respect between the film-makers

and Calton Athletic would last long after the film was released. Eighty group members viewed the film in the Glasgow Odeon prior to the premiere and gave it a standing ovation at the closing credits. Their only gripe was with the scene where Johnny Swan puts an unconscious Renton into a taxi and sends him to the local A & E – apparently such altruism between dealer and addict is rare.

The proceeds of the premiere went to the group, and the film cast and crew later played a couple of fund-raising football matches for Calton. These games, along with the later fundraising efforts of the *Trainspotting* gang, helped to raise hundreds of thousands of pounds to help recovering addicts. A lot of nonsense has been written about Irvine's book and the subsequent play and film 'encouraging' drug use, so it's perhaps apt to note here that it probably saved the lives of a lot of addicts through these fundraising efforts. Calton's director, Davie Bryce, wrote an excellent book, *Alive and Kicking*, which goes into more detail about their battles with authority and the way that *Trainspotting* helped them. Irvine became a good friend of Bryce and wrote the foreword for the book.

Irvine visited the set on 27 June to film his cameo role as Mikey Forrester, the drug dealer who supplies Renton with the opium suppositories. Mikey is one of the sleaziest characters in a tale that is full of disreputable chancers, so Irvine was honoured to have been given the part, later describing it as nice typecasting. He flew in from Amsterdam and gave a performance that was never going to give De Niro sleepless nights. After a nosey around the set and an interview which later turned up as a DVD extra, Irvine flew back to the 'Dam.

Andrew Macdonald says the moment the whole project fell into place was when he and Danny read John Hodge's 'worst toilet in Scotland' section. It was a tough day's shooting for McGregor, and he was desperate for it to end. Hodge's script initially had a montage of clips to accompany the moment when Renton sits on the pan – a lorry on a building site dumping a load of bricks, B-52s shedding their load on Vietnam and the legendary clip of the *Blue Peter* elephant misbehaving in the BBC studio. Sadly, the montage never made the final cut. The part where Renton swims to collect the suppositories was filmed on the final morning of the Glasgow shoot at the local Nautical College. Hodge says he was inspired by the scene in *A Nightmare on Elm Street* where the character Nancy, played by Heather Langenkamp, is pulled down the plughole by Freddy Krueger.

The disco scene culminating in Renton tapping off Diane was shot at the Volcano Club in Benalder Street at the foot of Byres Road in Glasgow's west end on Tuesday, 30 May. The two and a half minutes of film seen on screen took almost fourteen hours to get right. The fellow in the blue frilly shirt who tries to chat up Diane as she leaves the disco was Hugh Reed, who fronted the wonderfully named Glasgow rock band Hugh Reed and the Velvet Underpants. Hugh, who now lives in Zhichunlu, China, told me: 'On the day Danny Boyle talked me through the part, and I stood with Kelly. There wasn't much in the way of conversation as I could tell she was nervous, even more so than me.' Kelly Macdonald confirmed in her interview on America's NPR that she was so shy and nervous she used to hide in the toilets when she wasn't required on set. The scene where she and Renton make love was shot on the day that Kelly invited her family on to the set. 'It shows how young and daft I was . . . So, my poor mum and brother had to sit on the catering bus the whole day, and luckily they didn't get to see me working that day.'

The whole temper of the film changes 37 minutes in with the death of baby Dawn. McGregor signals the switch in mood with the chilling voiceover, 'But the good times couldn't last for ever.' It's an intensely emotional scene to watch, and it brought the best out of the young actors. The outstanding Susan Vidler later commented: 'Even though I knew the baby and knew nothing had really happened to it, I don't think I could go through it again.' Special-effects experts Grant Mason and Tony Steers worked for over a month making the baby out of silicone rubber. Grant told me: 'Danny Boyle asked us to make the baby move in a similar way to the small doll that was used in *Shallow Grave*. It was to look like the real kid that was in the film, obviously, but larger and bloated.' Baby Dawn would reappear later in the film, when she terrifies Renton as she crawls along his bedroom ceiling while he is going through withdrawal. Grant recalls how they worked for a whole day on that scene: 'There was a meeting beforehand, and various ways were discussed about how we should do it. Eventually, it was decided to run it on a railway-style track. We were above the set, operating it on a backpack rig with levers on it that had been made so it could be operated through bicycle-type cables. That made the baby's arms and legs move. We went to the Wills factory early in the morning and set it all up . . . meantime the rest of the crew were filming the underwater bit from the toilet scene at the water tank at Glasgow Nautical College. Then they all came back, and I think it was just before lunchtime that we made a start on the Baby Dawn scene. It was shot on the very last day of filming in Glasgow. There was a bit of pressure on us all that day, and Danny Boyle did get a bit frustrated. I think he realised that things maybe weren't working out as good as he thought with that baby. I think he wanted to shoot a lot more stuff on the scene, but basically they had run out of time. It was getting very strenuous.' Despite the reservations on the day, the scene turned out well and is one of the most memorable moments in the film.

James Cosmo and Eileen Nicholas gave strong

performances as Renton's parents in the scene where their son goes through withdrawal, both confused about what was going wrong in their son's life but equally determined to stand by him and help him kick his habit. James had first worked with Danny Boyle on the BBC Northern Ireland production *The Nightwatch*, and the director approached him directly to play the key role of Renton's dad. James, who was born in Clydebank, told me: 'Even though it was set in Edinburgh, the story was very familiar to me. I had known people like Mr and Mrs Renton all my life. Although drug addiction – other than alcohol – was pretty rare when I was growing up, I still knew the psyche of these people and how they tried to cope with what was going on. I felt quite at home playing the character.' That scene ends in the surreal quiz-show exchange between Mr and Mrs Renton (answering questions on the HIV virus) and the perma-tanned host of *Supermarket Sweep*, Dale Winton. 'Dale was a very nice guy. The two things I remember most about him were his orange tan, and he also had massive hands like a navvy!' recalled James.

Boyle got the balance between scaring and amusing his audience just right. The violent scene when Begbie glasses a drinker in a London pub left nothing to the imagination. The camera angles and sound effects give a sense of realism, but Boyle doesn't stay too long on the carnage caused by Begbie or use close-ups. For lighting reasons, Boyle had to shoot the extras' frightened reactions first, but they weren't authentic enough. Carlyle asked him to let him do his bit first, and was so realistic that the extras were genuinely scared. Carlyle later said that even he was scared by the way he became Begbie. As Davie Bryce of Calton Athletic wrote: 'What Irvine Welsh caught brilliantly and Bobby did in the role was that alcohol is responsible for more crime, violence and drug addiction than anything else.'

The final scene where Renton heads for Amsterdam, hoping to clean up and find redemption, drew some criticism for being too saccharine, especially when he leaves money for Spud. The money part of the scene was a last-minute decision by Danny Boyle, and it certainly ends the film on an optimistic note.* It shows that friendship can survive the horrors of addiction. As with *Shallow Grave*, the soundtrack for *Trainspotting* was crucial in getting the right mood, with music playing as important a role as it does in Martin Scorsese's films. The music reflected the changes in Renton's (and Irvine's) life, from the glam-rock of Lou Reed and Iggy Pop through Heaven 17, acid house, Leftfield and Underworld right up to the Britpop of Blur, though sadly there was no place for John Carmichael's Ceilidh Band this time around.

Looking back on the film, David Aukin says, 'There is something very exciting about being involved with a film that is a game-changer in the sense that it divides generations. With *Trainspotting*, most of the people I knew over the age of 40 thought it was terrible or disgusting, but the

---

* An additional ten minutes of footage was left out of the film. It wasn't until seven years later, with the release of a two-disc Definitive Edition DVD, that fans got the chance to see the full, uncut version and, with the aid of digital technology, reinsert them into the original where they were intended to be. The original film is one of the few films that are actually too short. I could happily have sat through another 30 minutes. The excellent Peter Mullan (Swanney) had a couple of scenes cut. They showed how, after jacking up once too often, he has a leg amputated. Renton visits him in hospital, where Swanney makes bold predictions that he will soon be in Thailand selling dope. The reality is shown later when he is seen pretending to be a Falklands veteran and begging for money. Both scenes reinforce the message that drugs will fuck you up in the long run, but perhaps the film-makers felt they had made that point forcibly enough through Tommy's story. Boyle later said it was tough to cut these scenes, especially as Mullan did such an amazing job. Elsewhere, Renton's job interview and part of Spud's interview were also binned, as were some other scenes with Diane, Renton and Sick Boy.

enthusiasm from just about everyone under 40 for the film was phenomenal. *Shallow Grave* and *Trainspotting* were that type of film and are always indissolubly linked in my head. I remember when I first saw the completed version I called in one of my colleagues, John Willis, who was the director of programmes at Channel 4, because at that point I was a bit concerned that it might not be allowed to be shown on television. John just adored it and said, "Don't worry, we'll fight for this one." In the end there was a small furore over *Trainspotting*, but nothing serious.'

18

Poster boys

Not a moment is wasted; each and every second of the film fizzes with madly inventive direction, crackling dialogue and pitch-perfect performance.

Ian Nathan, *Empire*

It might be perceived as a rebel, anti-establishment film, but *Trainspotting* was at the centre of a very calculated and carefully planned promotional campaign. The marketing budget put up by a confident PolyGram was a whopping £800,000 – more than half the £1.5 million Film4 invested in the making of the film. Danny Boyle and Andrew Macdonald were very marketing-aware and knew exactly how to make a film that would match with the target audience, how the film should look, the soundtrack to use and in which cinemas the film should play. Work on selling the picture started long before it hit the cinema screens with PolyGram bringing representatives of the big cinema chains to the set in Scotland. The film poster, which was central to the campaign, was sent out to student unions prior to the film's release and was also used as part of a railway marketing campaign where students who bought a Railcard got a voucher which they could exchange for a poster.

In January 1996, a film tie-in edition of the book was brought out, complete with a new cover featuring a photo of Ewan McGregor wi' the sweat lashin' offay him. A sound-track album also hit the shops, as did the excellent audio-book. The main trailer was shown at cinemas at much the same time as massive posters were placed at main railway stations, including one at London Charing Cross which was 100 feet long. Teaser posters of individual characters appeared first on escalator panels and bus shelters, followed by the massive group posters. The iconic poster for the film featured five of the film's stars; Peter Mullan missed out, as did Kevin McKidd, who had gone on a £250 package holi-day to Tunisia to recover from the rigorous film shoot. McKidd would later say that he felt a bit of an idiot when he returned to the UK to be greeted by a giant *Trainspotting* billboard at Waterloo Station which did not feature him.

The poster was the creation of Rob O'Connor and Mark Blamire from London-based design company Stylorouge, with the photos taken by Lorenzo Agius, who has since gone on to become a leading celebrity photographer. Back in the mid-1990s Stylorouge were already known for designing stunning album covers for bands like Blur. They were approached by PolyGram, who were looking for visuals that emphasised the *Trainspotting* characters as a close-knit posse. Rob told me: 'PolyGram thought it worth considering a buddy-movie approach, and that it would be a good idea to create something that reflected a group of people in a gang who all lived their lives together and indulged in this subcul-ture together as a band of friends.'

PolyGram showed them a still from *Backbeat* – Iain Softley's excellent 1994 biopic of Stuart Sutcliffe and the Beatles – as a visual guide. Rob recalls: 'There was one

particular image of the campaign for *Backbeat* which was
this iconic shot of those four guys in silhouette on the docks
at Liverpool, which perfectly evoked the spirit of the band
and the background of their early years. They were looking
for something like that, something instantly recognisable as
a bunch of mates.' It took a while, but Stylorouge eventually
concluded that such a shot wasn't ideal for a story of a bunch
of back-stabbing chancers like Sick Boy and Renton. Instead,
they suggested alternative ideas, and Andrew Macdonald
warmed to the notion of each actor posing in the style of the
character they played in the film, with each individual
numbered and named on the poster (an idea not dissimilar to
the promotional posters for two other great 1990s films,
Reservoir Dogs and *The Grifters*). 'The novel was written
from the multiple points of view and in the voices of each of
the main characters, and we felt it was important to stress the
individuality of those personalities,' says Rob.

The photo-shoot was done on the last day of filming in
London at a studio in the East End. The actors had been
filming final pick-up shots at dawn that day and turned up
looking rough, tired and less than enthusiastic about the idea
of posing all day for the poster. They were all ready to head
off to work on other films, so there was pressure on Stylorouge
and Lorenzo Agius to get it all done on the day. Robert
Carlyle was also eager to shave off his Begbie moustache.
Rob says, 'We had done a test shoot with Lorenzo some time
before, with Stylorouge staff and the photographer's assistants standing in for the actors, to demonstrate the ideas to
the client and be prepared for the actual shoot.' On the big
day they tried a couple of matey group shots with the actors
all dressed in black, but it soon became apparent that that
didn't work.

Rob explains: 'There had obviously been a lack of commu-
nication between the film company and the actors in terms of

what they were expected to do. So, after breakfast the first thing we had to do was to go through all the visuals with them and say, "This is what we are doing." The main detractor from this plan was Jonny Lee Miller, who couldn't understand why everyone was being asked to wear black for one of the shots. That, though, was purely a stylistic thing to make them look like they were all in a band together. We wanted a strong black-and-white image with the actors' bodies merging into a large area of black, from which all the text could be reversed out, but this image was never used.

'Bobby Carlyle was great. He was saying to them all, "Look, this is what you have to do sometimes in the film business. It's PR, and let's be professional about it. If someone wants you to wear black and that's the idea that has been approved, then we wear black!" He was incredibly helpful to us on the day. After that it was just a case of doing the individual shots, and everyone really got into that part. What made it easier was that they were still in character, and all we really wanted them to do was play to that; they had all been a bit out-there during the film shoot, so when it came to the photos it was almost like an extension of the shoot. It helped that they were a bit knackered. They did look genuinely drained.'

Lorenzo Agius coaxed the best out of all the actors, with Robert Carlyle in particular really going into character, sticking up two fingers to the camera. Rob says, 'Carlyle was a real star on the day. His performance in front of the camera was a real masterclass. He really went into character, it was amazing to watch.'

By early evening the shoot was over, and for Stylorouge the real work began, producing the famous stills and original poster for the film, with orange lettering (as used in dangerous chemical warnings and British Rail signage), a white background, railway station announcement terminology

('This film is expected to arrive . . .') and some of the most
memorable film photos ever taken. The images were then
used on giant billboards at railway stations throughout the
land. The design concept behind the poster went on to sell
everything from Virgin trains to packets of Jelly Babies in
Odeon cinemas.

February 1996 saw Scotland in the grip of *Trainspotting*
fever. Two Edinburgh charity premieres were held at the UCI
cinema in Kinnaird Park and the Cameo cinema on 15
February. Later that evening at 8.15 p.m., a third world
premiere was held at the Glasgow Odeon, with the cast plus
Angelina Jolie, Robbie Coltrane, Damon Albarn and Jarvis
Cocker in attendance. All of the proceeds from the showings
went to Calton Athletic. When tickets for the Glasgow Odeon
went on sale, queues formed at 5 a.m. and all the seats sold
out in 90 minutes. Through in Edinburgh, the Cameo
premiere sold out two weeks in advance, even though the
title of the film to be shown was a secret. The cinema had
given out a series of cryptic clues over the previous month to
the identity of the mystery film. Among the clues were:
'Where James Osterberg meets van Gogh' (alluding to Iggy
Pop's 'Lust For Life').

Irvine invited a squad of his old friends – including Dave
Todd and Sandy Macnair – to the Cameo showing. On the
night, they all met for a few pints in the King's Arms across
the road from the cinema. Dave recalls: 'Irvine was very laid-
back about it all, and we got into the cinema just before the
film started. We had seats reserved right in the middle with
Irvine and Anne. But there were no big Hollywood-style
announcements before the film. All the big stars and Danny
Boyle were through in Glasgow. People loved it, and there
was a round of applause at the end.' An *Evening News* vox-
pop found that everyone was raving about the film; the

general opinion was that it was funnier than the book, and that it didn't glamorise heroin, but neither did it portray the drug as evil. Among those interviewed was one 'salesman Sandy Macnair of Haymarket'. The 11.45 p.m. showing on the first day at the Cameo was interrupted when police raided the cinema after the cash register was plundered. The auditorium was cleared and a number of people were arrested before the show restarted. One cinemagoer commented that 'they picked several people from the crowd; they seemed to be looking for people with long hair'. The film went on to smash *Shallow Grave*'s record for box-office takings at the Cameo.

Dave Todd remembers: 'When we got outside there was a single-decker bus waiting to take us all through to the party in Glasgow. We all piled into the off-licence to get a carry-out for the bus. Irvine tried to get on and the driver says, "Nae standing on the bus, pal", so Irvine just went through on the train instead. Then the driver told us all, "Nae drink on the bus", but we were all drinking away anyway. The party was held in an old warehouse which had been turned into a club. As soon as you went in there were girls offering you glasses of champagne, and there was a free bar of course. So we just started knocking back the champagne. There was soup and stovies too. We spoke to Danny Boyle and also to Robert Carlyle. He was a really nice guy. I complimented him on his Edinburgh accent and he seemed really pleased that Edinburgh folk thought that he had got it right.'

Eight days later, the film went on general release on the same weekend as Ang Lee's *Sense and Sensibility*, Martin Scorsese's *Casino* and the Antonio Banderas film *Desperado*. They were all strong films, although perhaps only *Casino* was really aiming for the same market and competing for lead reviews on press and TV. PolyGram were confident that the buzz surrounding Boyle's reputation would ensure that *Trainspotting* got the bulk of publicity.

The early reviews were uniformly glowing, with comparisons drawn with classic films like *A Clockwork Orange* and *Goodfellas*. Glasgow's *Herald* sent *six* of their writers to review it, and though there were some reservations the overall impressions were strong. Allan Laing thought that 'the sheer honesty of *Trainspotting* delivers more of an anti-drugs message than any well-intentioned government health warning could ever hope to achieve'. *Empire* magazine's Ian Nathan hailed it as the best British film of the decade, saying it would not disappoint fans of the book. He captured the spirit of the time when he concluded, somewhat optimistically: 'Hollywood come in, please, your time is up. Not only can we compete, we can knock you straight into the ground.'

Critics attending the press screening at the Cannes Film Festival greeted the final credits with bemused silence, but many praised it later. Irvine, Ewan McGregor, Andrew Macdonald, Danny Boyle and John Hodge attended the festival. UK Heritage Secretary Virginia Bottomley viewed a special screening and liked it, saying she was moved after watching the shocking scenes and that she backed the message of the film. At a press conference, Irvine, resplendent in a Hibs top, talked candidly about his heroin days. David Aukin told me: 'I don't know why, but they would not put it into competition at Cannes. Maybe they felt they were too new to the game. Anyway, they gave it a special screening instead in the main festival hall. PolyGram organised a party afterwards and it was the event of the festival that year, an amazing event.'

The film hit the US in July, with David Bowie and his wife Iman hosting a glitzy American premiere with a fundraiser for the American music industry's Aids charity Lifebeat. Strangely, Welsh wasn't there on the night, preferring instead to attend a mate's birthday bash down by Leith docks. It was the second time he had passed on a chance of meeting the man he considers to be the ultimate rock star, having previously declined a lunch appointment. The prospect of finding out that his hero was just an ordinary, down-to-earth guy rather than the otherworldly star possibly scared him. The film took New York by storm, with long queues outside cinemas no doubt attracted by the publicity blitz that included a full page in the influential *New York Times*. The film did well in the States, eventually earning almost $16.5 million, which put it at number 97 in the US box-office charts for the year. A bit of perspective is given by the fact that the number 1 film, *Independence Day*, took over $306 million. *Variety* magazine later reported that *Trainspotting* was proportionately the most profitable film in the world for 1996, earning £45 million, a profit ratio of more than twenty to one.

19

Welshmania

I'll sleep when ah'm dead, ya know?

The astonishing success of the film had a massive impact on *Trainspotting*'s book sales, though exactly how many books were sold and when is difficult to tell. Unfortunately, the sales figures from the book industry's monitor, Nielsen, aren't conclusive, as sales weren't tracked comprehensively before the millennium and didn't include export figures and library copies. Neither Irvine nor his publisher Robin Robertson could give me exact figures, so it's guesswork to a certain extent on my part, but the book had gone into fourteen reprints even before the film sent sales rocketing around the world. The Scottish bestseller list – although not entirely reliable, as it usually focused on the sales of just one book chain – reveals how dominant an author Welsh was in his native land. On 31 July 1997, *Trainspotting* was at number 1 and Irvine also had numbers 3 and 4 in the list with *The Acid House* and *Marabou Stork Nightmares* respectively. Only Iain M. Banks, with his science fiction novel *Feersum Endjinn* at number 2, could challenge Welsh's dominance.

The book was flying off bookshop shelves, and it also became the most stolen title by shoplifters. Most readers, though, used more conventional and legal means to get a hold of *Trainspotting*. Alan Warner tells a nice tale that sums up how popular the book was. 'I recall the day I knew everything had changed. Walking down to east end Waterstone's on Princes Street and a workie came out of Waterstone's: he had his hard hat on and overalls covered in paint, and in his arms he had five copies of *Acid House* and five of *Trainspotting* . . . for his mates back on the site . . . just like the books were fish suppers. That was actually the moment for me . . . maybe the best high of all as a Scottish writer.'

By 1996 the *Evening News* was calling Welsh a millionaire. But Irvine rebuffed this, saying he had certainly not made a million through book sales. He told *Dazed and Confused* magazine in March 1996: '*I sold about 200,000 books in three years, which is about 60p a book, which is maybe 120 grand over three years. Take the deductions off that, and you've got £70,000, so that's about twenty grand a year, which is just about the same as I was making when I was working for Edinburgh Council before. It's a far cry from being a millionaire. I must be the only millionaire that lives in a two-bedroomed tenement flat.' *The Times* later reported that Irvine came second in the list of top-selling authors in the UK for 1996, behind Terry Pratchett. Yet Pratchett had 21 books in print, whereas Irvine only had four. The paper stated that Irvine's sales were worth £1,562,003, of which he got around ten per cent (according to Book Track). Irvine was well ahead of long-established literary heavyweights such as John Grisham, Stephen King and Catherine Cookson.

---

* Presumably this refers to combined sales for *Trainspotting*, *The Acid House* and *Marabou Stork Nightmares*.

A day spent searching through the back issues of the trade journal *The Bookseller* helps to put some scores on the board. There's no mention of Irvine that I could find prior to January 1996, but previewing the release of Welsh's third book, *Marabou Stork Nightmares,* the magazine stated that Welsh was 'very much a cult sale', though 'enormous in the right area'. Later that month, a list of the paperback bestsellers of 1995 put *Trainspotting* at number 72, selling 130,113 copies at home and 4,110 abroad. This total of 134, 223 grossed £803,960. Impressive though this is, it is put into perspective by the fact that John Grisham's *The Chamber* was number 1 on the list, selling a total of 1,130,533 and grossing nearly £7 million.

It was the launch of the film in early 1996 that really shifted Irvine to another level sales-wise. *Trainspotting* made its first appearance in *The Bookseller* Top 15 paperbacks in early February of that year, and the following month it was joined by the film tie-in. By 15 March Irvine had three books in the UK Paperback Top 10, the two *Trainspotting* titles and *Marabou Stork Nightmares. Trainspotting* never got to number 1 in the list, and the film tie-in peaked at number 2 on 29 March. It was held off the top spot by Jostein Gaarder's *Sophie's World.* Don't feel too sorry for Irvine, though, because on 7 June *Ecstasy* went straight in at number 1, ousting Joanna Trollope's *The Best of Friends* from the top slot.* The other high new entry that week, Stephen King's *The Green Mile,* could only make number 4. This was probably the high point in terms of weekly sales in the UK, though Irvine continued to have one or two books in the charts every week until late July. As to how many copies these books were selling per week, again it's guesswork. Frustratingly, *The*

* The American trade journal *Publishers Weekly* reported that *Ecstasy* 'sold 100,000 copies on its first day of sale in the UK. What a rush.'

Bookseller only introduced weekly book sales figures on 26 July – the week that Irvine disappeared from the top 15. But a look at the charts for 1997 shows that Nick Hornby's *High Fidelity* was selling about 4,500 copies a week when it was at the top of the charts. One would guess similar numbers were being sold for *Trainspotting* back in the halcyon days of the spring of 1996. The annual paperback chart for 1996 shows that *Trainspotting* came in at number 51, selling 170,112 at home and 26,074 abroad, giving a total of 196,186 and a gross of £1,959, 898. The film tie-in didn't make the charts, but would no doubt still have sold tens of thousands of copies that year.

The highpoint of Welshmania probably came when *The Times* in November 1997 reported on a poll of the twentieth century's greatest books. *Trainspotting* was number 1, ahead of classics like *Lord of the Rings, 1984* and *Catcher in the Rye*. *The Acid House*, which I doubt even Irvine's most loyal fans would claim to be one of the greatest books ever written, was at number 29. The poll was carried out over two months in July and August of 1997. Over 15,000 customers in 79 Virgin Megastores across the UK were surveyed. Meanwhile the selling of *Trainspotting* continued apace, with the film spawning a boom in sales of related items such as T-shirts, posters and soundtrack albums. This commercialisation of a book that had a critique of consumerism as one of its central themes was not without irony.

Irvine's publishers, Cape, released his fourth book, *Ecstasy*, in August 1996 on the back of an award-winning £10,000 marketing campaign, with lots of London underground advertising and features in hip magazines like *The Face* and *GQ*. Cape's press officer, Stephanie Sweeney, told *The Bookseller* that the campaign was precisely planned in every detail from the jacket image to the events programme. 'We felt there were two kinds of customer for a new Irvine Welsh.

The author's fan base is a cult and club audience, but with the release of the film *Trainspotting* he was moved into a mass audience. Everything we did was a cost-effective way of keeping the former and gaining the latter.' Reflecting this two-pronged approach, that month Irvine read to a literary audience of more than 900 people at the Queen Elizabeth Hall on the South Bank at 7.30 p.m., then sped across town to a packed Blue Note jazz club in Hoxton for a midnight reading. 'These few hours brought all our plans together,' Rachel Cugnoni, Cape's publicity director, told *The Bookseller*.

Irvine's American book tour of 1997 saw him make a triumphant return to the States. Just fourteen years previously he had visited some of those same cities as a somewhat lost youngster, pounding the streets of Los Angeles, getting drunk in dodgy bars, still dreaming of being a someone. It was on these trips, of course, that he first started writing *Trainspotting*; now he was returning triumphant, being touted as the hottest thing on the UK literary scene. Against all odds, *Trainspotting* had become a hit in America (Irvine was shocked by his success in the US; he didn't think the book would translate from Edinburgh to Glasgow, let alone to America). The big push in America started in July 1996, with Irvine's US publisher rushing out 50,000 copies of *Trainspotting* in a new edition with a glossary explaining the more arcane Scottish words and phrases. This came in the same month as the film opened in New York and Los Angeles, and was part of a feverish cross-media promotional campaign that saw film posters sent to bookstores nationwide. The book was sold in Tower and Virgin music stores, and the book, film and soundtrack were promoted in the US clothes chain Urban Outfitters, which catered primarily for the young and fashionably disaffected. Profiles of Irvine appeared in magazines such as the *New Yorker, Spin, Vogue, Newsweek* and *Entertainment Weekly*, and an interview appeared on NPR's *Morning Edition* programme.

Irvine's UK publisher, Cape, had sent the galley proofs of *The Acid House* to the venerable New York publisher W.W. Norton in 1994, and they subsequently signed Irvine up. It was Norton who sponsored the 'Great Scots Tour' of America which featured Irvine, James Kelman and Duncan McLean. All three writers objected to the constrictive label given to the tour, and there were occasional awkward moments when radio presenters resorted to playing bagpipe music or using other clichéd representations of Scottish culture. Irvine later wrote in *Loaded* that 'the media stuff though definitely suffered from the "Great Scots" bollocks and too often descended into "what-do-you-guys-wear-under-your-kilts?"'. Jim, Duncan and I got on well; they were excellent gadges to travel with.'

After a standing-room-only event at the Borders store in downtown Boston, on 1 May the tour moved to New York, where the writers stayed at the TK Hotel on 59th Street. Irvine did a DJ stint at a local radio station and then gave an expletive-laden interview for NPR radio. Told he could not use the f-word, Irvine instead made merry by using the c-word. Then it was on to the main event at a Barnes & Noble bookstore downtown, where Irvine was on fine form reading from *Marabou Stork Nightmares*. He then embarked on an epic drinking session with Scottish comedian Phil Kay. Norton's editor Gerald Howard, who organised the tour, wrote that the pub crawl resembled 'the Scottish substance abuse Olympics'. Our hero partied all night, ending up in what was possibly a crack den in the Lower East Side. Miraculously, he arrived back at the hotel with minutes to spare for the departure to LaGuardia airport for the flight to California.

Welsh continued the bacchanalian frenzy in San Francisco, attending an all-night rave organised by the Scottish Cultural and Arts Foundation, where the good feeling was enhanced by news that back home the Tories had been trounced in the General Election. Loaded on E and Guinness, Irvine didn't sleep for the next two days. At a post-gig party for the Chemical Brothers, he entered the club to be met by a Japanese *Trainspotting* fan who was wearing a Hibs strip. Welsh still managed to give a storming reading at the Edinburgh Castle pub on Saturday night, giving the seething mass of punters a treat by reading 'Traditional Sunday Breakfast'. A reporter for *Salon* magazine, Sara Baird, left him lying prostrate on the pool table, asking 'What's next?' The following evening it took a chemical charge to get him onstage at the Cowell Theater, where after giving his reading he was asked from the crowd what impact the drug ecstasy was having on young people. 'Well, it's working pretty great for me right now' was Welsh's reply. Thereafter the tour moved on to Seattle, but there's no record of what Irvine got up to there. He probably slept a lot.*

---

* Intriguingly the US tour was filmed by the publisher Peter Kravitz and cameraman Michael McDonough for a documentary which has never been released. Surely someone at BBC Scotland or STV could obtain the footage and broadcast the documentary, which chronicles a very important episode in Scottish literary history?

20

The train keeps a-rollin' . . .

I'm probably clapped out now in terms of what I can do in the same vein. You've only got a certain shelf life and I don't want a fucking writer's career. I don't want to have loads of my books on the fucking shelf and . . . be touted as one of these fucking kind of greats.

Q interview, 1996

One night, while I was writing the passage in this book where I recall getting slung out of a bar with Irvine sometime in the late 1970s, I looked up to see the same man on my TV screen. Irvine was sitting all alone in a TV studio in Edinburgh, trying gamely to debate Britain's future role in Europe with *Newsnight* host Jeremy Paxman and various politicians hundreds of miles away in London. After a bright opening, Irvine started to toil under the pressure of Paxman's line of questioning and eventually seemed to resort to reading from notes, never a good idea on live TV. I gave up watching after Ukip's Nigel Farage appeared to find common ground with what Irvine had just said, but watching Irvine that night was proof positive of just how much his life had changed since those drunken days back in the 1970s.

I lost regular contact with Irvine around 1985, seeing him only occasionally at Easter Road and in the usual pubs for a quick chat. Even at these brief meetings it was difficult to get close to him. He always seemed to be surrounded by people with the evil eye, eager to be seen with Irvine Welsh though strangely unwilling to buy a round. It's been fascinating to watch from far, far away Irvine's life changing. The most obvious difference to note is that he seems finally to have found his true vocation in life. Despite what he said in the introductory quote to this chapter, and the occasional disparaging remark about the profession, he has settled on a writer's career. He has grown to enjoy the whole process of writing, working out all the ideas in his head and the storytelling. Since the release of *Trainspotting* he has written eleven other books, several stage plays and screenplays, and he has been a regular contributor to newspapers, websites, blogs and Twitter. Nowadays he is almost as obsessive about writing as he once was about football and rock music. He thinks it's a respectable profession for an ageing punk. Initially, he wasn't so keen; it took him a long time to actually admit that he was a writer. But he persevered, because he's good at it, and compared to some of the 'proper' jobs he's endured in the past, writing offers easy money and lots of it.* He also believes the old proverb that the devil makes work for idle hands; when he's not writing, he tends to fall into his old bad habits.

Of his subsequent books *The Acid House* was enjoyable, as was *Filth*, though one did feel an urge to take a shower

* In the late 1990s he was thought to be earning over £1 million a year. As late as 2003, the *Daily Mirror* estimated he had raked in £375,000 in the previous year.

after reading the latter. Neither was as downright hilarious or indescribably sad as parts of *Trainspotting* were, but his later books were never likely to have the same shock value, cultural impact or sales success as his debut. Writing is a job to him now, not the exciting gamble it was at the beginning of his career. He says he has neither the time nor the patience to spend years creating a polished literary jewel that sparkles with descriptive writing and metaphors. He does his best with every book, then sends it to the publisher, parties for a while and moves on to the next one. He once commented, 'When you write a book it's a way of getting rid of something that you don't particularly want back. Like dain' a shite.'

Irvine says he doesn't care enough to read reviews of his own books; he just gets his publisher to send him the best ones for the book's dustjacket. It's probably just as well; his reputation among some highbrow critics has nosedived over the years. I remember a journalist friend telling me of a literary editor on the newspaper he wrote for – who had raved about *Trainspotting* on its release – throwing the press copy of one of Irvine's books into the waste-paper bin after having read just a few pages, muttering something about 'sexist garbage'. The criticisms are always along the same lines: once he moves outside his familiar milieu he is exposed as an ordinary writer; he can't write descriptive prose like he does monologues; he cannot write convincingly about women; the swearing and violence in his later books are gratuitous and nasty rather than funny. Another familiar accusation is of 'misery tourism' – living the high life in America but still writing about the poor downtrodden schemies back in his native land.

Some of the reviews have been savage. *The Times* said his sixth novel, *The Bedroom Secrets of the Master Chefs,* was so awful that 'it invents its own category of awfulness'. But the *Financial Times* thought that the same book 'flickers with the dynamism, black humour and imaginative bravado that is Welsh at his best'. One review of *Ecstasy* called it 'the literary equivalent of a drug coma'. Not that it bothered Irvine or his fans much. The book went straight to number 1 on the UK bestseller list and had sold nearly 200,000 copies by the end of 1996. Irvine says that it was around the time *Ecstasy* came out that he first realised he was a 'proper writer'. He had two books in the Top 10 and was trading blows with middle-class Oxbridge writers such as Julian Barnes and Martin Amis. A similar divergence among the critics came for *Porno*, the sequel to *Trainspotting*, in which Sick Boy has moved into the porn business. It was described by the *Scotsman* as 'flaccid reading, pitiable evidence of a past-it writer failing to capture his literary libido'. But *The List* thought it was a 'highly entertaining, fast-paced page turner of a beach novel'. It was nominated for Scottish Book of the Year in 2002, only to lose out to Janice Galloway's *Clara*. No writer is ever going to please every reviewer; I suspect Irvine probably got a much bigger buzz discovering that cricket legend Andrew Flintoff's favourite book is *Filth* than from getting a positive review in one of the broadsheets.

In the summer of 1998 Irvine bought a smart apartment in Edinburgh's New Town. Coincidentally, his new home was next to the one where part of Danny Boyle's *Shallow Grave* was filmed. Irvine still has this home and uses it whenever he returns to the capital. From his front window he has a splendid view of the tower blocks of Muirhouse. But ever since 2002 he has been resident elsewhere, leading an itinerant life and dividing his time between Dublin, London, Miami and Chicago, where he taught creative writing at Columbia College. He met his second wife, Beth Quinn, when she worked as a waitress in a Chicago sushi restaurant. Contrary to what has been written elsewhere, Beth was never a student at Columbia College. Irvine told me: 'I met her in an Irish bar called Rosie O'Grady's. I went up to her and tapped her teeth and said, "You've got brilliant big American choppers." She replied, "You're Scottish, aren't you? Do you guys have any teeth?" When we met, she knew very little about me and hadn't read any of my books, though she had seen the movie.' As ever, he keeps domestic affairs private. But I did like his comment that Beth, an attractive, blue-eyed Irish-American who is a good few years younger than him, had been 'good for my posture'. The couple shared a home in Dublin for a number of years, a three-storey Victorian red-brick building near Rathmines Bridge. Views are obviously important to Irvine; this apartment looked out to the Dublin Mountains.

Sometimes the new and old sides of his life meld together in bizarre fashion. In March 2007 he flew into the UK from 90-degree heat in Miami wearing a T-shirt and jeans, arriving in freezing Glasgow just in time to witness a rare Hibs success in the League Cup final. After watching a 5–1 caning of Kilmarnock he partied in Leith till the early hours before jetting back to Florida, where he had a large Bloody Mary in a favourite Miami Beach deli and read the match reports from that morning's Scottish newspapers. Strange life. In 2012 he left business at the Cannes Film Festival to witness Hibs's Scottish Cup final mauling by the dreaded Hearts. He retains an interest in Hibs, but despairs at the state of the game in Scotland and the way it has lost touch with its working-class roots.

He says he stays grounded by keeping in contact with his genuine friends from way back. Whenever he is in Edinburgh he tries to meet up with old mates who have known him since primary school. They have a beer and maybe go to Easter Road. If he ever gets too carried away by his success, these guys soon cut him down to size.

Sandy Macnair told me: 'Success doesn't seem to have changed him markedly. He maybe talks about his work more than most of us would do when in company, but then that's quite understandable. He still frequents the same sort of sleazy pubs with the same group of sleazy mates when he's back in Edinburgh. And he is still an unpredictable radge when sauced up.' Despite the occasional lapse into the old bad habits Irvine keeps trim these days. He enjoys tennis, horse-riding and running though he says 'marathons are beyond me now though, but I keep fit by doing the boxing training, though I had to stop sparring as young guys have too much hand speed.'

Robin Robertson says, 'Nowadays he's very successful, very busy, very confident, without any of the problems that are usually associated with success. He's loving it. He's hugely generous and great fun with an enormous enthusiasm for what he is doing. He probably never had any plans to be an author and certainly didn't have any plans to be a film-maker or work in television, but these things are happening. I cannot keep up with all his projects. He seems very happy with his life, and Beth is a great foil for him.'

Alan Warner has remained in touch with Welsh ever since the early days. He told me: 'As the years went by, I think he would agree we became much closer – probably email had a lot to do with that. Our wives became pally – going shopping together in Cannes and all that, which I'm doubtless still paying off. I remember Irvine and Beth and a bit of a posse came down to stay with Hollie [Alan's wife] and I in Spain once, where I was living at the time. Johnny Brown, the singer from the Band of Holy Joy, was there, and we went to these mad South American salsa places. I can't get rid of the guy! He even followed me to Ireland. And he hasn't changed at all. That's the problem. He's much tougher than me. He can meet you for a porridge breakfast at fucking 9 a.m. That's pretty tough. I do remember Irvine and me noised up Bret Easton Ellis quite badly in Dublin, at U2's hotel, singing to him and stuff. We had been in the pub and were five hours late. We were in this pub with this Irish writer and the guy was continually going, "Irvine, Irvine, they keep calling me sub-Irvine, what can I do? I'm not that influenced by you. Sub-Irvine they say. Do you think I am sub-Irvine? Irvine?" Irvine was nodding at him tolerantly. When this geezer went for a piss, Irvine turned to me and said, "Warner, why does he keep telling me his writing is fucking suburban? What's that got to do with me? What the fuck can I do about his writing being suburban?"

'I love the garish, almost cartoon-like nature of Irvine's later work. I always read his latest book and I always enjoy it. Irvine has made his own universe as a writer; people take it for granted now, but he has staked out his own territory, sort of Jackie Collins meets the Jackie/Junkie Massive. Ha ha. Immense. It's such great fun. I think *Filth* is my favourite Welsh novel. But *Trainspotting* had a slightly different atmospheric; a rawness and maybe a real emotion remains there. There's always a strong moral sense about Irvine's writing, like in *Marabou Stork Nightmares* – despite all the middle-class tutting and raising of eyebrows at his writing.

'You know lots of folk have a go at Irvine for living abroad when he could be soaking up the sunshine in Leith, but they overlook the fact that after *Trainspotting* he could have written nothing more, just ridden around in a fucking Ferrari for the rest of his days and gone a bit George Best. But he didn't. He can't even drive! He kept writing, he kept interested in the culture around him. I would be floating dead in a swimming pool if I had had Irvine's fame and success. Everyone is affected by success, but not necessarily changed by it. Irvine was mature when success and fame came, so he coped. And we writers are all permitted our Diva Day once a year, darling. I've been through a tiny bit of that success thing too, though nothing compared to what Welshy went through. It's all just like the wise old Joe Walsh song, "Life's Been Good". "It's tough to handle, this fortune and fame, everybody's so different but I haven't changed."'

Trainspotting continues to have an incredible impact. Just as it was read by many people who had seldom bought a book before, it also encouraged many young people to try to emulate Irvine's success. As Robin Robertson said at the height of *Trainspotting*'s success: 'Ten years ago, the stuff I was being sent was pastiche Kelman; now it's pastiche Welsh.' He remains a source of inspiration to many younger writers. Thriller writer Louise Welsh picked *Trainspotting* as her favourite Scottish book of the twentieth century. Hugh Reed, who played Diane's suitor in the film's disco scene, told me there is a *Trainspotting*-themed bar/restaurant in Beijing. Harry Gibson sent me a letter that included a flyer from the WaterAid charity with the slogan 'Choose Life'. The same slogan has also been used in government anti-drugs campaigns, much to Welsh's amusement.

Of course, the nagging question of whether *Trainspotting* encouraged drug abuse will never really go away. Did reading the book, seeing the play or film, inspire impressionable youngsters to take drugs? Well, yes, it probably did in some cases. The early part of the film in particular, with its handsome lead star, pounding soundtrack and dark humour gave drug-taking a seductive rebel-romance quality. For some people that might override all the negative stuff: the dead baby, the overdose, the court appearance and the fatalities. Yet, back when we were kids, bands like the Rolling Stones, singing about 'sweet cousin cocaine' in 'Sister Morphine', gave drug use a mystical allure. On balance, I think *Trainspotting* shows the reality of drug abuse. There are a lot of good times. They will make you feel superhuman for a few hours. But, in the long run, unless you are very careful or very lucky, they will destroy you. Heroin in particular can degrade you in unimaginable ways.

Of all the people I spoke to or read about for this book, the two most telling contributions to this debate came from two guys who knew quite a lot about heroin abuse. I never met Calton Athletic's Davie Bryce; sadly, he died before I could interview him, but his own book makes some very interesting points. Writing about the film, he said: 'Some people said it glamorised drugs. Nonsense. It deglamorised drugs. How? It highlighted the HIV issue. Anybody who saw the film and hadn't used drugs before and afterwards said, "I think I'll start injecting heroin", must come from another planet. It showed the realities of drug use. It wasn't all doom and gloom. There are the funny bits. There are the kicks. But it took you to the dark side, the withdrawals, the infections and the cot deaths.'

Dr Roy Robertson, through his work in the Muirhouse community, has seen first-hand the devastation heroin brings to lives, but he gives short shrift to those critics of Irvine's book and the subsequent film who say that it encouraged drug use. 'That is absolute rubbish; Irvine was telling it like it was. I remember interviewing a guy years later that I had known for twenty years, who by that stage had HIV and was really quite ill. I asked him what he thought about Irvine's book, and he suddenly became animated, saying, "I hate that guy, I hate him! He stole my story . . . that was me. I don't know how he did it, but he stole my personality."' And it's true, Irvine did capture those personalities, you look at the people on the *Trainspotting* poster and they look just like those kids. It was a very good portrayal. That's what those kids were like, quite different from now, where we are dealing with a rather sad lot of 50-somethings. I still see about 50 of that original group. We still have young drug users, but they don't behave like that any longer. If you think about Irvine Welsh's characters, they are young people who are not a million miles away from the first-year undergraduates that most people know, skinny young kids behaving badly whether with alcohol or drugs.

'Anyway, people are not stupid; I think the book would

scare most sensible people away from drugs . . . The only thing, and this is not meant as a criticism of the book, is that I think it did not say that this is a chronic disease . . . but it's not a medical book, is it? If I were writing a medical book it would talk about it like any other chronic disease, which can be cured in some people, but mostly people will go on with the consequences of the disease for most of their lives. That is what we see now, people at all stages of the disease. I have people who say, "Oh, you knew my granddad, he died of Aids." These are young girls, aged 21, injecting heroin.

'The people who inject heroin are usually people who have had bad things happen to them in childhood. They've maybe been sexually abused or had childhood misconduct problems, alcoholic parents or single parents – that's why they use heroin. This is a part of a spectrum of disorder that we refer to as deprivation and poverty. It's something we don't fully understand the full implications of. It's not like people are making this decision as a lifestyle choice. It's just there, like alcohol is there. I mean why do people become alcoholics?'

As for the future, well, *Trainspotting* is now so embedded in Scottish and British culture that it's never going to go away. In 2003 customers of the book chain Ottakar's voted it their number 1 favourite Scottish read, ahead of *Sunset Song* and *Kidnapped*. Every now and then things go quiet, but then a new production of the play appears, or a significant anniversary of the book or the film comes around, or Irvine emerges from hibernation with a new book, and the whole circus comes alive again. Irvine told me how the release of *Skagboys* had effectively relaunched *Trainspotting*, that when he went on a US tour he was amazed to see how many young kids had become new fans of the book. As I was working on this final chapter, a news report told how Danny Boyle intends to reunite the original film cast to make *Trainspotting 2*. This is one train that will just run and run.

Bibliography and sources

Books

Laidlaw, William McIlvanney, Hodder & Stoughton, 1977
Scream, if you want to go faster (New Writing Scotland 9), Hamish Whyte & Janice Galloway (eds), Association for Scottish Literary Studies, 1991
Trainspotting, Irvine Welsh, Secker & Warburg, 1993
Shallow Grave & Trainspotting, John Hodge, Faber and Faber, 1996
ahead of its time, Duncan McLean (ed.), Jonathan Cape, 1997
Pandora's Handbag, Elizabeth Young, Serpent's Tail, 2001
4 Play, Irvine Welsh, Vintage, 2001
In-Yer-Face Theatre, Aleks Sierz, Faber and Faber, 2001
Sword of Honour, Evelyn Waugh, Chapman & Hall, 1952–1961
Gordon Strachan, Leo Moynihan, Virgin Books, 2005
Pimp, Iceberg Slim, Canongate, 2009
Caught by the River: A Collection of Words on Water, Jeff Barrett, Robin Turner & Andrew Walsh, Cassell Illustrated, 2009 (contains essay by Irvine Welsh)
Carspotting: The Real Adventures of Irvine Welsh, Sandy Macnair, Black and White Publishing, 2011
We Are Hibernian, Andy MacVannan, Luath Press, 2011
Never Give Up: A Community's Fight for Social Justice, North Edinburgh Social History Group, 2011
Skagboys, Irvine Welsh, Jonathan Cape, 2012

TV, newspaper and magazine articles

Edinburgh Evening News (Pink edition), 13 February 1982, 'Hibs fan killed in bus horror'

Glasgow Herald, 15 July 1982, 'Self-help the key for communities in the addiction trap', Kerron Harvey

The Scotsman, 20 June 1983, 'Edinburgh "A major centre for drugs"', William Paul

Edinburgh Evening News, 19 April 1984, 'Getting rich on misery', Ian Burrell

British Medical Journal, vol. 292, 22 February 1986, 'Epidemic of AIDS related virus (HTLV –111/LAV) infection among intravenous drug users', J R Robertson *et al*

Scotland on Sunday, 26 April 1992, 'Rebel Inc.'s revolutionary sell fights the slump', Jonny Jacobsen

The Herald, 31 July 1993, 'Fear and Lothian' book review by A.C.

Big Issue in Scotland, 23 July–5 August 1993, 'The write to life, liberty and happiness', Neil Trotter

Scotland on Sunday, 8 August 1993, 'Through the eye of a needle', Kenny Farquharson

The Guardian: Edinburgh Festival Supplement, 14 August 1993, 'Blood on the tracks', Elizabeth Young

The Sunday Times, 15 August 1993, 'Cruising for a bruising', book review by Lucy Hughes-Hallett

The Scotsman, 18 September 1993, 'Objects of Desire', column by Irvine Welsh

Rebel Inc., issue 4, 1993, The Ecstasy Interview by Irvine Welsh and Kevin Williamson

The List, 25 February–10 March 1994, 'Chill out club', Sue Wilson

The Scotsman, 26 February 1994, 'Acid drops', Catherine Lockerbie

The Independent, 5 May 1994, '*Trainspotting*, Citizens Theatre, Glasgow; Horror gets laughs', Keith Bruce

The Independent, 5 April 1995, '*Trainspotting*, Bush Theatre, London', Carole Woddis

The List, 7–20 April 1995, 'Home in a strange town', Eddie Gibb

The Independent, 15 April 1995, 'The not-so-shady past of Irvine Welsh', John Walsh

Sunday Times, 16 April 1995, 'Voices from the edge', Chris Savage King

Scotland on Sunday, 23 April 1995, 'Four letters that still spell out "hype"', Iain S Bruce

The List, 16–29 June 1995, 'Forever in high heels', Fiona Shepherd

The Sunday Times Scotland, 23 July 1995, 'Colourful language', Alan Chadwick

The Big Issue, October 1995, 'Interview with John Hodge', David Milne

Edinburgh Herald and Post, 25 January 1996, '*Trainspotting* set to smash box office records in the capital', Brian Ferguson

Time Out, 31 January 1996, 'The other side of the tracks', Tom Charity

The Scotsman, 3 February 1996, review of *Trainspotting* film by Lynn Cochrane

Scotland on Sunday, 4 February 1996, 'Smack in the face', Allan Hunter

The Scotsman, 6 February 1996, 'Trainspotters in rush for tickets', Dani Garavelli

The Scotsman, 8 February 1996, 'Primal scream', Brian Pendreigh

The List, 9–22 February 1996, 'Trainspotters of the world unite' and 'Training session', Fiona Shepherd

The List, 9–22 February 1996, 'On the right tracks' and 'Novel approach', Alan Morrison

The List, 9–22 February 1996, 'Say it loud', Deirdre Molloy

The List, 9–22 February 1996, 'The big score', Thom Dibdin

The Irish Times, 17 February 1996, 'Well spotted', Michael Dwyer

The Scotsman, 17 February 1996, 'Spotting image', portrait of Irvine Welsh

Edinburgh Herald and Post, 22 February 1996, 'They are off the rails', Allan Hunter

The Scotsman, 23 February 1996, 'Needle points', Angus Wolfe Murray

Empire, March 1996, 'First class return', Caroline Westbrook

Empire, March 1996, 'Now wash your hands', John Naughton

Empire, March 1996, 'The writing on the wall', Caroline Westbrook

Central Times, March 1996, 'An actor's life for me', Graham Parsons

Dazed and Confused, March 1996, '*Trainspotting*: Irvine Welsh', Fiona Russell Powell

Evening News, 7 March 1996, 'Muirhouse and proud'

New York Times, 31 March 1996, 'The Beats of Edinburgh', Lesley Downer

Big Issue, 29 March–11 April 1996, 'The confessions of Irvine Welsh', Irvine Welsh

Publishers Weekly, 13 May 1996, '*Trainspotting*: Can it repeat UK success?', Jonathan Bing

The Scotsman, 16 May 1996, 'Welsh adds heroin to his list of hits'

The List, 31 May–13 June 1996, 'The agony and ecstasy', Kathleen Morgan

The Scotsman, 1 June 1996, 'Hackneyed gab', Ian Bell

Publishers Weekly, 5 August 1996, 'Behind the bestsellers', Daisy Maryles and Dick Donahue

Bomb 56, summer 1996, 'Irvine Welsh', Jenifer Berman

Q, July 1996, 'Who the hell does Irvine Welsh think he is?', John Naughton

Edinburgh Evening News, 26 August 1996, 'Welsh stories earn him a magic million', Mark Campanile

The Bookseller, 6 December 1996, 'Singing a sombre music'

The Scotsman, 1 January 1997, 'Irvine Welsh in his natural habitat', Barry Didcock

The Times, 11 January 1997, 'Top earning authors of 1996'

Salon, 13 May 1997, 'Media circus: Scot on the rocks', Sara Baird

Boston Phoenix, 15–22 May 1997, 'Scotched', Chris Wright

Publishers Weekly, 16 June 1997, 'On the road with . . . Great Scots', Julie Moline

Loaded, September 1997, 'Irvine Welsh: the *Trainspotting* author hits the streets of San Francisco'

Big Issue, 11–17 December 1997, 'My kind of town'

Edinburgh Evening News, 16 June 1998, 'Bestseller Irvine spends £159,000 on a writing pad'

Scotsman Weekend, 25 July 1998, 'Scenes from the life of Irvine Welsh', Duncan McLean

The Herald, 21 December 1999, 'Face of the Day', Robert Carlyle profile, Dominic Ryan

Sunday Mail, 3 December 2000, 'A long Leith of life; the *Trainspotting* reunion'

Scotland on Sunday, 2 December 2001, 'Drama in a different class', Mark Brown

The Scotsman, 6 February 2002, 'Theatre's best shot in the arm', Joyce McMillan

The Times, 12 April 2002, 'Feeding of the naked lunch', Irvine Welsh

Sunday Herald, 2 June 2002, 'Hibs superfans Welsh and Scott pay tribute to sacked French hero', Bridget Morris

Daily Telegraph, 29 June 2002, 'Out of the shadows', Irvine Welsh

The Scotsman, 24 August 2002, 'Brain rotting', *Porno* review by Tom Lappin

Daily Telegraph, 17 March 2003, 'From America', Irvine Welsh

Scotland on Sunday, 25 May 2003, '*Trainspotting*: director's cut is the deepest', Brian Pendreigh

Sunday Mail, 28 September 2003, 'Irvine Welsh splits from secret wife', Lorna Hughes

Edinburgh Review 113, 2004, Irvine Welsh interview, Aaron Kelly

Archives of Internal Medicine, vol. 164, 14 June 2004, 'Changing patterns in causes of death in a cohort of injecting drug users 1980–2001', Lorraine Copeland *et al*

spikemagazine.com, 1 December 2005, '*Trainspotting* the play: Harry Gibson: 10 years on', Chris Mitchell

The Observer, 4 December 2005, 'I'd rather look at the hills than get wasted', Sean O'Hagan

The Independent, 29 December 2005, 'Ten years on, just as shocking', Charlotte Cripps

The List, 1 January 2005, 'The 100 Best Scottish Books of All Time – *Trainspotting* chosen by Louise Welsh'

The Herald, 7 January 2006, '*Trainspotting* at 10', Neil Cooper

Daily Telegraph, 16 July 2006, 'I did well out of Thatcherism', Nigel Farndale

Scotland on Sunday, 16 July 2006, 'Welsh would be happy to choose life under Tory leader Cameron'

The Guardian, 12 August 2006, 'Mellow fellow', Stuart Jeffries

The Herald Magazine, 21 April 2007, Andrew Macdonald interview by Bob Flynn

Scottish Studies Review, spring 2007, 'Speaking Welsh: Irvine Welsh in conversation with Ian Peddie'

The Guardian, 16 June 2007, 'School's out', James Campbell

The Observer, 19 August 2007, 'My Week: Irvine Welsh'

The Sunday Times, 19 August 2007, 'I chose to choose life', interview by Emma Wells

The Observer, 16 September 2007, 'The Record Doctor: Irvine Welsh', interview by Paul Mardles

Journal of the Royal Society of Medicine, November 2007, 'Heroin injecting and the introduction of HIV/AIDS into a Scottish city', Roy Robertson and Alison Richardson

The Cult, 31 January 2008, 'Snarl, grunt, Welshy ya cunt', Garrett Faber

The Herald Magazine, 12 January 2008, Kelly Macdonald interview by Alastair McKay

The Herald, 19 April 2008, 'What the poster boy did next', Neil Cooper

The Independent, 16 May 2008, 'Jeff Torrington: author of *Swing Hammer Swing!*'

The Herald Magazine, 24 May 2008, 'Train stopping', James Mottram

The Guardian, 21 June 2008, 'Fighting talk', John Mullan

The Herald, 22 June 2008, 'Sex, drugs and crime . . .', Paul Dalgarno

Sunday Herald, 30 June 2008, 'Talking Welsh', Stephen Phelan

The Guardian, 5 July 2008, 'My mentor', interview with Deany Judd

The Sunday Times, 10 August 2008, 'My hols', Sian Thatcher

The Herald Magazine, 15 November 2008, 'The edge', Susan Swarbrick

Bafta Guru, 5 December 2008, 'Robert Carlyle: a life in pictures'

The Herald Magazine, 13 December 2008, Danny Boyle interview by Teddy Jamieson

Movie Connections: Trainspotting, 26 January 2009, BBC

The Scotsman, 27 January 2009, 'What I know about women', Irvine Welsh

The Herald Magazine, 24 January 2009, 'The aim of the game', Teddy Jamieson

The Guardian, 14 March 2009, 'Up from the street', Irvine Welsh

The Herald Magazine, 11 April 2009, Kevin Macdonald interview by Will Lawrence

The Herald ABC, 11 April 2009, 'Spotting a good thing', Susan Swarbrick

The Times Magazine, February 2010, 'Significant others. The relationships that make a life', Alexia Skinitis

Literator: Journal of Literary Criticism, Comparative Linguistics and Literary Studies, 1 April 2010, 'Alienation in Irvine Welsh's *Trainspotting*', B.A. Senekal

Financial Times, 12 June 2010, 'I'm a pretty noisy person to be around', York Membery

The Herald, 15 June 2010, 'Paul Reekie: poet, writer, iconoclast', Neil Cooper

The Herald Magazine, 29 January 2011, Kelly Macdonald interview by Susan Swarbrick

The Herald, 24 February 2011, 'Writer Welsh explored his drug battle in *Trainspotting*'

Creative Review, 7 March 2011, '*Trainspotting*'s film poster campaign, 15 years on', Gavin Lucas

The Herald, 7 April 2011, 'Never one for moaning', Alison Rowat

The Courier, 20 June 2011, '"Just let it wash over you" – actress Susan Vidler on the surreal *Knives in Hens*', Jack McKeown

The Skinny, 30 June 2011, 'Love's rebellious joy – a tribute to Paul Reekie by Irvine Welsh, Vic Godard and Gordon Legge'

Bush Post, 6 July 2011, 'Archive treasure no. 7: *Trainspotting*', Emma Stoffer

Addiction Research Report 2012, 'Early life influences on the risk of injecting drug use etc.', John Macleod *et al*

The Herald, 18 August 2012, 'Drug deaths in Scotland reach highest ever level', Jody Harrison

The Guardian, 19 August 2012, 'Irvine Welsh tears into the Booker prize', Charlotte Higgins

Fresh Air from WHYY, 20 September 2012, 'Kelly Macdonald: strong woman on the *Boardwalk*' radio interview by Dave Davies

Sunday Times Scotland, 2012, 'After heroin, flesh is the new drug of choice' Irvine Welsh profile

Bella Caledonia, 10 January 2013, 'Scottish independence and British unity', Irvine Welsh

Picture credits

Thanks are due to the following for the images in the plate section: page 1, courtesy of David Todd; page 5, courtesy of Sandy McNair and David Todd; page 6, courtesy of Robin Robertson; page 7, courtesy of David Harrold; pages 8 and 9, courtesy of David Todd; page 10 (top), courtesy of the Gunnie Moberg Collection at Orkney Library & Archive; page 10 (bottom), courtesy of Herbie Knott, Rex Features; page 11, courtesy of Robin Robertson; page 13, courtesy of Lorenzo Agius/Contour by Getty Images (thanks also to Rob O'Connor and Mark Blamire, Stylorouge); page 15, courtesy of Fiona Hanson/PA Archive/Press Association Images. Thanks to Dave Harrold for the cover photograph, which is from the photo shoot for the first edition cover of *Trainspotting*.

Index